In the Rebel Cafe

Interviews with Ed Sanders

Edited by Jennie Skerl

Beat writing is one of the most formative poetics of the mid- to late twentieth and twenty-first centuries. Its connections to emerging postmodernisms—which collapsed boundaries among genres such as fiction, verse, diary, and memoir; between private and public pronouncements; between fact and invention; between and among sexual identities and desires—coincided with social justice movements in the United States and abroad. This series, created through an alliance with the Beat Studies Association, will bring recognition to the decades of serious scholarship devoted to Beat literature and writers.

Ed Sanders. Photo Credit Joseph M. Giordano

In the Rebel Cafe

Interviews with Ed Sanders

Edited by Jennie Skerl

Clemson University Press

First Edition, 2020
This paperback edition published 2025

ISBN: 978-1-942954-95-8 (hardback)
ISBN: 978-1-63804-171-9 (paperback)
eISBN: 978-1-942954-96-5 (e-book)

Published by Clemson University Press
in association with Liverpool University Press

For information about Clemson University Press,
please visit our website at www.clemson.edu/press.

Library of Congress Cataloging-in-Publication Data
Names: Sanders, Ed, interviewee. | Skerl, Jennie, editor.
Title: In the rebel cafe : interviews with Ed Sanders / edited by Jennie Skerl. Other titles: Interviews. Selections
Description: Clemson : Clemson University Press, [2020] | Series: Beat studies series | Includes bibliographical references and index. | Summary: "A collection of interviews with Ed Sanders with a critical introduction to Sanders's life and work, a chronology of Sanders's career, a bibliography of his publications, and a discography of the Fugs and Sanders albums. The interviews constitute a career biography of Sanders as a writer, musician, and activist"-- Provided by publisher.
Identifiers: LCCN 2020003889 (print) | LCCN 2020003890 (ebook) | ISBN 9781942954958 (hardback) | ISBN 9781942954965 (ebook)
Subjects: LCSH: Sanders, Ed--Interviews. | Poets, American--20th century--Interviews. | Musicians--United States--Interviews. | Political activists--United States--Interviews. Classification: LCC PS3569.A49 A6 2020 (print) | LCC PS3569.A49 (ebook) | DDC 811/.54 [B]--dc23
LC record available at https://lccn.loc.gov/2020003889
LC ebook record available at https://lccn.loc.gov/2020003890

Typeset in Minion Pro by Carnegie Book Production.

Contents

Acknowledgments

I am grateful to Nancy M. Grace and Ronna C. Johnson for encouraging this project from the beginning. This book would not exist without the assistance of Jennifer O'Leary and Neal Kenney in the Interlibrary Loan department at Francis Harvey Green Library, West Chester University, and Timothy D. Murray and the Special Collections staff at Morris Library, University of Delaware. I thank Joseph M. Giordano for allowing the use of his recent photograph of Sanders. Marian Mollin generously permitted the inclusion of her previously unpublished telephone interview and provided an informative introduction. At Clemson University Press, Alison Mero's guidance has been most helpful. I offer a heartfelt thank you to Ed Sanders for taking time to answer my questions and for inspiring this book. As always, thanks to John L. Hynes for his day-to-day, year-to-year encouragement and support.

Introduction

All hail to the Rebel Cafe

We'll have to keep on
opening and closing our
store fronts, our collectives,
our social action centers
till tulips are in the sky

The cafes come The cafes wane
but the best and final rebel cafe
is inside the human brain

All hail to the Rebel Cafe
All hail to the Rebel Cafe
Rebel Cafe

—Ed Sanders, "Hymn to the Rebel Cafe"[1]

Ed Sanders's multifaceted artistic career began when he read Allen Ginsberg's "Howl" as a high school student in Kansas City, Missouri. Inspired by Ginsberg's poetry and his powerful dissenting voice, Sanders hitchhiked to New York in 1958 to enroll at New York University and become part of the Beat poetry movement. Sanders soon became enmeshed in the Lower East Side poetry and arts scene—a distinctive avant-garde of the early sixties peopled by second-generation Beat, New York School, and Black Mountain poets who read in coffee houses, painters who founded cooperative galleries, underground film makers, and performance artists who created Off-Off Broadway shows and new art forms such as the happening. From the late fifties until the mid-sixties, the Lower East Side became an epicenter of artistic ferment, and Ed Sanders, a self-proclaimed "beatnik," was a central figure in what John Gruen called the new bohemia.[2]

In the crucible of the New York City avant-garde scene, Sanders was part of a younger generation that drew from the poetics of the Beats, Charles Olson's projective verse, and the New York School, as well as a vibrant arts community that produced hybrid works that did not conform to traditional genres and hierarchies, giving birth to pop art and postmodernism. Artists disseminated their work through new, do-it-yourself media such as the mimeograph machine, rock music, comics, underground film, and improvisational performances. As a prominent member of this arts community, Sanders performed in many formats—print, poetry readings, music, visual art—and created his own venues as a publisher, bookseller, and band leader of the rock group the Fugs. Much of his early work can be seen as postmodernist, avant-pop, punk, and performance art *avant la lettre*. In his later work, based in Woodstock, New York, he continued to innovate via a newspaper, television program, website, microtonal instruments, musical/poetic/dramatic works, glyphs, and a new poetics called investigative poetry. Sanders's work has always been informed by principled political stances, from the sixties counterculture of peace, free speech, sexual freedom, egalitarianism, and sharing of abundance to his later role as a historian and a citizen involved in environmental issues in his region. Sanders is a social critic who is also a patriot committed to American ideals: as he said in his introduction to *Tales of Beatnik Glory* (2004), his generation realized "there was oodles of freedom guaranteed by the United States Constitution that was not being used."[3]

Sanders's avant-garde artwork has been a life-long project of innovation while maintaining accessibility to reach readers/audiences with a message for social change. Sanders identified as Beat from the beginning of his career, and he has remained linked to his Beat Generation origins through his many friendships with Beat writers and through teaching at the Jack Kerouac School for Disembodied Poetry at Naropa University (founded by Allen Ginsberg and Anne Waldman) and at the Schule für Dichtung (School for Poetry) in Vienna, (which is modeled on the Naropa program. He continues his Beat artistic practice through oral public poetry, demotic diction, setting poetry to music, formal experimentation, and challenging mainstream culture and politics.

Sanders's poetry has been recognized through fellowships and awards and by inclusion in key anthologies and encyclopedias. The fame of the Fugs and Sanders's role in the counter culture continues to the present day. However, the academic world has been slow to follow up with scholarly criticism. Undoubtedly, one reason for this lack is academe's disdain for Beat writers, with the exception of a few who achieved renown in the fifties (Allen Ginsberg, Jack Kerouac, William S. Burroughs). Sanders is often name-checked only in broader critical surveys of the Beat Generation. Another factor is Sanders's work across media and genres. Critics tend to classify artists into particular generic or stylistic categories in order to place the individual within a defined context. Avant-garde artists like Sanders—who defy categories, who work in several genres and mix them up, and create unique forms such as glyphs or invent their own instruments—cannot be pigeonholed, and thus are often overlooked.[4] Perhaps this collection of Sanders's interviews will provide a context useful to future critics

This book presents a decade-by-decade selection of important interviews with Sanders, beginning with his first interview in the *Village Voice* at the age of twenty-five. Interviews have been selected for historical significance and for the quality of the discussion of his work. Read in chronological order, the interviews constitute a career biography of Sanders as a writer, musician, and activist. In his own words, Sanders chronicles his transition as a poet from lyric to historical narrative to epic, the development of his fiction and journalism, the creation and revival of the Fugs, his role in the artistic and countercultural movements of the sixties, his subsequent historical assessment of the era, and his continuing social commitments.

This introductory chapter provides an overview of Sanders's life and work; however, as the interviews demonstrate, Sanders is his own best critic as he discusses his influential mentors, his growth and development as an artist, his purpose and techniques in specific works, and his political activities.

The Lower East Side in the Early Sixties

The Lower East Side arts/bohemian community was aware of the older Beats and earlier avant-gardes and built on their achievements, but they also introduced new ideas and a new artistic style that signaled what Marianne DeKoven calls "emergent postmodernism."[5] Perhaps the most prominent characteristic of this avant-garde was the democratization of the arts.[6] Artists sought to create accessibility through low-cost materials or performances and an ethic of equality among artists and between artists and their audience. Democratization supported a drive toward eliminating hierarchies, both aesthetic and social. The combination of materials from popular, mass culture along with the traditions of high culture—including the classics—was part of this style, as was incorporating taboo subject matter and language, especially references to the body, sexuality, and drugs. Media and genre boundaries were also broken down by Lower East Side artists in an interdisciplinary style that combined word and image, sound and performance, and communal interaction among artists across media. Stylistically, erasure of boundaries was conducted in a spirit of play and spontaneity; thus, the work-play boundary was also challenged. Sanders captures the principle in this passage from *Tales of Beatnik Glory*: " … it was the best of times, it was the worst of times, but it was *our* times, and we owned them with our youth, our energy, our good will, our edginess. So let's party. . . . Poetry was a party. Work was a party. When I put out an issue of *Fuck You/A Magazine of the Arts* … that was a party. Fugs rehearsals were a party. Even demonstrations and long meetings planning the revolution."[7]

Physicality, the body as the focus of art, was also a mark of this avant-garde, especially its emphasis on the sexual body as the ground of a new aesthetic and an imagined social utopia. Nudity and explicit sexuality in the performing arts and film presented the shameless sexual body as a force for liberation, and poetry, such as Sanders's, included explicit sexual references and formerly taboo language. Terence Diggory has commented on the sexual energy underlying both Beat and New York School poetry in the sixties, providing not only a basis for social and artistic freedom, but also a vision of society expressed by the counter-culture.[8] Similarly, Sally Banes, in her analysis of this artistic community, discusses the sexual body as the "locus of liberation, abundance, and community."[9] According to Beth Bailey, transgressive sexuality, obscenity, and vulgarity became countercultural identity markers, explicitly equated with a larger ideal of freedom, and she identifies Sanders as an advocate of sexual excess as a weapon of cultural revolution.[10]

This same bohemian community was also the home of many political activists in the anti-nuclear, anti-war, and civil rights movements which in the sixties were linked to movements for free speech, sexual liberation, and the legalization of marijuana. The political and artistic were intertwined in that many artists were also politically active or contributed their art to benefit political causes. Indeed, it is the mark of this early sixties generation that political protest was integrated into their art—in contrast to the comparative withdrawal of the earlier generation of Beats and other bohemians in the late forties and early fifties. Group activity in politics and art fostered a strong sense of community, and the fusion of the aesthetic and the political created a utopian belief in the power of the avant-garde to change society by creating an alternative model. Sanders expressed this ideal as "Goof City," a concept introduced in his first published poem, "Poem from Jail," and described in *Tales of Beatnik Glory* as "a place of great freedom, affordability, cheap rents, adequate wages, wild times, plenty of leisure, guaranteed access to thrills and art, with streets so safe a person, man or woman, could walk naked at 4 a.m. and not be bothered or touched."[11]

Sanders in the New Bohemia: Early Poetry

No other artist of that time and place better exemplifies the sixties Lower East Side avant-garde than Ed Sanders: poet, publisher, musician, peace and free speech activist. His art was inseparable from his politics and was a form of both protest and changing consciousness. Sanders's style in poetry, prose, and music employed the breakdown of hierarchies typical of arts of the period and was very much a part of the avant-garde program of democratization and accessibility. His work playfully combined elements from popular culture (such as cartoons, rock and roll, stand-up comedy), avant-garde art (such as open poetic forms, happenings, and mixed media), and the poetic tradition of the lyric going back to the ancient Greeks, producing an idiosyncratic collage of high and low culture, an inter-art mix of verbal and visual elements, accessible language, and his own characteristic humor made up of comic hyperbole, satire, slang, and neologisms. The sexual body as the site of cultural struggle was prominent in Sanders's work, as displayed in some of his early poems, the title of his poetry magazine—F*uck You/A Magazine of the Arts,* and the sexual comedy of the Fugs. At the same time, ancient Greek literature informed his writing and music: during this time he was also studying the classics at New York University, completing a degree in Greek in 1964. In addition, he studied ancient Egypt and learned to read hieroglyphics, which also entered his work.

In spite of his multifarious activities across genres and art forms, Sanders saw himself as a poet (as he is primarily known today), and especially as a performance poet, one of the dominant modes of postmodern poetry.[12] Poetry readings were central to the Beat aesthetic which continues to influence performance poetry and poetry slams to this day. Early on, Sanders was a participant in coffee house poetry readings, entering the world of Beat-inspired public poetry events and honing his craft in Lower East Side venues such as the Cafe Le Metro, the Five Spot, and the New York Poets Theatre. He was associated with the St. Mark's Poetry Project from its founding in 1966, which became a center of anti-war resistance as well as poetry. According to Daniel Kane, by linking poetry to rock and roll Sanders anticipated and inspired the Poetry Project's rock/poetry programming, thus marking the transition from the Beat poetry/jazz scene to the more broadly popular rock music of a younger generation.[13] The young Sanders also educated himself in contemporary avant-garde poetry through his magazine and bookstore, placing himself in the context of Donald Allen's *New American Poetry*, choosing Ginsberg and Olson as his mentors, and also adopting their chosen forerunners, William Blake and Ezra Pound.[14] Ginsberg and Olson led poetry movements that resisted mainstream ideology and promoted experimentation with form—both traits which define Sanders's poetry. The erudition of Pound, Olson, and Ginsberg appears in Sanders's poetry also in his allusions to ancient Greek and Egyptian texts and myths.

Sanders's first published poem (and the first that he considered worthy of publication) was "Poem from Jail" (1963). It was introduced by Lawrence Ferlinghetti's City Lights Press, giving him recognition from the most famous publisher of Beat poetry, and officially established Sanders as a younger poet in the Beat movement. Indeed, he was often called a "second generation" Beat. The poem, as in much of Sanders's art, brings together artistic experimentation with his political commitments and real-life activism: it was written while Sanders served a sentence in Connecticut for protesting nuclear submarines by attempting to interfere with the launch at the New London naval base as part of a demonstration organized by the pacifist Committee for Nonviolent Action (CNVA). The poem's visionary intensity shows the influence of "Howl," but the form is Sanders's own: short lines with a pounding rhythm based on Greek meters,[15] overt political protest against nuclear weapons and war, ancient Greek and Egyptian myths combined with Christian references providing a structure for a spiritual journey, and the ideal of Goof City, "where every choice is allowed." Similarly, Sanders's "Cemetery Hill," on the subject of his mother's death and written at the same time as "Poem from Jail," recalls Ginsberg's "Kaddish," but again the verse form and the vision of the Egyptian death barge represent Sanders's own sensibility.

In addition to these and other early visionary/political poems, Sanders was known for his explicit, often comic, poems about sexuality, which appeared in *King Lord/Queen Freak* (1964), *The Toe Queen Poems* (1964), and *Peace Eye* (1965). In *Thirsting for Peace in a Raging Century: Selected Poems 1961-1985*, Sanders included only few of these poems: "Sheep Fuck Poem," "Elm Fuck Poem," "This is the Prayer Wheel and Vision," and "Holy Was Demeter Walking the Corn Furrow." These poems are part of Sanders's sexual liberation and free speech agendas, but they also make a serious argument about human sexuality as part of the natural world and connected to a divine life force as conveyed in ancient mythologies. The Demeter poem is a tour de force that imagines sex between a human (the poet himself) and a goddess, inspired by the myth about Demeter and Iasion. This poem is an early move into the narrative mode that is prominent in Sanders's later poetry and convincingly portrays intercourse with a goddess who is also dirt and corn sprouts, silk, sheaves, and husks—an experience both literally dirty and ineffable. From these beginnings, Sanders developed his own idiosyncratic voice and a flexible style that could be visionary, transgressive, colloquial, humorous, narrative, or lyrical.

Fuck You: Sanders and the Mimeograph Revolution

From 1962 to 1965, Sanders was also an influential promoter and disseminator of avant-garde poetry through his self-published poetry magazine, *Fuck You/A Magazine of the Arts*, part of what Sanders called the mimeograph revolution. Sanders personally typed, duplicated, and stapled thirteen issues of his magazine. He stenciled the covers, which introduced the contents of the issues amongst a collage of Egyptian hieroglyphics combined with graffiti-like or cartoon images of penises, copulation, peace symbols, the eye of Horus (which Sanders called the Peace Eye), hypodermic needles, mimeo machines, and other images of both Sanders's art and the bohemian scene. Sanders saw his word-and-image format as carrying on the tradition of Blake. This "do it yourself" magazine published many of the most prominent Beat and other avant-garde poets of the period: Carol Bergé, Ted Berrigan, Paul Blackburn, Gregory Corso, Elise Cowen, Diane Di Prima, Lawrence Ferlinghetti, Ginsberg, Le Roi Jones, Lenore Kandel, Denise Levertov, Michael McClure, Frank O'Hara, Olson, Joel Oppenheimer, Gary Snyder, John Weiners, and more. The magazine also served as a manifesto for pacifism, free speech, sexual liberation, and the legalization of marijuana. The first issue announced a publication dedicated to "pacifism, unilateral disarmament, national defense thru [*sic*] nonviolent resistance, multilateral indiscriminate apertual conjugation, anarchism, world federalism, civil disobedience, obstructers and submarine boarders, and all those groped by J. Edgar Hoover in the silent halls of Congress."[16] Seeking submissions, Sanders proclaimed, "I'll print anything," and writers responded.

Sanders's Fuck You Press also published monographs, which were stapled pamphlets similar in format to the magazine. These included a collection of poems about Marilyn Monroe on the occasion of her death, Bergé's "Vancouver Report," summarizing an important 1964 poetry conference in Vancouver that brought together Beat and Black Mountain poets, Pound's previously unpublished Cantos 110–116, and the first publication of Burroughs's "APO-33, A Metabolic Regulator." The press also published monographs that other publishers wouldn't touch because of obscenity issues, such as Burroughs' "Roosevelt after Inauguration" and W. H. Auden's "The Platonic Blow."

In 1964, Sanders opened the Peace Eye Bookstore, which sold small press poetry publications and provided a base for Sanders's diverse activities—the press, poetry, art shows, rehearsal space for his rock band, work on his experimental films, and political organizing. According to Butterick, "For its time, Peace Eye was as vital as Lawrence Ferlinghetti's City Lights Bookshop had been on the West Coast during the previous decade."[17] The bookstore was raided by police in 1966 and Sanders was charged with obscenity based on issues of *Fuck You*. Charges were dismissed in 1967, but Sanders was advised by his ACLU lawyers to cease publication. Thus, Sanders, like many other writers (especially Beat writers) and artists who were pushing boundaries at the time, became the target of official censorship and part of the fight against it.

The Fugs: Music, Politics, and Exorcism

The culmination of Sanders's border-crossing and communal art during the sixties was his band, the Fugs, cofounded with another bohemian poet, Tuli Kupferberg. The group was named after the euphemism that Norman Mailer was forced to use in his World War II novel, *The Naked and the Dead*, flaunting the unspoken obscenity and the censorship that the band defied. Writing their own songs, the Fugs combined music with poetry, political protest, social satire, sex comedy, and an anarchic style that usually ended performances with a Dionysian kind of happening, with Sanders, in his own words, playing the role of "a modern-day American Bacchus."[18] Like most rock and roll bands, the Fugs sang about sex, but their songs were more graphic and satirical of the genre, such as "Group Grope," "Wet Dream Over You," and "Coca-Cola Douche." Popular anti-war songs included "Kill for Peace" and "Wide

Wide River," which described contemporary political discourse as a "river of shit." The Fugs also set to music poetry by Blake, Swinburne, Auden, and Ginsberg, among others. Musically, The Fugs were influenced by the popular music of their time—folk, rock, jazz, civil rights songs, as well as the avant-garde experiments of the Dada movement and contemporary performance art. Their eclecticism, erasure of genre hierarchies, and inter-art mix epitomized the art style of the sixties Lower East Side and also signaled the emergence of the postmodern pop avant-garde. Although the term "punk rock" had not yet been invented, Daniel Kane, in *Do You Have a Band*, identifies the Fugs' experiments with rock and poetry, avant-garde and pop, as "proto-punk."[19]

The Fugs had a cult following in New York and beyond. Six albums were recorded between 1965 and 1969. The core players during this period were Sanders, Kupferberg, and Ken Weaver.[20] They also had a political role beyond protest songs, often playing to benefit the anti-Vietnam War movement or activists who had been arrested. Perhaps their most famous performance/protest was their exorcism of the Pentagon during the 1967 anti-war march in Washington, D.C., included in Mailer's account of the event in *Armies of the Night* (1968).[21] Not so well-known was their exorcism at Senator Joseph McCarthy's grave in Wisconsin a few months later. In 1968, Sanders, with anti-war activists and Yippie[22] movement founders Jerry Rubin and Abbie Hoffman, organized a rock festival called the "Festival of Life" to take place in Chicago during the Democratic National Party Convention as a counter-cultural demonstration against the war in Vietnam. Another antiwar activist coalition, the National Mobilization to End the War in Vietnam (known as "the MOBE"), planned demonstrations at the same time. The Chicago police force violently broke up these gatherings, and several organizers (who came to be known as "the Chicago 8") were put on trial for conspiracy to cause civil disruption. Sanders was not charged but was called to testify for the defense in 1969.

At the end of the sixties, The Fugs disbanded; Sanders wanted to devote more time to writing poetry and running his bookstore, rather than spend his days managing a band. But that was not the end of The Fugs. After the election of President Ronald Reagan in 1980 and the resurgence of the conservative political ideology he represented, Sanders and Kupferberg decided to revive the band, with new members

Steve Taylor, Scott Petito, and Coby Batty. Reunion concerts began in 1985 and continued for fifteen years, and new albums were released. Notable concerts included an anti-space war opera called *Star Peace* performed in 1987 as a counter to Reagan's "star wars" missile defense plan, a "Real Woodstock Festival" in 1994 (the twenty-fifth anniversary of the original event) and again in 1999 (thirtieth anniversary), and an "Exorcism of the White House" in 2017 after the election of President Donald Trump, fifty years after the Fugs' exorcism of the Pentagon.

"The case that won't go away": Sanders and *The Family*

As the sixties closed, Sanders's life and work took a new turn. In 1970 he went to California to report for the *Los Angeles Free Press* on the Manson Family murders. The sensational murders fascinated and horrified the nation, and Sanders wanted to investigate and write about it. Initially, in the media, the Manson group appeared to some to be a kind of hippie commune, and Sanders wondered if the hippie values of individual freedom, free sex, drug trips, and questioning authority had somehow led to a grotesque murder cult. Ultimately, he discovered that the Family was a group of young people who had lost their individual freedom and moral compass by turning over their lives to a psychologically manipulative lifetime criminal who claimed absolute authority over his followers. To Sanders, the murders illustrated the existence of evil in the world and the necessity of maintaining independence from authoritarian leaders. As Sanders says in the interview with Stambler, "The only claim the book makes is to encourage people to be anarchists. For people not to follow leaders, to challenge every directive."[23]

Sanders devoted almost two years to researching and writing about the crime and the subsequent trial. He conducted hundreds of interviews, visited crime scenes and Family hangouts, collaborated with a private investigator, and sat through the trial. The book that resulted, *The Family: The Story of Charles Manson's Dune Buggy Attack Battalion* (1971; revised editions, 1990 and 2002) is a lengthy, detailed, chronological narrative of the crimes, the victims, the perpetrators, the police work, the lawyers, the death threats, and the Hollywood gossip that swirled about the case (about an underworld of sadistic sex, satanic rituals, and drugs). While the original edition did not cover the trial, later expanded versions about "the case that won't go away" covered the trial, the verdicts, and the aftermath—appeals, probation hearings, and the later lives of those connected with the case; in 2016, Sanders published a biography of one of the victims, *Sharon Tate: A Life*. *The Family* received renewed attention when popular media revisited the Manson killings fifty years later in 2019, most notably in Quentin Tarantino's film *Once Upon a Time . . . in Hollywood*.

The prose in *The Family* is a straightforward factual narrative, although sprinkled with Sanders-style slang or neologisms. (For example, he originated the term "snuff film," and sometimes punctuated the horror with "oo ee oo" or "ur-sleaze.") Sanders's immersion in his subject and his presence in the narrative, describing his investigation and injecting his personal reactions, paralleled some of the techniques of what was then known as the "new journalism," a postmodern genre. However, Sanders's emphasis was on laying out all the facts, not on a subjective account, fictional reconstructions, or stylistic flourishes as practiced by some of the new journalists.

Investigative Poetry

A few years after publishing the Manson book, Sanders and his family settled in Woodstock, New York, where he continued to work as a poet, short story writer, activist, journalist, and musician. His experience as an investigator, researcher, and manager of massive amounts of data led Sanders to develop a new poetics, which he defined in his prose manifesto, *Investigative Poetry* (1976), and its counterpart in verse, *The Z-D Generation* (1981). The manifesto was also influenced by the public revelations in the seventies of government malfeasance, such as the Pentagon Papers, Watergate, the CIA's secret experiments with mind control and participation in the drug trade, and the FBI's counterintelligence program which illegally surveilled and disrupted political organizations connected to the civil rights, anti-war, and Black Panther movements. Once again citing Blake, Pound, Olson, and Ginsberg as forerunners, in *Investigative Poetry* Sanders takes courage from Ginsberg's line: "Now is the time for prophecy without death as a consequence."[24] He conceives of investigative poetry as devoted to history and politics—the poet as chronicler of historical reality—supported by scholarly research and data-gathering, and presented in modern poetic forms that can also include new technologies and performance. The manifesto calls for poets "to assume their rightful / positions as chroniclers / of the Time Track, / of the historical moment / whether century, aeon, hour / or microsecond" with the goal of "making freedom," a new reality.[25] Sanders outlines the techniques of investigative poetry, influenced by Olson's projective verse as well as the tools of his own research: opening case files, employing Q-lists (lists of questions), relentlessly pursuing and organizing data, using footnotes. He highlights the importance of the poet's persistence in the face of derision and the use of non-violent direct action. Sanders's manifesto also calls for the presentation of data using both traditional and non-traditional poetic verse forms, including typographies, visual images, performance art, chanting, singing, music, and new technologies. Sanders envisions contemporary poets as "the Diogenes Liberation Squadron of Strolling Troubadors & Muckrakers," using "*every* bardic skill and meter and method of the last 5 or 6 generations, in order to describe *every* aspect … of the historical present, while aiding the future, even placing bard-babble once again into a role as shaper of the future."[26] *The Z-D Generation* provides additional literary models (Zola and Diderot), defines the War Caste and the Right Wing Nut, and encourages the modern poet to "refuse the proffer'd hemlock."[27] The impact of the theory of investigative poetry has been recognized by other poets, such as Robert Creeley and Kristin Prevallet.[28]

Investigative Poetry provides a kind of blueprint for Sanders's subsequent development as a poet. His later work includes long narrative poems, book-length biographical and historical works, invented microtonal instruments, and performance poetry. He moved away from Ginsberg's rhetorical style toward Olson's concept of the poem as an open field, and toward both Pound and Olson's proposals for the poem that evokes history. Through his friendship with his Woodstock neighbor Alf Evers (the author of several histories of the Catskills region), Sanders learned how historians work, drawing on this knowledge in later narrative poems that took as their subjects artists and activists that he admired. Notable examples of these include "Sappho on East Seventh," "Yiddish Speaking Socialists of the Lower East Side," "Cassandra" (a companion piece to the musical drama with the same title), "In Praise of William Morris," "Ode to Rachel Carson," and "Rothschild's Fiddle" (based on Chekhov's story). He also produced book-length biographical and historical narrative verse, including *Chekhov, A Biography in Verse,* (1995), *1968: A History in Verse* (1997), *The Poetry and Life of Allen Ginsberg* (2000), *A Life of Olson* (2018), and his longest poem: *America: A History in Verse* (five volumes on the twentieth century published 2000–2009, followed by four more volumes on the seventeenth through the nineteenth centuries, as yet unpublished). His most ambitious work, *America*, has been praised by historian Douglas Brinkley as history in the popular tradition of Carl Sandburg and Walt Whitman and by Jim Vernon as emancipatory in the Hegelian sense—a history that affirms humanity's ability to build a better world, providing examples of persons and events that contributed to human freedom.[29]

A detailed discussion of *America* cannot be undertaken in this relatively brief essay, but Sanders's *1968, A History in Verse* illustrates the style and strategies of the larger work.[30] *1968* provides a chronological month-by-month narrative of the events of that pivotal year in American history, combining the personal and the political. Sanders chronicles major political events—the anti-war movement, FBI and CIA disruptions of anti-war and civil rights protests, right-wing Cuban terrorist attacks in New York City, the Columbia University student uprising, the assassinations of Martin Luther King, Jr. and Robert F. Kennedy, the presidential campaign—and makes occasional references to events in other countries and in popular culture. These are interwoven with Sanders's own activities that year: Fugs concerts, family events, his work with the Yippies in planning the "Festival of Life" in Chicago, and the subsequent police disruption of anti-war protests during the Democratic National Convention. The Chicago events provide the dramatic climax to the narrative, as Sanders gives an exciting day-by-day account from his perspective as a participant. Sanders's direct involvement in this historic event effectively fuses his individual experience with the nation's conflict over the Vietnam War and the 1968 presidential campaign.

Stylistically, Sanders alternates brief prosy statements of fact with dramatic sweep of action and lyrical moments. The first thirty-five pages introduce all the major story lines, so that the reader can then follow each thread throughout the work. Within the larger monthly chronological structure, the poem's form consists partly of passages that put together brief references, as in a newsreel effect, alternating with extended passages, or set pieces, treating a particular event in a longer narrative—the events in Chicago in are the longest of these. Sanders sometimes inserts drawings and photographs—and there are footnotes. Prevallet points out that Sanders's use of historical facts and data is an example of sampling, an innovation that differs from avant-garde collage by preserving the reference and presenting it as a piece of information that interacts with other references.[31] *1968: A History in Verse* is an example of Sanders crossing generic boundaries in a work that is historical, autobiographical, narrative, dramatic, prosy, lyrical, documentary, verbal, and visual. It is both a factual history and a powerful personal statement by a writer committed to "the struggle/for freedom/& a just, sharing world."[32] Robert Creeley praised the poem as "an extraordinary accomplishment—personal, particularizing, revealing, documenting. I can think of nothing quite like it."[33]

Even as he turned toward narrative poems in the seventies, Sanders continued the oral performance tradition of the Beat poets. He continued to write a variety of shorter lyrics, composed to be read aloud, sometimes chanted or sung, and often set to music using his invented instruments. His two volumes of selected poems show the range of his poetry over time: *Thirsting for Peace*, 1987, and *Let's Not Keep Fighting the Trojan War*, 2009. Crossing genres is a constant, as when poems written for oral presentation with music, such as "Hymn to the Rebel Cafe" or "The Cutting Prow" (for Henri Matisse), appear in print, or when *Poems for New Orleans* is published simultaneously in print and on a music CD. Comedy continues to be a hallmark of his work, as in "Sorrentinobiblophobia," which begins by defining the title as the fear of being savaged in a Gilbert Sorrentino novel. Sanders's translations of Sappho and his *Tribute to Sappho*, a performance poem that is also a product of scholarly research, are also important contributions.

Sanders's Fiction: Novels and Short Stories

Another new direction in Sanders's career after 1970 is his work in fiction. *Shards of God* (1970) tells the story of the formation of the Yippies and their participation in the events surrounding the Chicago Democratic Convention in a fantastical, hyperbolic style combining contemporary popular culture and eclectic references to Buddha, Jesus, the Gnostic Aeon, and ancient Greek and Egyptian Gods. In this narrative, Yippie leaders Hoffman and Rubin are portrayed as superhuman heroes and sexual athletes fighting against the capitalist economic system, militarism, support for the war in Vietnam, and a corrupt political culture represented by the mayor of Chicago, Richard J. Daley. While their actions sometimes parallel episodes in the *Iliad* and the *Odyssey*, their weapons are sex, drugs, computers, and the aid of the gods and aliens from outer space. Sanders, the author, is also part of the fictionalized narrative. The stated goal of the Yippies is a future society built around liberty, sharing, and equality, in the words of the author's introduction: "a socialist computer-worshiping government inspired by I-mouth saucerlings and based on principles of enforced sharing."[34] He also calls each chapter a "magic rite," for the narrative turns what was a defeat (the disruption of the Chicago protests by police) into a symbolic victory.[35] Kasia Boddy calls the novel a song of triumph, comparable to the Pindaric ode which celebrates an ephemeral athletic victory.[36] As Sanders says: "Forty years from now the Yippies and those who took part in the Peace-swarm of 1967–68 will be recognized for what they are, the most important cultural political force in the last 150 years of American civilization."[37] This early work of fiction is postmodern in its mix of genres, high and low cultural references, historical and fictional characters, and the participation of the author in the narrative.

Sanders's second novel, *Fame & Love in New York* (1980), is a satire on the Soho art scene of the seventies, which succeeded the bohemia of the sixties Lower East Side and was quickly exploited by art dealers and real estate developers. The novel consists of a series of four linked stories with overlapping characters, and, like *Shards of God*, merges references to both high and low culture with science fiction inventions, detective stories, and cartoonish characters. Several comic plots are set in motion as an installation artist, a group of writers (the Balzac Study Group), the owner of a rare books store (The Lantern of Knowledge), and a rock band (J'Accuse) try to accumulate funds to support construction of a shrine to Hart Crane on Mars, and to meet the "glorious deadline" of establishing socialism in the United States by the year 2000. *Fame & Love in New York* includes a variety of illustrations, pages from manuscripts, sketches, footnotes, numbered lists, cross-referenced items and events, musical notations, lyrics, and diagrams of dance steps—all giving the work the playful feel of a game or improvisational performance. The commodification of creating and selling art, the cynical pursuit of celebrity on the poetry-reading circuit, the competition for the possession of rare manuscripts, the stylistic evolution of rock genres in a constant quest for best-selling albums are all lampooned in a postmodern pastiche; however, even though the artists are flawed by egotism, rivalry, commercialism, and buffoonery, they are redeemed by their devotion to building a better society. Sanders maintains a utopian desire that is not undercut by paranoia or repression; rather, the hope for a better world balances the cynicism of art as a business and the sinister forces of opposition. According to Lance Olsen, in this novel Sanders prefigures avant-pop, a form of literary post-modernism that draws heavily on popular culture.[38]

Also in the seventies, Sanders wrote volume one of *Tales of Beatnik Glory*, which became a thirty-year project, resulting in four volumes of interconnected short stories. In the introduction, Sanders says he began writing the stories as a form of healing after his immersion in the Manson case. In 1973, he began researching ancient Egypt for a poem about artistic rebels in the past, and from that inquiry grew the inspiration to write about his own rebellious generation and to explore the history of the Lower East Side. *Tales* is a fictionalized memoir, chronicling the Beat and subsequent hippie counterculture of the Lower East Side from 1957 to New Year's Eve, 1970. Structurally, the stories proceed chronologically with a few exceptions for flashbacks and glimpses of the future. Sanders creates a numerous cast of writers, artists, and political activists; imaginary characters interact with real people and respond to major historical events of the era, as well as fictional events such as "the great Tompkins Park beatnik-to-hippie conversion ceremony." Sanders himself enters the narrative through two characters who serve as his alter egos (an underground filmmaker and a dramatist who was once a graduate student in Greek) and a nameless character who owns the Peace Eye Bookstore and who often functions as an observer of the scene. The New York bohemian milieu below 14th Street, known as "the set," is described in thick detail—the "pads" in old tenements, the cafes, bars, bookstores, theaters, and the two squares (Washington and Tompkins)—with forays to Washington D.C. and Mississippi for political protest and, in later stories, to a commune in Kansas and Hollywood's rock music scene. As Sanders remarks, "Some locations in these tales, such as Stanley's Bar and the Charles Theater, actually existed, but others such as the Total Assault Cantina, the House of Nothingness Café, the Luminous Animal Theater, the Mindscape Gallery, the Café Perf-Po, the Anarchist Coal Collective, and of course the Aura of Health Trans-Truckstop Chow Crib should have existed, but never did."[39] Stylistically, the work is a mock epic in postmodern hybrid form that merges fact and fiction, realism and fantasy, the classical tradition and popular culture, prose and poetry, drawings, and an idiosyncratic but very accessible comic style that uses neologisms, compound word constructions, hyperbole, satire, and broad comedy. Sanders aptly describes a community that combines idealism with the ridiculous, making the point that flawed human beings can yearn for and work towards a better world. An important innovation is the "sho-sto-po" or short story poem—chapters that narrate entirely in verse. These long poems prepare the way for Sanders's book-length biographical and historical poems of the nineties to the present.

In paying tribute to his generation, Sanders sought to ground his work and his vision of a bohemian community within a historical context that links the transitory art world that existed for a few years to traditions spanning centuries or millennia. Thus, in *Tales*, he claims precursors in the work of earlier activists (such as the Yiddish socialists of the early twentieth century), prior avant-gardes (such as the Cabaret Voltaire of the Dadas), and great writers of the past, especially the ancient Greeks. Two of his short story poems, "Sappho on East Seventh" and "Farbrente Rose," are impressive poems that combine narrative and lyric and bring into the sixties history that can be used. Sappho is invoked as a muse by a classics student and writer to endorse the bohemian community's values of sexual pleasure, innovative art, compassion, sharing abundance, and the collapsing of hierarchies that promotes equality. Rose Snyder represents the "*farbrente meydelekh*," or "burning young women" who fought for workers' rights and a socialist future before World War I, bringing together past and present activists on the Lower East Side. The two stories are linked by their poetic form to give equal weight to two ideals: empowerment through erotic passion and the passion for social justice. Sanders's fictional places also link rebels of past and present, as the site of the Anarchist Coal Collective in the 1890s becomes the House of Nothingness in the early sixties and later the Café Perf-Po in the eighties. Unlike Sanders's novels, *Tales* ends with a more realistic assessment of the successes and failures of the sixties generation. For example, in the penultimate chapter, set in the future, the cast of characters have a party on the twenty-fifth anniversary of the closing of the House of Nothingness in which they share past events of which they are ashamed, while the last chapter, which takes place on New Years' Eve 1970, has the characters saying goodbye to their utopian dreams as they face a foreseen future of "grasping, greed, and war." Nevertheless, they are proud of their art and their desire to change the world "without a drop of blood," retaining hope for a future era of social change.

Sanders's Work in Journalism and Visual Media

Following their move to Woodstock in 1975, Sanders and his wife, Miriam, became active in community affairs, especially environmental issues and controlling development. Together they began publishing a newspaper, the *Woodstock Journal*, in 1995, which appeared bi-weekly until 2003. The newspaper covered local/regional news and selected national news, advocated for protecting the environment, especially Woodstock's water, argued for a national healthcare system, and published poetry, book reviews, and arts news. The diverse subject matter included reportage and local history pieces by Tinker Twine and Ed Sanders, as well as a column on local flora and fauna, written by Miriam Sanders. Regular features included Andrei Codrescu's humorous column, newspaper co-founder Alan Sussman's column on legal issues, political columns by Jim Hightower and Andrew Cockburn, and cartoons by Tom Tomorrow. *The Journal* published poetry by Ginsberg, Robert Creeley, Lawrence Ferlinghetti, Anne Waldman, Robert Bly, and Enid Dame. Sanders also contributed some of his own work, including portions of *1968* and *America: A History in Verse*. The paper's motto, "Refuse to Be Burnt Out (*Noli in Spiritu Combueri*)," was printed on the top of page two, where announcements about community events were made. This maxim has been often repeated by Sanders in subsequent work. After the newspaper ended publication Sanders created a website, also entitled the *Woodstock Journal*, which serves some of the same purposes as the print version. In addition to these forays into print and digital media, beginning in 1993 Ed and Miriam Sanders produced television programs on the Woodstock public access channel, featuring similar content to the *Journal*. These programs, addressing local and sometimes national issues, continue up to the present.

In recent years, Sanders has received recognition for his contribution to the visual arts. In fact, visual art has been part of his work from the beginning. In addition to festooning the cover pages of *Fuck You* with his imagery, Sanders's early poetry often included drawings, some inspired by his study of Egyptian hieroglyphs. In 2008, while on a trip to Florence, Italy, Sanders bought a notebook and used it to draw one "glyph" with colored pencils on one page each day, for a total of 72 pages/glyphs. The completed *A Book of Glyphs* was published in facsimile in 2014. The author's note to this publication defines the glyph as "a drawing charged with literary, emotional, historical or mythic, and poetic intensity" and points out that these glyphs have appeared in his poetry since the sixties.[40] In 2015, Poets House in New York sponsored *Seeking the Glyph: An Exhibition of the Glyphic Work of Ed Sanders*, showing selected drawings and daybooks created by Sanders from 1962 to the present. The glyphs are word-and-image drawings in colored pencil, conveying their messages with humor in a cartoon-like style. They can be seen as small, visual lyrics that address some of the same subject matter as Sanders's poems, such as homage to other poets or friends, criticisms of militarism and right-wing politics, and responses to the natural world. In fact, one section of Sanders's 2009 poetry collection *Let's Not Keep Fighting the Trojan War* is "A Sequence of Glyphs." Glyphs continue to appear on Sanders's website and in his poetry.

The Interviews

The interviews from the sixties reflect Sanders's prominent role in the arts and controversies of the time, and the interviewers themselves were also participants in shaping media reception of the growing counterculture. John Wilcock was one of the original founders of the *Village*

Voice, and his interview recognized Sanders's impact on the avant-garde scene. William F. Buckley, Jr., was an influential conservative voice whose television show (*Firing Line*) was a cultural institution for decades. This particular episode is often cited in Kerouac biographies and often viewed on YouTube, but few have paid attention to Sanders's sensible, measured response to Kerouac's belligerence and Buckley's conservative bias. Barry Miles was a friend of Ginsberg and Burroughs (later their biographer) and himself an important part of the countercultural scene in London. Both the Miles and Buckley interviews occurred shortly after the August 1968 events in Chicago, recording Sanders's immediate reaction.

Perhaps because of Sanders's move away from New York City and the attention of its media, only one interview from the seventies was found. It is significant because it provides Sanders's commentary on his Manson book soon after it was published. Sookie Stabler's interview appeared in *WIN*, a magazine published by the War Resisters League, reflecting Sanders's pacifist connections. There were also few interviews in the eighties, but the two included here by literary critics Tandy Sturgeon and myself, are the first to provide in-depth discussions of Sanders as a writer.

In the nineties, Sanders began to be interviewed more frequently as his cumulative body of work gained more notice, particularly *Thirsting for Peace in a Raging Century* (1987), which won the American Book Award, *Tales of Beatnik Glory* (volumes 1 and 2 published in 1990), and *Hymn to the Rebel Cafe* (1993). In 1999, the *Review of Contemporary Fiction* published a special issue on Sanders's fiction, edited by Brooke Horvath. At the time, Horvath said that Sanders's fiction was being overlooked in comparison to his poetry and the Manson book, a situation which may have been reversed somewhat after the publication of the complete *Tales* in 2004. Interviews in the nineties by poets in poetry magazines (Sean Thomas Dougherty, Steve Luttrell, Lisa Jarnot), a literary critic (Horvath), the founding editor of a magazine devoted to the Beat Generation (Kevin Ring), and the publisher of one of the first online music publications (Jason Gross) show the range of audiences Sanders reached and led to expansive discussions of recently published fiction, poetry, and the Fugs, as well as Sanders's current projects and political concerns. Historian Marian Mollin contributed her previously unpublished 1998 interview, which was part of her research on the American pacifist movement, providing the only detailed discussion of Sanders's pacifist activities in the sixties.[41]

Sanders's major publications since 2000 have led to interviews that review Sanders's history in the context of the broader history of our times—the very subject of his later work. Bob Reidel's interview in *Beat Scene* follows the publication of the complete *Tales of Beatnik Glory* (2004), the discussion linking Sanders's political activism past and present. Steve Paul's interview ranges over Sanders's varied literary career culminating in *America, A History in Verse*. Interviews with Marc Schultz and Daniel Maurer took place after the publication of Sanders's memoir of the sixties, *Fug You: An Informal History of the Peace Eye Bookstore, the Fuck You Press, the Fugs, and Counterculture in the Lower East Side* (2011). Both interviewers seek to establish connections between earlier and contemporary protest movements, as well as the Lower East Side, then and now. Markus Brandstetter's interview illustrates the type of courses that Sanders has taught at the Schule für Dichtung and Sanders's reputation beyond the United States. Longer interviews by Alan Bisbort and Jennifer Seaman Cook provide more in-depth reflections on the sixties.

This collection of interviews provides invaluable insight into Sanders's evolution as an artist, activist, and historian. A remarkable autobiographical career narrative emerges as Sanders discusses past and present work, his aesthetic principles, creative process, mentors, friendships, political commitments, and more. This volume is intended to bring renewed critical attention to a still-active artist whose avant-garde artwork combines innovation with a message for social change. Sanders's story should be of interest to students and scholars of the Beat Generation, postmodernism, and the cultural history of post World War II American society.

Notes to the Introduction

1 Edward Sanders, "Hymn to the Rebel Cafe," *Hymn to the Rebel Cafe* (Santa Rosa, CA: Black Sparrow, 1993), 15.

2 John Gruen, *The New Bohemia: The Combine Generation* (New York: Grosset & Dunlap, 1996), 6.

3 Edward Sanders, *Tales of Beatnik Glory*, Volumes 1–4 (New York: Thunder's Mouth Press, 2004), 2.

4 Sanders himself alludes to this issue in his interview with Kevin Ring. See page 97

5 Marianne DeKoven, *Utopia Limited: The Sixties and the Emergence of the Postmodern* (Durham: Duke, 2004), 8.

6 Ronald Sukenick, *Down and In: Life in the Underground* (New York: William Morrow, 1987), 127; Sally Banes, *Greenwich Village 1963: Avant-Garde Performance and the Effervescent Body* (Durham: Duke University, 1993), 6; and Hans Bertens, *The Idea of the Postmodern: A History* (London: Routledge, 1995), 5.

7 Sanders, *Tales of Beatnik Glory*, 277.

8 Terence Diggory, ed. "Introduction," *Encyclopedia of New York School Poets* (New York: Facts on File, 2009), viii.

9 Banes, *Greenwich Village 1963*, 219.

10 Beth Bailey, "Sex as a Weapon: Underground Comix and the Paradox of Liberation," in *Imagine Nation: The American Counterculture of the 1960s and '70s*, ed. Peter Braunstein and Michael William Doyle (New York: Routledge, 2002), 307, 312.

11 Sanders, *Tales of Beatnik Glory*, 429.

12 See Paul Hoover, ed., "Introduction," in *Postmodern American Poetry: A Norton Anthology* (New York: Norton, 1994), xxv–xxxix.

13 Daniel Kane, *All Poets Welcome: The Lower East Side Poetry Scene in the 1960s* (Berkeley: University of California Press, 2003), 72.

14 Donald M. Allen, ed. *The New American Poetry* (New York: Grove, 1960).

15 Butterick suggests that the narrow lines may have been shaped by Sanders writing the poem on "cigarette guts" in his jail cell, although Sanders mentions toilet paper in interviews. George F. Butterick, "Ed Sanders," in *The Beats: Literary Bohemians in Postwar America, Dictionary of Literary Biography*, Vol. 16, ed. Ann Charters (Detroit: Gale Research, 1983), 475.

16 Quoted in Butterick, "Ed Sanders," 474.

17 Butterick, "Ed Sanders," 477.

18 Edward Sanders, *Fug You: An Informal History of the Peace Eye Eye Bookstore, the FuckYou Press, the Fugs, and Counterculture in the Lower East Side* (Boston: Da Capo, 2011), 293.

19 Daniel Kane, *"Do You Have a Band?": Poetry and Punk Rock in New York City* (New York: Columbia University Press, 2017), 19-39. Sanders asserts in *Fug*

You (404) that he was the first to use the term "punk rock" in an interview with Robb Baker in the *Chicago Tribune*, March 22, 1970, F4.

20 See Sanders's *Fug You* for all the musicians who played in the band in the sixties.

21 Sanders described the event in detail much later in *Fug You*, 277–82. Michael William Doyle sees the levitation as part of the guerrilla theater movement in the 1960s. Michael William Doyle, "Staging the Revolution: Guerilla Theater as a Countercultural Practice," in *Imagine Nation: The American Counterculture of the 1960s and '70s*, ed. Peter Braunstein and Michael William Doyle (New York: Routledge, 2002), 71–97. Joseph P. Laycock proposes that, although most have considered this event a piece of political theater or simply a joke, the levitation of the Pentagon can be seen as a genuine magical ritual employing occult knowledge with the aim of altering reality by changing public consciousness. Joseph P. Laycock, "Levitating the Pentagon: Exorcism as Politics, Politics as Exorcism," *Implicit Religion* 14, no. 3 (2011): 295–318.

22 Officially founded in 1968, the Youth International Party (whose members were known as Yippies) used theatrical tactics and political pranks to protest the Vietnam War and encourage countercultural activism.

23 See Stambler interview in this volume, page 43.

24 The source of the quotation is Allen Ginsberg's translation of a line from Apollinaire's "Les collines" ("The Hills"), which appears in the Ginsberg poem "Death to Van Gogh's Ear." Edward Sanders, *Investigative Poetry* (San Francisco: City Lights, 1976), 11.

25 Sanders, *Investigative Poetry*, 19, 9.

26 Sanders, *Investigative Poetry*, 11.

27 Edward Sanders, *The Z-D Generation* (Barrytown, NY: Station Hill Press, 1981), n.p.

28 Robert Creeley, "Tell the Story," *Review of Contemporary Fiction* 19, no. 1 (Spring 1999): 58–60; and Kristin Prevallet, "Investigating the Procedure: Poetry and the Source," in *Telling It Slant: Avant-Garde Poetics of the 1990s*, ed. Mark Wallace and Steven Marks (Tuscaloosa, AL: University of Alabama Press, 2002), 115–29.

29 Douglas Brinkley, interviewed on *All Things Considered*, National Public Radio, March 21, 2001; Jim Vernon, "Hegel, Ed Sanders, and Emancipatory History" *Clio* 41, no. 2 (2012): 27–52.

30 Edward Sanders, *1968: A History in Verse* (Santa Rosa, CA: Black Sparrow, 1997).

31 Prevallet, "Investigating the Procedure: Poetry and the Source," 125.

32 Sanders, *1968*, 246.

33 Creeley, "Tell the Story," 60.

34 Edward Sanders, *Shards of God* (New York: Grove, 1970), x.

35 Sanders, *Shards of God*, ix.

36 Kasia Boddy, "*Shards of God*: An Epicinian to the Heroes of the Peace Swarm," *Review of Contemporary Fiction* 19, no. 1 (Spring 1999): 61–80.

37 Sanders, *Shards of God*, n.p.

38 Lance Olsen, "Divining the Avant-Pop Afterburn: *Fame & Love in New York*," *Review of Contemporary Fiction*, 19, no. 1 (Spring 1999): 99–100.

39 Sanders, *Tales of Beatnik Glory*, 1.

40 Edward Sanders, *A Book of Glyphs* (New York: Granary Books, 2014), n.p.

41 Mollin cites her interview with Sanders and also refers to *Tales of Beatnik Glory* in her book, *Radical Pacifism in Modern America: Egalitarianism and Protest* (Philadelphia: University of Pennsylvania Press, 2006).

Chronology

1939
Born James Edward Sanders, August 17, 1939, in Kansas City, Missouri, to Lyle David Sanders and Mollie Cravens Sanders.

1957
Death of Mollie Cravens Sanders in March. Sanders reads "Howl" as a high school senior.

1957–58
Attends University of Missouri.

1958
Inspired by "Howl" and *On the Road*, hitchhikes to New York in the summer and enrolls in New York University, majors in Greek, and also studies Egyptian hieroglyphics. Works as a clerk in a Times Square cigar store.

1961
Marries Miriam Kittell.

Active in the pacifist movement. Participates in protest against above ground testing of nuclear weapons at the Russian Mission to the United States. Joins in San Francisco to Moscow Walk for Peace sponsored by the Committee for Nonviolent Action (CNVA). Participates in a peace vigil and the Polaris Action, protesting nuclear armed submarines, by swimming out to a submarine (twice) in New London, Connecticut. Sanders's civil disobedience results in his arrest and imprisonment in the Montville State Jail in Uncasville, Connecticut, August 8–24.

Writes *Poem from Jail* while in jail in Connecticut.

1962

Works in NYU purchasing department.

Participates in a sit-in at the New York branch of the Atomic Energy Commission, arrested for disorderly conduct and serves sentence of ten days. Participates in Walk for Peace from Nashville to Washington, D.C.

Begins publishing *Fuck You/A Magazine of the Arts,* which published many of the avant-garde poets of the 1960s. (There were 13 issues from 1962 to 1965.) Fuck You Press also published poetry and other literary monographs. Inspired by the underground film scene, begins experimenting with film with advice from Jonas Mekas and Harry Smith.

1963

Sanders rents an apartment in a back building on Avenue A which was used for Fuck You Press and as a studio for underground films, designated as "a secret location on the Lower East Side" in the Press's publications.

Participates in the Great March on Washington, D.C. for civil rights and economic opportunity in August.

Poem from Jail published.

1964

Daughter Dierdre born. Receives B.A. in Greek from NYU.

Active in Lower East Side poetry readings at Le Metro, Five Spot, Diane di Prima's New York Poets Theatre. Opens Peace Eye Bookstore, located on East 10th Street between Avenues A and B. Meets Allen Ginsberg, a lifelong friend and mentor. Founds LeMar (organization promoting the legalization of marijuana) in New York with Allen

Ginsberg. Begins correspondence with Charles Olson, his later lifelong friend and mentor.

King Lord/Queen Freak and *The Toe Queen Poems* published. Sanders's Fuck You Press publishes William S. Burroughs's "Roosevelt After Inauguration" as a monograph, a collaboration with Allen Ginsberg.

The Fugs, a satirical folk-rock band, is founded by Sanders and Tuli Kupferberg to set poetry to music. The band's most active years were between 1965 and 1970, when they toured extensively in the United States and Europe, often appearing at anti-war activities and other political events. During that time, they had a run of over 700 performances at the Players Theatre in New York City. Six albums were recorded between 1965 and 1969. The core players during this period were Sanders, Kupferberg, and Ken Weaver.

1965
Sanders is one of the poets who reads at the Berkeley Poetry Conference, a seminal event for the younger generation of poets influenced by the Beat, Black Mountain, and San Francisco Renaissance movements. In the spring, Sanders is invited to read at SUNY Buffalo by Charles Olson where he meets Olson for the first time.

Police raid the "secret location," looking for marijuana, and take all of Sanders's films, which are never recovered.

Peace Eye published with introduction by Charles Olson. *The Complete Sex Poems* published. Final issue of *Fuck You/A Magazine of the Arts* published. Two issues of the *Marijuana Newsletter* published.

The Fugs Song Book! published. The Fugs first album, *The Village Fugs*, released.

1966
Peace Eye bookstore is raided by police. Sanders is charged with obscenity based on copies of *Fuck You/A Magazine of the Arts* found in the bookstore. He is defended by the ACLU.

Sanders receives a National Endowment for the Arts Fellowship.

The Fugs second album, *The Fugs*, released.

Sanders's poetry, magazine, and the Fugs are featured in John Gruen's *The New Bohemia: The Combine Generation.*

1967

The Fugs participate in the Week of the Angry Arts in which New York artists staged a variety of public performances to protest the war in Vietnam.

Sanders is on the cover of *Life* magazine, February 17, for an article on the underground culture, called by *Life*, "the other culture." The Fugs interviewed on *David Susskind Show.*

May 22, obscenity case against Sanders dismissed.

Participates in the October march on the Pentagon protesting the war in Vietnam and in the exorcism of the Pentagon as part of the demonstration.

Sanders's Fuck You Press publishes *Cantos* 110-116 by Ezra Pound. Sanders receives the Frank O'Hara Prize from the Modern Poetry Association.

Virgin Fugs album released.

1968

In January, Yippie (Youth International Party) founded with Abbie Hoffman and Jerry Rubin. In February, with other Yippies, Sanders plans the "Festival of Life," a rock festival and youth/hippie gathering to take place in Chicago as a counter-demonstration to the Democratic National Convention. Democratic National Convention takes place in Chicago in August. The Yippie festival is disrupted by Chicago police.

Peace Eye moves to former office of the *East Village Other* on Avenue A near 9th Street.

Sanders appears on William F. Buckley's *Firing Line* with Jack Kerouac and sociologist Lewis Yablonsky, September 3, 1968.

"The Hairy Table" published in *San Francisco Earthquake* 1 (summer/fall 1968), 39-44.

In November, Sanders organizes what may have been the first underground comics exhibit at Peace Eye bookstore.

Fugs albums *Tenderness Junction* and *It Crawled into My Hand, Honest* released.

1969

"The Hairy Table" selected for an NEA/Viking Press anthology (*The American Literary Anthology*/3), awarded $1000 prize from NEA. Sanders is asked to withdraw from the anthology to save NEA from feared cuts by Congressional representatives.

Belle of Avenue A released. The Fugs are disbanded.

Death of Jack Kerouac.

1970

Sanders and his family move to the West Village. He closes the Peace Eye bookstore.

Sanders testifies at the Chicago 7 trial.

Sanders goes to Los Angeles to research the Manson Family killings, writes about Manson trial for *Los Angeles Free Press* from May to November.

Shards of God published.

Sanders included in *Anthology of New York Poets*, edited by Rod Padgett and David Shapiro.

Golden Filth released. *Sanders Truckstop*, his single album, released.

Death of Charles Olson.

1971

The Family: The Story of Charles Manson's Dune Buggy Attack Battalion published. Revised editions published in 1990 and 2002.

1972

Vote!, co-authored with Abbie Hoffman and Jerry Rubin, published.

Single album, *Beer Cans on the Moon* released.

Sanders is included in Allen De Loach's anthology *The East Side Scene: American Poetry, 1960-1965*.

1973

Egyptian Hieroglyphs published.

1974

Sanders and his family move to Woodstock, New York.

1975

Tales of Beatnik Glory, Volume I, published.

Fugs Four, Rounders Score released. *Two Toughs: Ed Sanders and Michael Brownstein* released.

1976

Investigative Poetry and *20,000 A.D.* published.

1977

Teaches classes in the summer at Naropa University, off and on, from 1977 to the present on investigative poetry, theory and practice of writing book-length poems, on operating small town newspapers, and setting poems to music.

Sanders begins to invent small electronic instruments he calls the EBS (Electronic Bard System), used to accompany poetry readings.

The Party: A Chronological Perspective on a Confrontation at a Buddhist Seminary published. *Love and the Falling Iron* published.

1978

Municipal Power Cantata is performed in Woodstock.

1979

The Silkwood Cantata is performed at the Creative Music Studio in Woodstock.

1980

Fame & Love in New York published.

1981

Z-D Generation and *The Cutting Prow* published.

1982

Sanders's poetry is included in *The Postmoderns: The New American Poetry Revised*, edited by Donald Allen and George F. Butterick.

Proto-Punk: The Fugs' Greatest Hits Vol. One released.

1983

Sanders awarded Guggenheim Fellowship for poetry. Delivers the Charles Olson Memorial Lectures at State University of New York at Buffalo in March.

Sanders is included in the *Dictionary of Literary Biography*, volume 16, *The Beats: Literary Bohemians in Postwar America,* edited by Ann Charters.

1984

A Fugs reunion band is formed in Woodstock (including Sanders, Kupferberg, Steve Taylor, Scott Petito, Coby Batty), performs annually for next 15 years in the United States and Europe. The NRS studio, in Woodstock, New York, owned by Petito, becomes the Fugs headquarters.

1985

Hymn to Maple Syrup and Other Poems published.

Fugs's albums *Refuse to be Burnt Out* and *Baskets of Love* released.

1986

The Fugs perform *Star Peace* as a response to Reagan's "Star Wars" plan. The opera is produced at the Syracuse Stage in Syracuse, New York, and at the Oslo International Poetry Festival. A two-disk album released.

Fugs album *No More Slavery* released.

1987

Sanders receives a National Endowment for the Arts Fellowship.

Thirsting for Peace in a Raging Century, Selected Poems 1961-1985 published, receives American Book Award in 1988. *Poems for Robin* published.

Star Peace released.

1988

Sanders chairs a committee to rewrite the Woodstock zoning law.

1989

The Fugs Live in Woodstock released.

1990

Tales of Beatnik Glory, Volumes I & II, *Ocean Étude and Other Poems*, *The Family* (revised), published.

Songs from a Portable Forest (best of the 1980s reunions) released. Sanders's single album, *Songs in Ancient Greek* released.

1991

Sanders included in *Out of this World: An Anthology of the St. Mark's Poetry Project*, 1966-1991, edited by Anne Waldman.

Sanders's single album, *Yiddish-Speaking Socialists of the Lower East Side* released.

1992

Sanders included in Viking anthology, *The Portable Beat Reader*, edited by Ann Charters.

1993

Ed and Miriam Sanders produce a local news and commentary program on the Woodstock public access channel from 1993-1997: "The Sanders Report" and "The Woodstock News."

Hymn to the Rebel Cafe published.

Cassandra, a musical drama, is produced by the Woodstock Guild in August/September.

1994

Cracks of Grace published.

Sanders included in the Norton anthology *Postmodern American Poetry*, edited by Paul Hoover.

The Fugs organize the Real Woodstock Festival (on the twenty-fifth anniversary of the original event), held in August. *Fugs Live from the 60s* released.

Sanders produces "The New Amazing Grace," with contributions from over 100 American poets and musicians, at the Poetry Project in St. Mark's Church, New York (published on his website).

1995

Teaches classes at the Schule für Dichtung (Vienna Poetry School) off and on from 1995 to the present. Courses offered on biographies in verse and the poetics of Sappho, Allen Ginsberg, and Jim Morrison.

Ed and Miriam Sanders begin publishing the *Woodstock Journal*, a bi-weekly newspaper. After eight years, it is transformed into a website.

Chekhov, A Biography in Verse published.

The Real Woodstock Festival, 2-CD set, released.

1996

American Bard, single album released.

1997

Awarded a fellowship by the Foundation for Contemporary Performing Arts. Receives a Writers Community residency sponsored by the YMCA National Writer's Voice through the Lila Wallace Readers Digest Fund.

Gives a talk at the Rock and Roll Hall of Fame as part of a special exhibit "I Want to Take You Higher: The Psychedelic Era 1965-1969."

1968: A History in Verse published.

Death of Allen Ginsberg.

Death of William S. Burroughs.

1998

Sanders included in New York Public Library Exhibit, "A Secret Location on the Lower East Side," devoted to small press publishing of avant-garde poetry ("the mimeograph revolution") in San Francisco and New York.

Sanders included in anthology, *Poems for the New Millennium: The University of California Book of Modern & Postmodern Poetry*, volume 2, edited by Jerome Rothenberg and Pierre Joris.

Begins research for *America, A History in Verse.*

1999

Sanders performs "Thirsting for Peace in a Raging Century" at the American Festival of Microtonal Music at Columbia University.

The Fugs hold a reunion concert, The Real Woodstock Festival II in Woodstock (thirtieth anniversary of the 1969 festival).

The *Review of Contemporary Fiction* publishes a special issue on Sanders' fiction edited by Brooke Horvath.

2000

Writer in Residence, New York State Writers Institute, Albany, NY.

The Poetry and Life of Allen Ginsberg published.

Volume I and Volume 2 of *America: A History in Verse* published.

2001

"A Tribute to Sappho—A Talk with Music" performed at Poet's House, New York City, March 30 (published on Sanders's website).

Sanders included in anthology, *Beat Down to Your Soul*, edited by Ann Charters.

Death of Gregory Corso

2002

The Family (revised) published.

2003

Writer in Residence, New York State Writers Institute.

The Fugs Final CD (Part 1) released.

2004

Stanzas for Social Change published. Volume 3 of *America: A History in Verse* published. *Tales of Beatnik Glory*, Volumes I-IV, published.

Sanders included in *Civil Disobediences: Poetics and Politics in Action*, edited by Anne Waldman and Lisa Birman.

2005
Thirsting for Peace, single album, released.

2006
Ed and Miriam Sanders produce a local news and commentary program on the Woodstock public access channel from 2006 to the present.

2007
Poems for New Orleans released, awarded "Best Poetry CD for 2007" by About.com.

2008
Poems for New Orleans, *This Morning's Joy*, and *Revs of the Morrow* published.

Don't Stop! Don't Stop!—4-CD boxed set of early Fugs songs released.

2009
Let's Not Keep Fighting the Trojan War published.

CD-ROM released: *America, A History in Verse, the 20th Century*, Volumes 1-4, 1900-2000. Includes the booklet, "The Writing of *America, A History in Verse.*"

2010
"History of the Fugs" published on The Fugs official website.

Be Free: The Fugs Final CD (Part 2) released.

Death of Tuli Kupferberg.

2011
Fug You—An Informal History of the Peace Eye Bookstore, the Fuck You Press, the Fugs and Counterculture in the Lower East Side published.

2012
Receives PEN Oakland Josephine Miles Literary Award.

Boo-Hooray Gallery exhibit of full run of *Fuck You/A Magazine of the Arts* (New York City).

The Fugs Greatest Hits, 1984-2004 released.

2013
Sanders is included in *The Cool School: Writing from American's Hip Underground* edited by Glenn O'Brien.

2014
A Book of Glyphs published.

2015
Exhibition, "Seeking the Glyph: Edward Sanders" at Poets House, New York City, features Sanders' glyphic work from 1962 to the present.

2016
Sharon Tate: A Life published.

2017
The Fugs exorcise the White House on fiftieth anniversary of their exorcism of the Pentagon. The exorcism of the White House has its premiere performance at Cooper Union in New York City on April 30, 2017. The Fugs also perform a live version of the exorcism at a demonstration sponsored by Veterans for Peace at the Lincoln Memorial in DC.

2018
Sanders gives the Annual Charles Olson Lecture: "A Life of Olson, with Glyphs" at the Cape Ann Museum, Gloucester, MA.

Broken Glory: the final Years of Robert F. Kennedy and *A life of Olson: A Sequence of Glyphs on Points of His Life, Work and Times* published.

Premier of *Cassandra*, a multimedia poetic drama at the Burchfield Penney Art Center, Buffalo, New York.

Published and Recorded Works by Ed Sanders

Books

Poetry (including pamphlets, chap books)

Poem from Jail. San Francisco: City Lights, 1963.

KingLord/Queen Freak. Cleveland: Renegade, 1964.

The Toe Queen Poems. New York: Fuck You, 1964.

The Complete Sex Poems. New York: Fug Press, 1965.

Peace Eye. Buffalo, NY: Frontier, 1965. Rev. ed. Cleveland: Frontier, 1967.

Egyptian Hieroglyphics. Canton, NY: Institute for Further Studies, 1973.

20,000 A.D. Plainfield, VT: North Atlantic Books, 1976.

Love and the Falling Iron. Bolinas, CA: Yanagi, 1977.

The Municipal Power Cantata. With Eli Waldron, Ilene Marder, and Martin Fleer. Woodstock, NY: Poetry, Crime & Culture, 1978.

The Cutting Prow. Santa Barbara: Am Here Books, 1981.

The Z-D Generation. Barryton, NY: Station Hill, 1981.

Hymn to Maple Syrup and Other Poems. Woodstock, NY: Poetry, Crime & Culture, 1985.

Poems for Robin. Woodstock, NY: Poetry, Crime & Culture, 1987.

Thirsting for Peace in a Raging Century: Selected Poems 1961–1985. Minneapolis: Coffee House, 1987. Rev. ed. Minneapolis: Coffee House, 2009.

The Ocean Étude and Other Poems. Woodstock, NY: PCC, 1990.

Hymn to the Rebel Cafe. Santa Rosa: Black Sparrow, 1993.

Cracks of Grace. Kenosha, WI: Membrane, 1994.

Chekhov, A Biography in Verse. Santa Rosa: Black Sparrow, 1995.

1968, A History in Verse. Santa Rosa: Black Sparrow, 1997.

America, A History in Verse. Vol. 1, 1900–1939. Santa Rosa: Black Sparrow, 2000.

America, A History in Verse. Vol. 2, 1940–1961. Santa Rosa: Black Sparrow, 2000.

The Poetry and Life of Allen Ginsberg. Woodstock, NY: Overlook, 2000.

America, A History in Verse. Vol. 3, 1962–1970. Santa Rosa: Black Sparrow, 2004.

Stanzas for Social Change. Kathmandu: Shivaston, 2004.

Poems for New Orleans. Berkeley: North Atlantic, 2008.

Revs of the Morrow. New York: Libellum, 2008.

This Morning's Joy. Boise, ID: Limberlost, 2008.

America, A History in Verse. Vols. 1–5, America, the 20th Century. CD-ROM with descriptive booklet. Woodstock, NY: Blake Route, 2009.

Let's Not Keep Fighting the Trojan War: New and Selected Poems 1986–2009. Minneapolis: Coffee House, 2009.

Broken Glory: The Final Years of Robert F. Kennedy. With Rick Veitch. New York: Arcade, 2018.

A Life of Olson: A Sequence of Glyphs on Points of His Life, Work and Times. Woodstock, NY: Meads Mountain Press, 2018.

Fiction

Shards of God. New York: Grove, 1970.

Tales of Beatnik Glory. Vol. 1. New York: Stonehill, 1975.

Fame & Love in New York. Berkeley: Turtle Island Foundation, 1980.

Tales of Beatnik Glory. Vols. 1–2. New York: Citadel Underground, 1990.

Tales of Beatnik Glory. Vols. 1–4. New York: Thunder's Mouth, 2004.

Non-Fiction

The Family: The Story of Charles Manson's Dune Buggy Attack Battalion. New York: Dutton, 1971. Rev. ed. *The Family: The Manson Group and Aftermath.* New York: Signet NAL, 1990. Rev. ed. *The Family.* Boston: Da Capo, 2002.

Vote! With Abby Hoffman and Jerry Rubin. New York: Warner Paperback Library, 1972.

Investigative Poetry. San Francisco: City Lights, 1976.

The Party: A Chronological Perspective on a Confrontation at a Buddhist Seminary. Woodstock, NY: Crime & Culture, 1977.

Fug You—An Informal History of the Peace Eye Bookstore, the Fuck You Press, the Fugs and Counterculture in the Lower East Side. Boston: Da Capo, 2011.

Sharon Tate: A Life. Boston: Da Capo, 2016.

Edited Books/Pamphlets

Poems for Marilyn. New York: Fuck You, 1962.

Bugger: An Anthology of Buttockry. New York: Fuck You, 1964.

Despair: Poems to Come Down By. New York: Fuck You, 1964.

Roosevelt After Inauguration, by William S. Burroughs. New York: Fuck You, 1964.

The Vancouver Report, by Carol Bergé. New York: Fuck You, 1964.

A Variorum Edition of the Entire Extant Works of Thales! New York: Fuck You, 1964.

The Fugs' Song Book! With Ken Weaver and Betsy Klein. New York:

Peace Eye Bookstore, 1965. Detroit: Artists' Workshop, 1966.

Health Bulletin: APO-33, A Metabolic Regulator, by William S. Burroughs. New York: Fuck You, 1965.

The Platonic Blow. By W. H. Auden. New York: Fuck You, 1965.

The Cantos of Ezra Pound, 110–116. New York: Fuck You, 1967.

Fuck God in the Ass: A Response to the Napalming of Vietnamese Children. New York: Fuck You, 1967.

Magazines

Fuck You/A Magazine of the Arts. Poetry magazine, 13 issues. New York, 1962–1965.

Marijuana Newsletter. Publication of the Committee to Legalize Marijuana (LeMar), 2 issues. New York, 1965.

Newspaper

Woodstock Journal. With Miriam Sanders. Bi-weekly newspaper, 177 issues, Woodstock, NY, 1995–2003.

Website

Woodstock Journal. http://www.woodstockjournal.com.

Glyphs

A Book of Glyphs. New York: Granary Books, 2014.

Recordings (Music Albums and CDs)

The Fugs

The Village Fugs Sing Ballads of Contemporary Protest, Points of View, and General Dissatisfaction. Broadside-Folkways, 1965. LP. Reissued as *The Fugs First Album.* ESP and Base, 1966. LP. Reissued with additional tracks, Ace, 1993 and Fantasy Records, 1994. CD.

The Fugs, ESP, 1966. LP. Reissued with additional tracks as *The Fugs*

Second Album. Fantasy Records and Ace, 1993. CD.

Virgin Fugs. ESP and Base, 1967. LP.

Tenderness Junction. With Allen Ginsberg and Gregory Corso. Reprise, 1968. LP.

It Crawled into My Hand, Honest. Reprise, 1968. LP. Edsel, 1986. CD.

The Belle of Avenue A. Reprise, 1969. LP.

Golden Filth: Fugs Live at the Fillmore East. Reprise, 1970. LP.

Fugs Four, Rounders Score. With the Holy Modal Rounders. ESP, 1975. LP.

Proto-Punk: The Fugs' Greatest Hits Vol. One. Adelphi, 1982. PVC, 1983.

Refuse to Be Burnt Out. New Rose and Olufsen, 1985. CD. With additional tracks, Ace 1994. CD.

Baskets of Love. Olufsen, 1985. CD.

No More Slavery. New Rose and Olufsen, 1986. CD. With additional tracks, Ace 1994. CD.

Star Peace. New Rose and Olufsen, 1987. CD.

Fugs Live in Woodstock. Musik/Musik, 1989. CD.

Songs from a Portable Forest: The Best of the Fugs 1984–1989. Gazell, 1990. CD.

The Fugs Live from the 60s. Ace, 1994. CD.

The Real Woodstock Festival 1994. Ace, 1995. CD.

The Fugs Final CD (Part One). Artemis, 2003. CD.

Don't Stop! Don't Stop! Ace, 2008. CD.

Be Free, The Fugs Final CD (Part Two). Fugs Records, 2010. CD.

The Fugs Greatest Hits, 1984–2004. Fugs Records, 2012. CD.

Sanders Solo

Sanders' Truckstop. Reprise, 1970. LP.

Beer Cans on the Moon. Reprise, 1972. LP.

Two Toughs: Ed Sanders and Michael Brownstein. Naropa Institute, 1975. LP.

Songs in Ancient Greek. Olufsen, 1990. CD.

Yiddish-Speaking Socialists of the Lower East Side. Hyperaction, 1991. CD.

American Bard. Olufsen, 1996. CD.

Thirsting for Peace. Olufsen, 2005. CD.

Poems for New Orleans. Paris Records, 2007. CD.

An Interview with Ed Sanders

John Wilcock

Originally published in The Village Voice, *June 17, 1965, 2. Reprinted by permission of* The Village Voice.

The nearest thing that the rebel New York underground has as a headquarters is the shabby Peace Eye Bookstore near Tompkins Square on the lower East Side. Here, invariably surrounded by plotters, protesters, and pamphleteers, shaggy-haired Ed Sanders operates a rickety mimeograph machine turning out a non-stop series of brochures, newsletters, catalogs of esoterica, and a legendary revolutionary organ which has been euphemistically tagged (by the uptown glossy magazines) as *Love You*, and whose real title will be found in the interview that follows.

John Wilcock: How old are you?

Ed Sanders: Twenty-five.

Wilcock: What is people's first reaction to the title *Fuck You/a Magazine of the Arts*?

Sanders: Occasionally, a reader will go insane with rage. Tight-assed people sometimes giggle. Some let their eyes glaze over and look bored. At cocktail parties in Michigan they burn it. The Mexican border police register disgust. But most are friendly and very curious.

Wilcock: Do you ever bother to justify or explain it?

Sanders: Of course. I usually try to explain what I am doing: a word should have one basic meaning; a lovely word like fuck, or fuck you, should not have hateful, pejorative connotations. I try to explain about the LSD Communarium, freedom for hallucinogens, God through cannabis, grope for peace, etc., etc.

Wilcock: What is the philosophy that guides your choice of content?

Sanders: The philosophy of Total Assault on the Culture. I print the poetry I like plus occasional free-verse gutter doggerel. As for the editorials, notes on contributors, peace statements, and Egyptian freak-doodles, I pretend that the United States is a very permissive asylum and act accordingly.

Wilcock: You frequently make reference to a mythology I know nothing about, with your references to the Sun God Ra, etc. Whence?

Sanders: In the early '60s, I studied Plotinus, Poe, St. John of the Cross, telepathy, and Bop Kaballa. In 1957 I had certain religious visions of a solar (Sun God Ra) nature which created an interest in things Egyptian. In order to read certain cantos of Ezra Pound in 1961 I studied Egyptian hieroglyphics at the New School and on my own. When I started freaking out F.Y. in 1962, I sprayed my Egyptian studies into the editorial format.

Wilcock: You've moved the language forward in great strides, particularly with your 42nd Street freak-sex scene vocabulary—are your creating slang or recording it?

Sanders: Time Square has held my interest for many years; I've even worked at a cigar store at 42nd and Broadway for the last five. I synthesize and sometimes create slang, but more often I record it from the freak-language of my friends. I borrow from crooks, hustlers, queens, dope-freaks, amphetamine-heads, poets, Ginsberg, Professor Frank Peters, Charles Olson, the Ted Berrigan Conspiracy, and other sources. I've learned much from the brilliant techniques of William Burroughs.

Wilcock: You're married? Your wife is your private life?

Sanders: I keep my wife strapped into a Perfumed Garden at a secret 27th Street scene.

Wilcock: Who finances *Fuck You*?

Sanders: A leading Ezra Pound scholar, a millionaire painter, an uptown publisher, and a cartel of 17 Time Square toe queens.

Wilcock: Is there an official price? Do you charge anybody?

Sanders: I give *Fuck You/A Magazine of the Arts* away free, as they come out. Complete runs of all back issues I sell to university libraries and collectors to help finance new issues. Many of the major universities in the country have full sets.

Wilcock: Why did the FBI visit you?

Sanders: They think I'm wonderful.

Wilcock: Who are the Fugs?

Sanders: The Fugs are a rock and roll, folk, and poetry spew-singing group operating as an emanation of the culture of the lower East Side. All of their 40 or so songs are original creations or adaptations of poems. We believe in BODY POETRY. That is, the Fugs work through the genitals and the Big Beat to get to the brain, and through the brain and the Big Beat to get to the genitals, thus creating a thrilling cross-current. You can freak all this out in our forthcoming Folkways record album.

Wilcock: What are some of your other activities?

Sanders: Co-editor of the Marijuana Newsletter, formed to promote legalization of marijuana; I operate the Peace Eye Bookstore and Scrounge Lounge, in the lower East Side; I'm publisher and editor of several anthologies of poetry, among them *Banana*, *Despair*, *Bugger*, and *Suck*; I'm a veteran East Side bar creep. Currently I'm shooting short films at my secret movie studio to show with the Fug songs. That is, I'm creating a movie/music system called the Fugitone: among the first to be shot are "Coca Cola Douche," "Bull Tongue Clit," and the "I Saw the Best Minds of My Generation Rock."

The Hippies

William F. Buckley, Jr.

Originally broadcast on the television program, Firing Line *with William F. Buckley, Jr., September 3, 1968. The interview is available from the Hoover Institution at Stanford University, identified as* Firing Line *with William F. Buckley Jr., Program 113 "The Hippies," Hoover Institution Archives. This transcript was prepared by Jennie Skerl and printed with the permission of the Hoover Institution.*

William Buckley: Our topic tonight is the Hippies, the understanding of which we must, I guess, acquire or die painfully. We certainly should make considerable progress in the next hour because we have a professional student of hippies, and also someone who is said to have started the whole Beat Generation business, and finally a hippie type who can correct us, ever so gently please, if we're wrong.

Mr. Lewis Yablonsky is a sociologist who studied at Rutgers and took his doctorate at New York University and teaches at San Fernando State College in California, where he is chairman of his department. His first book, which focused on teenage gang life and drug addiction, prepared him for his magnum opus, which is called *The Hippie Trip: A Firsthand Account of the Beliefs and Behavior of Hippies in America.*

Mr. Jack Kerouac over here became famous when his book *On the Road* was published. It seemed to be preaching a life of disengagement, making a virtue out of restlessness. The irony is that when the book was belatedly published in 1958, seven years after it was written, Mr. Kerouac had fought his way out of the Beat Generation, and is now not exactly orthodox, at least a regular practicing novelist, whose thirteenth book, *The Vanity of Duluoz*, is widely regarded as his best.

Mr. Ed Sanders is a musician, a poet, and a polemicist. He is one of the Fugs, a widely patronized combo. He has published four books of poetry and has vigorously preached pacifism for a number of years. I'd like to begin by asking Mr. Sanders whether we have serious terminological problems. For instance, are you a hippie, Mr. Sanders, and if not, wherein not?

Sanders: Well, I'm not exactly a hippie. I have certain sentiments toward that, quote hippie movement, unquote, I would say that I differ from the hippies in that I would have a more radical political solution to the problems of this part of the century. And I have my roots more strongly in, say, the classical tradition and in poetry and literature rather than in dope and street sex.

Kerouac: And you published that magazine called what?

Sanders: Called *Gutter Expletive/A Magazine of the Arts.*

[Audience laughter]

Buckley: Do I understand from this, that we are supposed to make the inference that the hippies don't have a highly developed political schedule, a highly developed political ideology.

Sanders: The problem with the term like "hippie" is that they have a definition foisted on them by the media, and that the word "hippie" has been limited by the necessities of the type of journalists that promote it. You can't rely on the name "hippie" to include a human being, everything about a particular human being. It's a bad term, I think, because it has no meaning; you might think of hippopotamus. It has no other connection, spiritual or emotional, like say, the Beat Generation title has. It has other implications. The word hippie, you immediately think of—you don't have any good connections—

Yablonsky: I kind of disagree with that. I spent last year traveling around the country to various communes, to various—Haight Ashbury, the Lower East Side, various city scenes—and there was an identifiable—define a hippie as generally a young person—in several categories.

There's kind of a priestly type: I would include Allen Ginsberg and Tim Leary, and individuals like that in that category. People searching for some loving solutions to society's ills, trying to tune into the cosmos—whatever that means—we can explore that. Generally using psychedelic drugs. And then there's a whole cadre of individuals—

Kerouac: [interrupting] Cadré.

Yablonsky: —whom I term novices, who are attempting to achieve a certain transcendental state. Then there are teeny bopper kids who are sort of hanging on, and there are some ancient folks like Kerouac here who—

Kerouac: What do you mean ancient?

Yablonsky: Why couldn't you have kept quiet while I was talking? I'll keep quiet while you talk.

Buckley: I think that's fair enough.

Kerouac: You said cadres; it's cadrés.

Yablonsky: I apologize for my semantics.

Kerouac: And I showed thumbs down to Ginsberg over there in the back. [Ginsberg was in the audience.]

Yablonsky: He's a nice fellow.

Kerouac: Yeah, we'll throw him to the lions.

Buckley: Well, what about it, Mr. Kerouac? You're exercised about something, by something—

Kerouac: Restless, it's true. You had the right word, restless.

Buckley: What is it in your judgment distinguishes the hippie movement from, for instance, simply a routine radical—

Kerouac: [interrupting] Get your question over with!

Buckley: What distinguishes the hippie movement from simply an orthodox radical, say, Adamite movement?

Kerouac: Nothing! Adamite? Adam and Eve, or atom?

Buckley: Adam, as in Adam and Eve.

Kerouac: What's with Adam and Eve? What's with Adamite? Where they wear their hair long, in caves?

Buckley: Yeah, sort of back to nature.

Kerouac: Might have to in due time with "atomite"—the bomb.

Buckley: [laughing] Hey, that was good, wasn't it? Give that man a drink.

Buckley: Now, Jack Kerouac, what I wanted to ask is this: to what extent do you believe that the Beat Generation is related to the hippies? What do they have in common? Was this an evolution from one to the other?

Kerouac: I'm just [one of] the older ones. I'm forty-six years old. These kids are eighteen. It's the same movement. It's apparently some kind of Dionysian movement, in late civilization, in which I did not intend, any more than I suppose Dionysus did, or whatever his name was. Although I'm not Dionysus, I should have been.

Buckley: That's a point.

Kerouac: It's just a movement which is supposed to be licentious, but it isn't really.

Buckley: Well, licentious in what respect?

Kerouac: The hippies are good kids. They're better than the Beats. The Beats, Ginsberg and I, we're all in our forties. He [Ginsberg] started this, and the kids took it up, and everything, but a lot of hoods, hoodlums and communists jumped on our backs. Well, on my back, not his [points to Ginsberg in the audience], Ferlinghetti jumped on my back and turned the idea that I had that the Beat Generation was a generation of beatitude and pleasure in life and tenderness, but they called it in the papers the Beat Mutiny and Beat Insurrection, words I never used. Being a Catholic, I believe in order, tenderness, and piety.

Buckley: Well, then your point was that a movement which you conceived as relatively pure has become ideologized and misanthropic and generally objectionable.

Kerouac: A movement that was considered what?

Buckley: Pure.

Kerouac: It was, in my heart.

Buckley: What about that Mr. Yablonsky? Do you see that as having happened somewhere between the Beats and the hippies.

Yablonsky: I think there's in early '67 going back to around '64 or '65, there were a lot of people trying to return to sort of an Indian-style of life, or to relate to the land differently, trying to love each other, and communicate and be more open with each other, and I think recently it has taken a turn in a violent direction. A lot of the responsibility, I think, is due to drugs like methedrine and amphetamines, and perhaps the overuse; it's been around quite a while now, of drugs like LSD—

Kerouac: How about the herring?

Buckley: What is herring? Is that kind of drug?

Sanders: Cherry Herring.

[Audience laughter]

Yablonsky: Kerouac is still on alcohol. There are other drugs now.

Buckley: What about it, Mr. Sanders, is that out of tone?

Sanders: You mention misanthropic and objectionable. Many of the so-called misanthropic elements of this generation are due to the war, in that you have a surly generation of draft eligible but literate and articulate people who are confronted with the hideous probability of having to go to an Asian land war. So they have to go to war, and they're faced with this looming, gloomy future, and that rather than die in Vietnam, they'd rather prepare themselves to articulate a lifestyle in the streets and in the open that really reflects something they really want to do, rather than this other thing they have to do later on that they don't believe in, but they will do, because push comes to shove most kids go to war.

Buckley: But the trouble with that is it doesn't account, for instance, for the restlessness in, say, Paris, where they don't have that particular problem.

Sanders: That's the up-against-the-wall syndrome—

[segment ends]

Buckley: Mr. Sanders, I'm interested in trying to pin this point down, because a lot of us heard that the restlessness of so much of American youth, which has contributed to the growth of the hippie movement has to do with the trauma of Vietnam, but then all of a sudden a while ago in France it seemed like the entire student population exploded even though that particular provocation was singularly, in fact, conspicuously absent, France having been officially very pro-North Vietnam, very anti-America. How do you account for that, and has it caused you to perhaps to look into more generic sources?

Sanders: I think it's the nefarious occurrence on French civilization of Madame de Gaulle.

Buckley: Madame de Gaulle?

Sanders: Because she has exercised a noxious influence on French television, sitting up and personally censoring it.[1]

[Audience laughter]

No, it's absolutely true, and I think that when you have a type of obnoxious matriarchy that's evident in France, plus an encrusted, boring, boorish university structure, and the old man himself: there's a huge structure there to revolt against.

Buckley: Madame de Gaulle is roughly equal to Vietnam.

Sanders: She's Madame Nhu.

Buckley: Professor Yablonsky, what would you say if a student of yours told you that?

Yablonsky: I think in the United States, the hippies, with all the difficulties of defining them, come from the middle/upper classes, upper social economic situations. These are generally people who have tasted the best that American society seems to have to offer, they have access to all the goodies, and they're turned off by it, and they feel it's kind of a plastic society. There's no room for political change. I'm talking about the pure hippie. A pure hippie isn't particularly involved in politics. He retreats from that, he's withdrawn from it, and he's involved in—I mentioned the term—cosmic consciousness before. There is an experience one seems to get under LSD, that a lot of people talk about, as putting them in touch with all things, with all people. There's a kind of extremist effort at love that seems to dominate the hippie scene, a retreat from politics.

---

1 Madame de Gaulle campaigned against nudity and sex on television.

Buckley: Is there a causal relation between their adopting these attitudes and the Vietnam War? Or do you reject the Vietnam War as the proximate cause of the movement?

Yablonsky: I think the Vietnam War is part of it.

Buckley: If we had had no Vietnam War, we might have had the identical thing—is that your point?

Yablonsky: I think there's no single cause for a particular movement. I think part of it may have been the assassination of JFK. I think that people on the left felt that through the establishment, through political devices, the society could move in other directions.

Buckley: In what direction was it moving in 1963 that was pleasing to them?

Yablonsky: There was a movement towards greater welfare programs, towards resolving in some way the civil rights issues. There seemed to be some hope, and then this seemed to be sapped off, and a lot of kids who went to Mississippi—

Buckley: It's precisely the movement that didn't get passed in 1961, '62, and '63, the time you just enumerated, [that was] passed in '64, 65, 66. So it seems there was almost a negative correlation between civil rights legislation and welfare passages and the growth of the movement.

Yablonsky: I think you can cross-compare the limited JFK administration and the rather lengthy LBJ administration. I think the LBJ situation has been going through the motions of doing something. I feel and a lot of people have told me this, a spirit afoot in the country. There seemed to be a bit of a revival with Bobby Kennedy, and to some extent the McCarthy involvement. I think a lot of people are turned off from the political establishment because they don't see any hope for changing it. They use terms like "plastic," and more severe words about it; they are disengaged; they're uncommitted to it.

Buckley: How about that, Mr. Kerouac, does that make sense to you?

Kerouac: I lost the entire train of thought.

Buckley: Well, the train of thought has to do with whether in the last few years people have ceased to look at the political process as possible in terms of bringing on the kind of world we want to live in, and maybe that has something to do with the assassination of Kennedy, and that kind of thing.

Kerouac: No, that was an accident. I refer back to Count Leo Tolstoy, who wrote *War and Peace*, who said that at one time the hourglass, that's the sand that's coming down from one top of the hourglass onto the other, and that will be the end of war. I think that war will be over fairly soon, although I don't know for sure. That's what Tolstoy said. The guy who taught Gandhi and Henry David Thoreau.

Buckley: Taught them a lot of foolish things.

Kerouac: I didn't get the full context of your question.

Buckley: Well, the full context of the question is, are a significant number of Americans precisely [unclear] when we enunciated the Great Society?

Kerouac: Oh, Great Society!

Buckley: I.e., the society that was actually going to introduce politics [unclear]. Are they disillusioned, and does this have to do with the growth of the hippie movement?

Kerouac: I think the Vietnamese War is nothing but a plot between the North Vietnamese and the South Vietnamese, who are cousins, to get jeeps from the country.

[Audience laughter]

Buckley: They're not very good plotters, are they?

Kerouac: But they got a lot of jeeps!

[Audience laughter]

I think they're pulling the wool over our eyes. We're American lambs.

Buckley: They turned out to be more expensive than Sears Roebuck jeeps.

Kerouac: That's what I really think there. As for the Russian takeover of Czechoslovakia, that showed the world what they're like, what the Communists are really like—they're really fascists.

Buckley: Mr. Sanders.

Sanders: It was a terrible thing. If I were in Czechoslovakia, and a Czechoslovakian student, I would be putting out an underground newspaper, and doing my best—

Kerouac: Called what?

Sanders: Called—Gutter Expletive/A Magazine of the Arts.

[Audience laughter]

Buckley: Since you aren't in Czechoslovakia, Mr. Sanders, what do you consider it appropriate to do in the United States?

Sanders: During the presidential campaign?

Buckley: By way of protest against the Czechoslovakian situation.

Sanders: Well, I recommend sit-ins in front of the Russian mission—

Kerouac: What for?

Sanders: To vigorously and more forcefully yet nonviolently to witness against it. I would advocate writing articles, and I would advocate maybe going to Czechoslovakia. The Fugs are going to Europe in a couple of weeks.

Kerouac: [interrupting] Bring your carbines?

Sanders: We're going to the Essen Song Festival in Germany, and we may just try to freak into Czechoslovakia to visit Kafka's birthplace. So, we may have a homage to Kafka with our band.

Buckley: Do you draw any generalities on the basis of the behavior of the Soviet Union which instruct you in assessing other political situations?

Sanders: Yeah, like Mayor Daley in Chicago.

Buckley: What are those?

Sanders: Well, those are that when you attempt to essentially get together to press a point about a war, about a freedom, or about freedom of journalism; when you're confronted by people like the Soviet leaders and like the leaders in Chicago, namely Mayor Daley and Mr. Stahl and Mr. Barger of the Chicago municipal office; and that you're confronted with essentially the same position: you're not allowed, you're clubbed, you're maced, you're gassed, you're freaked, zapped, pushed over. If you're an old lady, you're thrown through a plate glass widow; if you're a cripple, you're thrown against a streetlight; if you're a peaceful, long-haired, loving protester, you're smashed and knocked down; if you're a cameraman, you're bricked, and your camera is destroyed, and your blood is splattered all over you. It's a nefarious thing, and there's all kinds of correlations.

And the lesson you would draw, would be to prepare yourself, in the sense of, if you're nonviolent as I am, and if you believe in pacifism, you would attempt to create a body of love and life, so that that thing can't happen, that there will be so may loving people there, that you will have a Festival of Life and all its attributes, and you can do that by praying together, by loving together. Allen [Ginsberg] was singing Om in the streets, which is the Hindu benevolent word. By getting together and creating love, I think it's a great force, at least in allowing you to demonstrate in the United States against Daley—who is, you know, like Al Capone.

Buckley: Yeah.

Kerouac: Beware of false prophets, who come among you dressed in sheep's clothing, and underneath they are ravening wolves.

Sanders: Who's that?

[Segment ends]

Buckley: Mr. Yablonsky, I would like to ask you this because you have studied very carefully the whole hippie mentality. I was in Chicago, and so were a lot of people who would not really have recognized what happened on the basis of Mr. Sanders's description. But I do think that Mr. Sander means it; I think that he really thinks the cops were looking for old ladies to maim and gentle people to savage. And I think the fact he thinks it is interesting. I would like to hear your analysis that they seem to feel it is compulsive to believe a Daley, who after all is a hero of John F. Kennedy and Bobby Kennedy, whom you associate with the best aspirations of the youth, how come they feel this way—what is it in their creed that requires this?

Yablonsky: First of all, I wouldn't hook Daley in with JFK. He's a big city boss. I just observed you and others on television in Chicago.

Buckley: Nothing bellicose about me.

Yablonsky: I think that if the people who were involved, the hippies, or the Yippies, had been permitted to sort of do their thing, and to chant, and to have a peaceful march—

Buckley: Their thing involved the assassination of a few Democrats, wouldn't it?

Yablonsky: Oh, no, not at all.

Sanders: Absolutely not!

Yablonsky: I think there were around maybe ten thousand young people who would have sung peace songs in the park.

Buckley: But, in fact, they threw bricks.

Yablonsky: I think there was apparently a lot frustration of their efforts to do something—

Buckley: Now, wait a minute. You know Tom Hayden. You know Rennie Davis. You know these characters. Everybody here knows them. And we know these are not sweet little old flower children. They were intending to make a scientific, ideological point, which is to engage the police in violence in order—

Sanders: [interrupting] Not at—

Buckley: I'll be right with you—in order to try to produce a wave of sympathy which they succeeded and they are absolutely elated; it would have been impossible for the police to withdraw in such a way as to satisfy them, because the only way they could have been satisfied is by a forcible encounter.

Yablonsky: You asked me about the hippies and the Yippies, and I was talking about what they would have done. I tend to agree with you that there were other segments of the population, possibly including the Blackstone Rangers, and other groups who were prepared to stir something up if it didn't happen, but I think there was such an overreaction, such a trigger-finger kind of situation, that these kids began to open the thing up, and before anything could get going, there was a lot of smashing. And then the others moved in. I think there would have been a kind of a love-in type of scene in Chicago by a large segment of the young people.

Buckley: If you could have separated the two.

Sanders: Well, because they were very clearly separated. There were two movements operating in Chicago. The Yippies wanted Lincoln Park, which is many, many miles away from the Amphitheater [where the Democratic Convention was held], and is many miles away from the Hilton [where many politicians and news media were staying]. They wanted to have a Festival of Life with rock music in the park, with theater classes, with guerrilla theater, with like various poets and people coming together for a Festival of Life.

Buckley: What is guerrilla theater?

Sanders: Guerrilla theater is a bunch of people who do not need props and who don't need a regular stage.

Kerouac: Crucified chickens?

Sanders: No, that's not guerrilla theater. But guerrilla theater just need themselves, and their own body makeup, and a few props like that. Anyway, we wanted Lincoln Park, and wanted to use the beach to swim and sleep at. And the Chicago authorities continually thwarted us throughout a whole six months of negotiations, refusing at any point to allow any demonstrations, so they literally drove Allen [Ginsberg], Jean Genet, William Burroughs, and even Clive Barnes of The New York Times—were driven out of the park at night by tear gas.

Buckley: Good. That's terrible.

[Audience laughter]

Sanders: That's true. So all these people were forced into the streets, with no place to go, except for the benevolence of a couple of churches, to sleep. There was a bus strike in Chicago, there was a cab strike, and there was no live TV coverage of anything, so they were forced into the street. The police attacked, pushed, mauled, maimed; and it's really what happened.

Now the other movement was the Mobilization movement—they wanted to march upon the Amphitheater. And that's Rennie Davis, and that's Tom Hayden, but also Dave Dellinger, who's an avowed pacifist, and benevolent leader of some standing. And they wanted to have a peaceful march on the Amphitheater, split up into groups, and those who wanted to march on would march on, and those who wanted to sit down would sit down. But there was never any violent confrontation planned. And when the Chicago people thwarted and frustrated constantly anybody's attempts to have peaceful demonstrations, naturally frustration, it mounted. But the amount of brick throwing was so negligible compared to the number of peaceful people there for a peaceful purpose, namely, to protest with their loving bodies what was going down at the alcoholic Amphitheater.

Buckley: What were you saying, Mr. Kerouac?

Kerouac: I said there are people who make a rule of creating chaos so that, once the chaos is under way, they can then be elected as the people who take care of the chaos.

Buckley: And you think this applies to the Chicago situation?

Kerouac: No, I'm not talking about Daley. I don't know anything about it. I wasn't there. I'm talking about his [Sanders's] idea of protesting and running around and making noise all over the place. If you create chaos, you can become the commissar of the control of chaos.

Yablonsky: I think there was a situation that was operative there. To go back to Prague, maybe to the thirties, a guy named Capek wrote a book called RUR—a great writer—related to the Universal Robot; what he was doing was making a statement about the fact that man is turning into kind of a machine, that there's no love, there's no communication, no humanity, and in Chicago we had a political machine which was airtight, plastic, solid as a rock, and here were some antagonists, but not really antagonists. They were people who were trying to be spontaneous, to do something else, to loosen the situation up, and we had these forces, kind of at opposite ends of the continuum, and a clash took place. I think this was part of the problem there.

Buckley: I think that's an interesting theory, but I'm not sure how convincing it is in light of the fact that the Democratic Party was by no means airtight. It may have been airtight up against people who want to storm the Amphitheater and burn it down, but it was certainly not airtight in term of the tussles going on with it. There was very spirited debate and there was a very high permeability for ideas that were fired in from about every Democratic philosopher in America. In other words, this was not a Tito-like neat little nominating session.

Yablonsky: There was a lot of lip service given to an open convention, but I think that, at the heart of the matter, it was all set—

Buckley: When it's all set, it can mean nothing more than people have made up their minds. If we decide in this room that our duties to free speech require us to listen to the nostrums of, let's say, the Labor Progressive Party, but, having listened to them, we then proceed to reject them, I don't think we have the right to say that our views were airtight. A lot of people had decided that they wanted Humphrey, and a lot of people were not shaken, which does not necessarily make a static convention.

Sanders: But you do not have to stack the galleries with "We Love Daley" signs; you don't have to shake down Mrs. McCarthy, and search her purse when she's surrounded by four Secret Service guards; you don't have to run people up to the wall, and smack them down.

Buckley: Ah, that's ineptitude. A lot of people say you don't have to publish the sort of stuff you publish in order to love people.

Sanders: Well, you know, why don't we just unite with the Russians and dance around?

Kerouac: You know what my mother calls Humphrey?

Buckley: I don't know.

Kerouac: Fat fake floogie with a floy floy.

[Audience laughter]

Kerouac: And you know what Agnew's real name is? "Agnotnostopolis," which means the son of the reader. In Messina, in ancient Greece, the Turks have taken over ancient Greece, Messina, and they said, "Don't read. You're censored." And his father read all the books. Very proud name.

Buckley: I say someday you'll become vice president.

Kerouac: My father, my brother, and my sister, and I have always voted Republican. We voted for Hoover. I was six years old, voting for Hoover.

[Audience laughter]

Sanders: The only thing that type police state repression forces upon us is—the next convention we're going to have to take ten thousand of us and run naked through the streets smeared with strawberry preserves.

Kerouac: Maybe I can lick it.

Sanders: My wife, maybe. They force you into an incredible position in the world when you want to protest or you want to make your voice known in a benevolent way, and yet at the same time, you're pushed and clubbed.

Kerouac: You make yourself famous by protest.

Sanders: Who does? Not me. I make myself famous by singing smut.

Kerouac: I made myself famous by writing songs and lyrics about the beauty of the things that I did, and the ugliness, too.

Sanders: You're a great poet.

Kerouac: You made yourself famous by saying, "Down with this! Down with that!" Go exit this, go exit that.

Sanders: I hope not. That's not what I want.

Kerouac: Take it with you. I cannot use your abuse. You may have it back.

Sanders: You're a great poet, we admire you, in fact, it's your fault—

[Segment ends]

Buckley: Now, Mr. Yablonsky, in your book, you list what you call the psychedelic creed. I take it that these are articles of faith to which most hippies would adhere. I think it would be interesting to check them out with Mr. Sanders and Mr. Kerouac. For instance, you say that "the hippie movement is a spontaneous evolution, it is not a heavily worked out plan."

Yablonsky: I would say that those creeds are kind of summarizations based on several hundred interviews with people on the scene, and what they say, it's not—

Buckley: I know—it wasn't handed out on some tablet—you infer it. Now then you say, "Drugs are a key to the gods in men, drugs are sacraments for a greater knowledge of the universe, drugs are a vehicle to a cosmic consciousness." Is there a considerable consensus at this point?

Yablonsky: A lot of people in the movement do take the position that every man is a god, and it's a very individualistic kind of a movement. Each individual should be free to do his own thing. It's rather anarchist actually, and I think here are the seeds of its failure.

Buckley: How are standards arrived at in hippie culture—on the basis of which one decides whether somebody's thing is insufferable?

Yablonsky: I saw someone assaulting someone at a commune up in Northern California. I started to intervene, and several people rather gently said, "Well, he's just going through his violence bag. Let him do his own thing." And I said, "What if he kills him?" Their position was that everyone should be free to do their own number. I don't share this view—but this is part of the philosophy.

Buckley: Do you endorse that particular impulse, Mr. Sanders?

Sanders: I've seen a lot of communes, and I've never seen a commune that really tolerated violence. I think that's one of the chief characteristics of a community of free people, that they're there to get away from violence. And when there's like drug-induced violence or other types of violence, in my experience, it's generally quelled.

Yablonsky: Every commune I went to I saw some degree of violence, anarchy, and chaos, and they would tell me about another one, and I went to around four. The last one I was way back in the hills, and I was rather frightened, because there was a rather high degree of violence. There were a lot of people freaked out on drugs. It was a rather chaotic scene.

Buckley: And how do victims of this violence characteristically react?

Sanders: Ouch.

[Audience laugher]

Yablonsky: Like most people do.

Buckley: But they have no mechanisms to which to appeal.

Yablonsky: Right, this was one of the few times in my life that I wished there were police around.

Kerouac: It was the black flag of anarchy.

Buckley: Would you say their leaders are quote "spontaneous," they're not pushy leaders who are self-appointed. They are selected by hippie constituents, because they are called "spiritual centers." How are they selected, and what authority, once selected, do they have?

Yablonsky: The philosophical theme would be that certain individuals are purer, more loving, more tuned into nature and other people and that people seek them out.

Buckley: What power do they have?

Yablonsky: They deny having any. And claim to have no power.

Buckley: So that a victim in one of these situations would get nowhere by addressing his complaint to the quote "leader," because the leader would have no authority to address those grievances?

Sanders: [interrupting] Are we talking about reality or not? I've never seen such a situation. He's talking about, say, a desert commune, or a commune that's isolated from the fabric of the police. And I'm familiar with the communes in New York City, for instance, where you're constantly reacting and relating to the so-called other world, and you're really never without police protection. You usually have a phone.

Yablonsky: Up in Big Sur and places like that—

Sanders: Yeah, well. The point is that we're emphasizing violence and it doesn't happen.

Kerouac: I was at Big Sur.

Buckley: You've written a book about it.

Yablonsky: When were you there, Jack?

Kerouac: Oh, get off it!

Yablonsky: Were you there lately?

Kerouac: I lived there alone; I lived with a mule up there.

Buckley: Is it okay for a hippie to call the police when he needs help, or is that considered anti-something?

Sanders: Sure, you got some snuffer that's going to get you, call the police, of course. Why not? You're attaching all these theoretical tags. That's the problem with using the word "hippie." It's a tag. You can't say they're anarchists. They all have middle-class equipment, a lot of them, and they can plug right back in. It's easy, gee, let's see, police, you dial them, you know, 911.

Yablonsky: Isn't one of the goals of a lot of people on the scene to turn off all middle-class values, and to tune into some other sense of reality?

Kerouac: Nixon's the middleman. Man for the middleman, and Agnew.

Sanders: What we're really involved in is the definition of the word "drop out." I think that thinking quote "hippies" are involved in a new interpretation of what dropping out means. You naturally retain some connection to the police, and the hospital, and the fire department—

Yablonsky: Isn't this a negative retention of things your parents laid on you?

Sanders: Hey, I'm glad they laid hospitals on me.

Kerouac: Hey, Ed.

Sanders: Huh?

Kerouac: Ed, I was arrested two weeks ago. And the arresting policeman said, I'm arresting you for decay.

Buckley: I assume he was able to prove it.

Yablonsky: Might be the start of a new movement.

Sanders: Decay-da?

Kerouac: He said decay.

[Audience laugher. End of segment. There were questions from the audience in the last segment. The audience consisted primarily of students from Bernard M. Baruch College, Columbia University, and Hofstra University.]

Question: Mr. Yablonsky, I'm interested in what kind of future you see for the hippie movement.

Yablonsky: I think a lot depends on American society. If it becomes more open, and less plastic, and more loving, and a lot of the rigidified institutions that have developed like a lot of our families and whatever, if things begin to change, there won't be any need for people to react in a rather extreme form, looking for love. It will be found in the regular social system. In that case, it will disappear, or it may grow if things become more rigidified, or Nixon gets elected—

Buckley: I'd like to comment on that. [Audience laughter] It may very well grow to the extent that we all encourage (a) intellectual irresponsibility, and (b) personal irresponsibility. It may very well be that the psychologists are correct who say that what precisely has encouraged the hippie movement to be irresponsible is a complete lack of leadership. Maybe when we start writing books about them, we ought even to muster up the courage to say certain things they do they ought not to be permitted to do. Yes, question over there—

Question: Would any of you regard the hippie movement not only as a reflection of the inadequacies of the society as a whole, but also as a manifestation of the psychological inadequacies of the individual hippies themselves?

Yablonsky: Well, there's such freedom within the framework of the movement, that people that society would classify as "psychotic" are allowed to do their thing and they live and eat and are taken care of by others and appreciated. In fact, to a great extent this is one of the interesting facets of the hippie movement, that there's a humane approach to people who society would label in some extreme fashion. And so, there are a lot of young people who don't make it through the usual channels that find a life for themselves on the hippie scene.

Buckley: But the question itself poses a methodological challenge, doesn't it, because it's hard to establish by mutually agreed upon means what normalcy consists of. Maybe Mr. Sanders is normal, for all we know.

Kerouac: Maybe I am, too.

[Audience laughter]

Yablonsky: If people get nude, as Ed described, and put strawberry jam on, and run through the streets—

Kerouac: Scatological there, Sanders.

Yablonsky: It's a movement. If one guy does it, he'll get arrested in a moment unless he gets some followers.

Kerouac: Why do you want followers?

Buckley: Did you want to comment on that, Mr. Kerouac? Sorry.

Kerouac: I was asking why he wants followers.

Buckley: Who? Mr. Sanders?

Kerouac: Abramowitz, or whatever his name is.

[Audience laughter]

Yablonsky: Don't get anti-Semitic with me. I happen to be Jewish. My name is Yablonsky.

Kerouac: I called you by your name.

Yablonsky: Why did you call me Abramowitz?

Kerouac: What is it?

Yablonsky: Yablonsky.

Kerouac: Oh, Yablonsky.

[Audience laughter]

Buckley: You didn't mean to be rude, did you? Come on, now.

Kerouac: No, no. I forgot his name.

Buckley: Now, did you want an answer to that question?

Kerouac: Which question? Yes, I'll answer that question over there about the methodological.

Sanders: What about emotional paraplegic.

Buckley: Here's one for you.

Question: As far as hippies and those who live in a commune, do they plan on making it a lifetime occupation? Are they just going to sit down and watch the world go by? Because they don't really do anything.

Sanders: That's not what they're doing. Everybody sits down part of the time and watches the world go by.

Question: Are they adding anything?

Sanders: It's like there are certain religious movements, like the Brethren or the Quakers, who don't believe in proselytizing but live by example. And you'll never get any queries from the Church of the Brethren to join their beliefs, but at the same time they try to live an exemplary life, and that's probably the main motivation behind a commune life. Rather than say, "Come here and join us," they would show an example and hopefully accrue—

Question: Do you plan to be a Fug when you're fifty?

Sanders: When I'm fifty, I plan to be an emotional paraplegic smoking peace-herbs.

Kerouac: Neurasthenic psychotic.

Buckley: Do you think that would be an improvement, Mr. Kerouac?

Kerouac: No, no. I was just kidding.

Buckley: Why should this particular impulse ever last? Why when you get around thirty or thirty-five you think, oh, I'm going to put my youth behind me and go to work for the First National Bank?

Yablonsky: A lot of the young people who are in this movement, they look up and see their fifty-year-old father, who did everything, has all the goodies, 2.8 cars and three houses, and whatever, and he's kind of miserable, and he's not communicating with his wife and whatever. And they say, well, if I go to the right schools, and do all these things, this is what is going to happen to me. I'm going to try something else. And I think that the hippie movement is partly this, a kind of a social experiment.

Buckley: Partly a social experiment that understands the likelihood of its own futility. Put it this way, will anybody be thinking about the hippies ten years from now—other than in the sort of a hula skirt sense?

Sanders: No, by then, the hippies will be in the command generation, and all the pot-smoking law students and all the young legislators who are introducing legalization of pot bills and all the young professionals who are quote "turned on" and articulate and who are aware of Mr. Kerouac's and Mr. Ginsberg's great contribution to America civilization.

Kerouac: [interrupting] You hope. I'm not connected to Ginsberg. Don't put my name next to his.

Sanders: Okay, Mr. Kerouac's contribution to American civilization, those people will be quote "the command generation," and hopefully retain some of the humane attributes—

Kerouac: Command generation!

Sanders: Well, that's what it's going to be. That's what *Time Magazine* calls it.

An Interview with Ed Sanders

Barry Miles

Originally published in Review of Contemporary Fiction *19, no. 1 (Spring 1999): 14–22. Reprinted by permission of the* Review of Contemporary Fiction.

In 1965 I was managing Better Books, an avant-garde bookshop on London's Charing Cross Road, which stocked as many American small-press poetry magazines as I could get. We carried *Lines*, *Mother*, *C*, *Birth*, and so on. I contacted Ed Sanders through Allen Ginsberg, who gave me his address, and we soon became the only shop in Europe to carry *Fuck You/A Magazine of the Arts* (edited and published by Sanders "from a secret location on the Lower East Side"). We sometimes sent Ed parcels of English books, such as George Andrews's *The Book of Grass*, for his Peace Eye bookshop in exchange for the publications of the Fuck You Press.

Toward the end of 1965, a woman called Betsy Klein arrived in London, carrying credentials from Ed to say that she was cool, "Fill her lungs with dope," and other attestations of her worthiness. Betsy was then living with Ken Weaver, the drummer with the Fugs, and when *The Village Fugs* was released on the Broadside label in January 1966, she put a copy in the mail to us.

By then, I had just opened a new bookshop called Indica Books on Mason's Yard, off Duke Street Saint James's, and was closely involved with the Beatles. Paul McCartney was in the shop helping to build shelves when the package arrived. Because we had no record player in the shop, Paul took the album and went next door to the Scotch Saint James's, which was then the "in" club for rock 'n' roll musicians. After a lot of banging on the door, the manager was finally persuaded to let us in—he had little choice really, considering that the success or failure of this type of club depended upon attracting famous names, and his take always rose enormously if one of the Beatles was present. A cleaner was wiping down the tables, and lit by normal-strength bulbs instead of being in almost total darkness, the club looked pretty tacky. Next to the dance floor was an old carriage of the sort that once transported young blades around the city, in which the DJ equipment was housed. Paul placed the record on the deck and "Slum Goddess" filled the club, played at top volume. The manager, who had been expecting the latest groovy sounds from Stax, could not believe his ears. "Why do you want to listen to such filth?" he asked Paul. "The Fugs," Paul told him knowingly, "are the next big thing!" For the next few months, whenever he was pestered for autographs by American tourists in nightclubs, he would always sign his name as Tuli Kupferberg, the percussionist with the Fugs, causing considerable consternation.

I always admired Ed Sanders because he was what we now recognize as a postmodernist figure. He bridged the gaps separating genres: he is a poet, novelist, editor, publisher, political activist, bookshop proprietor, songwriter, singer, and musician. He was the first to use rock 'n' roll as a vehicle to present texts by Swinburne, Blake, Burroughs, and Ginsberg; he wrote both poetry and song lyrics; he was an important publisher, breaking the dependence upon commercial houses by producing his own mimeographed editions from a clandestine press housed in a backyard building off Avenue A between 12th and 13th Streets in the Lower East Side. Because the press had no fixed address, Ed was able to print such things as the "Roosevelt Routine" chapter that City Lights Books cut from William Burroughs's *The Yage Letters* as well as such material as *Bugger: An Anthology*. His revolution extended from the production and promotion of literature into politics—with LeMar (the Movement to Legalize Marijuana), Sexual Liberation, and the Yippie Party—to give him a career in the arts that, in its scope, parallels that of André Breton.

This interview was conducted with Ed Sanders at my house in Lord North Street, Westminster, London, in October 1968, when the Fugs were touring Europe.[1] It was originally taped for the *International Times*, Britain's first underground paper, but for some reason was not used. This is its first publication.

Ed Sanders: I don't want to talk about the Fugs—just about the future. Everything is organized for me, finally, at least for the next year or so. I'm weak on theory and philosophy. I'm a practical man.

Barry Miles: Does it divide up at all into what you're doing with the Peace Eye, what you're doing with music, what you're doing with politics?

Sanders: The Peace Eye's reopened at the old EVO [*East Village Other*, New York's first underground newspaper] offices, with a big stock and energetic management. It's doing very well.

Miles: Do you issue catalogs?

Sanders: We've issued a catalog, although it's not a rare book catalog. It's a magical poetry catalog that's beamed essentially at the people who write letters to the Fugs. Kids at American high schools all over write to us, so I send them the catalog.

Miles: It's largely poetry and little magazines?

Sanders: Yeah, well, you know, magazines. "Due to the unsettling times," there's heavy interest in alchemy and magic, witchcraft and Satanism and Aleister Crowley and the related star data, crystal balls, astral projection, Scientology.

Miles: Is that very big over there?

Sanders: Well, Scientologists are so pushy; it's strictly an S&M scene in the United States anyway. So it either attracts stoned masochists or stoned sadists.

Miles: Everyone I've come across who went into it has stopped creating or whatever they were doing: artists stop painting, poets stop writing.

---

1 The Fugs's impact on London can be measured by their treatment in Jenny Fabian and Johnny Byrne, *Groupie* (1969; London: Omnibus, 1997), in which they play a prominent role.

William Burroughs hasn't written anything outside of Scientology since he's been involved with them.[2]

Sanders: It was interesting to watch Burroughs at the Chicago convention. He had a tape recorder with this certain type of noise that he claimed would create confusion, and the first thing he did upon arriving at the Democratic Convention at the amphitheater—he was admitted because he was covering it—was to turn on the tape recorder: sprayed it out over the galleries. So he sort of assumes part of the responsibility for the inner chaos of the Democratic Convention. And then, of course, he was right out there on the street. He, Jean Genet, Terry Southern, Allen Ginsberg, and Dick Seaver of Grove Press were all sitting down on the sidewalk in front of the police, and he was out there on that night with the tear gas.

So Scientology hasn't thwarted his social sense anyway. I mean, a lot of us view Scientology as … anyone who believes that there's a little two-inch being inside of your brain! I mean, you might as well go and read the Bible and run off to the Lutheran Bible school—it seems to make as much sense. See, its terminology is as simplistic as LSD terminology, which is essentially based on an airplane ride. Scientology seems to be based on typewriters: you know, being cleared and stops and engrams. Burroughs started to worry about his anal engrams: tricky anal problem, well, not a problem, but ain't no poetry in it, see?

Miles: I'm hoping he'll come back soon.[3]

Sanders: He was certainly a joy to see in the streets of Chicago, also Genet, who just walked clear up in front of the police. I saw the police charge him from my hotel window. He was trying to get to his car, and they chased him down the street throwing tear gas. He ducked into an alley that had a door, and about fifteen minutes later I saw him

---

2 Burroughs's involvement came to an end when the Scientologists placed him in a "condition of treason" for running "squirrel techniques" on himself with an e-meter. Auditing sessions with an e-meter were supposed to be conducted by a Scientology auditor. Burroughs was always opposed to L. Ron Hubbard's philosophy but was interested in his techniques for deprogramming the mind and identifying control systems.

3 Burroughs was visiting the States when this interview was conducted. His home was in London.

emerge from the door, look in both directions, and scuttle down the street. This lady journalist ran up to Genet and hugged him, and Genet turned to Ginsberg and said, "Be sure to tell her I'm a homosexual." That was really funny.

Miles: How successful do you think the demonstrations were in Chicago?

Sanders: Well, see, it wasn't really demonstrations. It was massing together and then trying to survive, en masse, for two or three hours without getting killed, given almost total violence. The only thing they didn't do was kill people or really maim them. Given the type of violence—violence that just bruises and cuts you—it proved that people can exist in such a situation and engage in paramilitary guerrilla runs and dodges, that we were just as smart as they were. We were able to survive under those conditions, which opens up the whole prospect of demonstrations in the United States because it's likely that they'll keep the conditions of limited snuff, limited violence, and if we keep our street tactics similar to Chicago, then we can run naked and crazy all over the United States. And we'll win or we'll do whatever we want. The next big test, of course, is the inauguration in January.

Miles: What's going to happen then? Anything specific?

Sanders: Well, we're going to apply for a permit in Washington to set up tents to show another lifestyle, festival-type thing. Our agents will be inside the inauguration, and there are so many of us that they can't keep us out unless they just refuse to invite anybody that has any liberal tendencies. We're going to get people inside the inauguration, some sort of theater, plays, theatrics. The Fugs sent a letter asking to play.

Miles: Are you concerned at all by the reception the media gave you?

Sanders: No. The Ginsberg generation has taken over the media. The beatniks turned journalists. People who were in graduate school and college during the fifties and were affected so strongly by the Beat generation are now moving into sensitive areas in the media. For instance, one of the chief NBC producers at the convention—whenever one would meet him in the streets in his helmet, in the C crew—he could talk to you on your own level, you know, in terms of drugs, pot, sex, and literature. One night he had to run back to his hotel room because he had gone and brought his acid out with him, and he wanted to stash it in case the police beat him up. And this was a key person—let's say—at the convention. So that's typical of the type of fortyish, Ginsbergian journalist that's around. They want to be of service and not just a lackey.

Miles: It's very strange to view America from here.

Sanders: Well, because it's insane, see? It's like if you have a psychotic aunt that you don't want to put away. You have to figure out how to get along with her—and especially if she has a gun—you have to figure out how she won't go nuts and shoot. The U.S. is a big problem, you know? All the religious maniacs in Europe went over there a hundred, two hundred years ago, all the soldiers of fortune and psychopaths and degenerates and all the freaks from Europe of that time went over there, and the combination of religious maniacs and killers—goons—just swept across the country like a bunch of army ants and killed everything they could find, killed the Indians' buffalo—anything they could shoot, man—and they occupied the territory and set up a civilization of maniacs.

And there we are. And four and five generations later, as a result of this incredible energy of our forefathers, we have a whole lot of energy and a whole lot of resources and money available to us. And power. Try to cut off the negative tentacles of American civilization, try to create something. Either cap it off so it doesn't hurt anyone anymore, or direct its energy into ways that aren't injurious to the world. It's a terrible task. I mean we got four thousand miles of maniacs over there.

Miles: Do you think it's possible for opinion from foreign parts to have an influence?

Sanders: That just pisses Americans off. World opinion just makes them more uptight, makes them more crazy.

Miles: How much connection is there between the underground and the big corporations in America? All the rock groups, for instance, are signed up to huge companies.

Sanders: Well, see, there's a pancake problem in the underground in that most people are really surface people. They didn't grow up in the underground and don't know the origins of the underground, don't know why there's an underground. They decide to associate themselves with the underground, and then they just flip themselves over—it's like a pancake, you understand—and then they're underground. I mean they're really there to make money. That's the problem with most of the groups … it's a cupidity problem. They're really in it, quite frankly, for the money, which, if William Blake's right, cuts away at their hearts like something savage, and that's where most groups are at. And the way to make a lot of money is to sign with a big company. Of course, another problem is that the small record companies in America tend to be crooks.

Miles: Have you found that the Fugs have managed to unite a lot of the old literary people?

Sanders: No. You see, the commercial literary set—Philip Roth, the *New York Review* crowd, Elizabeth Hardwick, and the Robert Lowell people—dig us, but the other people who have higher musical standards … frankly, up to now we hadn't got much sense of music. It's just now, particularly in the *It Crawled into My Hand, Honest* album, that we were able to take control of what we'd really like to do musically. But I don't know—our base is literary, most of our friends are literary, most devout Fug fans are in high schools in the Midwest. I know all the letters come from the Midwest, from kids mostly, young high-school kids.

Miles: I suppose there's nothing you can do about them—I mean in the Midwest.

Sanders: It's nice land. If it were just populated by civilized people. America is an incredibly beautiful land. It's incredibly diverse; any form of climate you like you can live in. You have your choice of everything. It's just the people and the traditions. So I would encourage people to stay in their communities unless they really want to go to New York to, say, study poetry. See, it's a matter of education. Young people should pick the places they want to go to in order to learn things. Civilization means that all young freaks should not study guitar.

Miles: What's the relationship between the underground and the Black Power people, the Black Panthers, for instance?

Sanders: Well, see, one of the good things about Chicago was that when you ran in the streets, you were side by side with the black brothers.

There were black people there. And people like Eldridge Cleaver are friends with Jerry Rubin, they're friends with the hippies. There's sympathy because there is this incredible phobia in the United States against heads. God, it's just incredible, you know, and so the hippies are the Black Power people, so it's like that.

Miles: They are usually reported as two completely separate things.

Sanders: Not at all. Black Power is a denial of the middle-class liberal; it's not a denial of the people who really want equality, who don't want a slave system. See, black people understand the situation without even having to contemplate it because there are vibrations, you know? And I think that some of the Black Panthers are able to get along with Jerry Rubin because Rubin is honest. He really believes in what he says, whereas a liberal might not: he might be a hypocrite. So I think the lines are very open for communication. I mean between the Peace and Freedom Party, Black Panthers, SDS, Marlon Brando.

The United States is really almost an open society. That's why I decided to do things like the Fugs and Peace Eye bookshop: to bring it out into the open, assuming that there is no real dualism in the message of the United States Constitution. You know you can create a format for presenting your views, so you have the strength in the electronic era by coming out into the open, no matter how freakish or revolutionary your views are. So being a pacifist, I realize that by not having anything to do with violence, I can't be brought into any sedition scene or any treason scene. It would only be somewhere, perhaps, in the obscenity area or some vague political theatrical area, so the dangers aren't great really. For instance, to me, a fine or those little jail terms don't mean anything—so the risks are small for someone like me, but the risks for someone like Jerry Rubin are considerable, or for Abbie Hoffman, who they really want to get.

The crucial point is the war and the draft. That's what so many people in my country don't understand. The whole reason the country is in turmoil is because of the draft and because of the war. No other reason. The country is wealthy, productive, energetic; there's no other malady but that.

Miles: What was the original impetus behind the Fugs—I mean, why did all of you literary figures decide to go into music?

Sanders: I organized the group. I opened up the bookstore in December and at the same time I was writing songs for a possible band. In my college days I had written a bunch of tunes to Blake songs: "Ah, Sunflower," "Oh Rose Thou Art Sick," "Long John Brown," "Little Mary Bell," and several other Blake things, and I wanted to sing. I didn't know how to sing. I had always read poetry in a kind of chanting, sing-song way, keeping one note, almost, when reading. I was inspired by listening to Ginsberg, Ferlinghetti, and Edward Dahlberg read in the fifties on MacDougal Street, and I read Pound and things—it all made sense. Being the victim of the Peace Walk generation, even trying to board submarines and just being a radical, I found it all made sense. So we started getting together.

Tuli wrote some songs, and I wrote some songs, and so there was Tuli and I. And Ken was in my bookstore all the time. He helped me put out *Bugger*, the mag, and some of the *Fuck You*'s, and then I learned that Ken played drums, had played in the El Campo High School marching band. And then I further learned that he had an old buffalo-hide drum, or something, and he got so he seemed natural to the routine. So there were Tuli and Ken and me. And then Steve Weber [guitar, vocals] and Peter Stampfel [fiddle, harmonica, vocals], who were in the Holy Modal Rounders. Peter and Steve started coming around to our sessions, and so it evolved, so we played around.

Miles: Do you have very much connection with the pop business generally?

Sanders: Well, see, pop newspapers tend to ignore us, but we have a vast network of connections in the States now. I can't stand the members of most groups, frankly, because they're atrophied souls. I mean they're so greedy that it defies description, or the content of their lives is so vapid and uninteresting to me, or they're so untrained in all the fields they should be trained in, like literature and writing and conversation, that they're just boring. Some of them are interesting. Joe McDonald is interesting and Janis Joplin. She's nice, smart. Charles Olson fell in love with her.

Miles: I'm glad he's getting around again. It's nice that people of that generation are getting involved with music.

Sanders: It's not necessarily the age of the person, but it's the dedication and the intelligence. It's a great era to be alive.

Miles: Do you still write poetry?

Sanders: Oh yes, I'm addicted to poetry. The problem is the way you think. I don't like to think in the thirty-two-bar music style. I'm trapped at the moment by the nature of the current Fugs music, and it tends to injure my poetry. I have a strong classical background in Greek meter, which is incredibly varied, and I wrote all my early poems in Greek meter—"Poem from Jail," for instance, is written entirely along the rigid lines of Greek meter—and so getting into rock music impaired my poetry a little bit. But I'm working on it. I just realized it happened a couple of months ago, and so I've been trying to rectify it.

Miles: So what kind of changes do you expect in your new poetry?

Sanders: I'm going to write a whole book of Blakean things—in the sense of real designing, a package. I like a book as an object of art, and I am going to design all the plates and do colored paintings, drawings, hand lettering, all very intricate, complicated, interesting. But there's got to be a way to make pop music more complicated, more surrealistic than it is. God!

Miles: Well, your extensions seem to be in the theatrical area.

Sanders: Yeah, well, I'm getting into it. I've been studying all these books on orchestration and how to write music notes. I've studied all that shit for the last couple of years. I get this music graph paper and just write simply—you write out lines and it's great, it's really fun. It's incredible, you have ten different layers of sound that can occur at the same time. You just figure out what goes through it. It's really fine. It's all learning just what an instrument can do and getting the right musical nomenclature, and then just writing what goes on in your brain on a piece of paper, which is great. Like I can listen to Beethoven in my brain and roughly write it like it is. It's just like learning Greek or something. It's like a language you've got to learn, a schoolboy thing. But once you do it, it's like you get onto a whole planet: the music planet.

Miles: How about the difference between live performance and recorded?

Sanders: Well, of course, you're limited. It's a Leonard Bernstein problem for a composer. You can spend all your time rehearsing, which is what a really top band does: they rehearse every day for four hours, even on the road, and they spend all their life, say, while they're on the road, practicing, eating, and playing. And that's a life form I don't want to get involved with. I concentrate on composition and poetry and a complex personal life.

"Sleezy Icky Yucky Mucky & Uck" An Interview with Ed Sanders

Sookie Stambler

Originally published in WIN *8 (January 1972): 6–10. Reprinted by permission of* WIN *and Sookie Stambler.*

What follows is the transcript of an interview with Ed Sanders, longtime peace activist and author of *The Family*, an account of the life and times of Charles Manson. Predictably, *The Family* is turning out to be one of the most controversial books ever written by one of us [i.e. pacifists]. Sookie Stambler conducted the interview on November 11.

Sookie Stambler: The style of your book is very factual. You've been criticized about all the dates and times and the excessive detail.

Ed Sanders: I knew that. Those were the criticisms we all anticipated and discussed at the publishers. And I decided that was the reality that built up. I was just laying out the facts and tried to keep myself out of it.

Stambler: Do you really think you did that?

Sanders: Not really. But I tried. I don't exist in the book. I just tried to coldly depict what I'd learned. If people find it boring, it is boring. But that's what life is all about. I wanted to demythologize the Manson thing. I wanted to depict it in all its boredom. It's a slow progression or transgression from the flower of 1967 to the pig of 1968 to the carnage of 1969, and I didn't want to make them heroes for anybody. So I coldly presented the facts. I put in a lot of aliases and facts and a lot of criminal police data. I was influenced by police reports. In certain ways I was writing like writers in the LA [Los Angeles] police department whose reports I saw.

Stambler: I remember your telling me that they had asked you to do the book.

Sanders: No. I would never be commissioned to do a book, ever. I decided to write a little thing about it. I didn't know if it was going to be a book or what, but something. I thought I could write a book quickly. This was in December of '69, right after everybody started getting arrested for all those killings. And they were trashing all those people as hippies, etc. And none of it seems to make sense. So I thought I could go out to LA and gather the data quickly and just do a thing. Sometimes I write very quickly.

Usually, I can just write something out and it doesn't take so long. I've been practicing my style for fifteen years. I felt competent to just do it. So I get out there, and I can't get any facts because everybody is paranoid and there are all kinds of death threats against—not me—but against various principals in the case. There's all kinds of weirdness and bribes and freakiness and nothing makes sense. So I wind up traveling all over the U.S. interviewing people with a little tape recorder. Talking to cops, to lawyers, to the Manson family.

Stambler: Did you get to see Manson?

Sanders: Yes. Most of my investigation I stayed away from him because he was very interested in projecting an image of his clan that was contrary to the reality of the situation.

Stambler: Which was what?

Sanders: Well, they thought they could manipulate the underground press toward adopting the position, the umbrella of which would cover Manson and his brutalities and his associates' brutalities.

Stambler: When you did get to see Manson, what was he like?

Sanders: I don't know how to answer that question because he just lectures. You don't get anything from him. My interest was information and the family's interest was not for anybody to know the story.

So when you go and see any of those people in jail, they just give you lectures. He's pretty glib, and he's very elegant in his phrases in a paranoid schizophrenic way. His interest was to give lectures on his flights of fancy. He wanted to get off. He thought he was going to get off.

Stambler: Why?

Sanders: At the end, he talked all the other defendants into testifying that he had nothing to do with it. But their lawyers wouldn't go along with it. There were all kinds of death notes, and one lawyer actually died.

Stambler: The one who went on the hiking trip?

Sanders: Yeah, we went in to his house after he died to see what was up because we thought he was murdered. So we found all these death notes. And there are circumstances about his death which are certainly weird. I'm still not sure if it was an accidental death.

Stambler: When Susan Atkins, a.k.a. Sadie Glutz, talked in prison, she seemed to tell those other women a lot of detail.

Sanders: Well, they were pumping her. She had a very eager mouth.

Stambler: Is she the one who got immunity?

Sanders: Originally, and then she changed her mind and Linda Kasabian got immunity and got off. She's now living in Canada trying to make a new life for herself.

Stambler: In the Tate-LaBianca murder, Manson didn't murder anyone. So who did he actually murder?

Sanders: In the California penal code first degree murder covers giving orders to murder. He went into the La Bianca house and tied them up, and everybody testified that he didn't participate in the crime. He just recently was convicted of a decapitation.

Stambler: Shorty Shea?

Sanders: Yeah. He got convicted for Hinman, too

Stambler: But he didn't do that.

Sanders: He hacked his ear. Well, I don't know. There's conflicting testimony. One other person who is now living says Manson did it. At this point, he's convicted of nine murders.

Stambler: You know the book, *In Cold Blood*, which has a totally different approach. It's a novelization. Most of your book was reportage.

Sanders: Right, Capote constructed conversations. I was overwhelmed by data. My book reflects one hundredth of the information. If I had the energy and the concern, I could have written a ten-volume day-by-day narration of events. I didn't. Capote did it. He had a different way of doing research.

Stambler: Were any of the articles you wrote for the *Free Press* part of the book?

Sanders: No, I wrote thirty articles on the trial. The book ends before the trial. If I were to have written about the trial I would have needed another 500 pages. The trial was really weird. Intrigue after intrigue, death threats, and weirdness.

Stambler: Not more interesting than the investigation?

Sanders: Oh, there should be a book about the trial, too, but in order to do it you'd have to step on some toes. There was a lot of intrigue, a lot of weirdness. I don't want to do it. I'm so sick of it.

Stambler: Did you like writing the book?

Sanders: Well, I didn't really write it. The facts just presented themselves. I wrote one draft and then rewrote it, and then they took the manuscript away and typeset it. I guess I wrote it. Some of my friends wanted me to continue to stylize it. I could have rewritten everything in a very snazzy style, but it would have taken me another year.

Stambler: Well, did you get sort of sick of the subject?

Sanders: Oh, God, I'm sick, sick, sick of it. I got caught in this routine, this project, and I got out of the thing the best way I knew how. I mean I got really trapped and nobody can know. I'll have to write a book someday about my experiences writing this particular book. The weird things I did to get information.

Stambler: There's a story about your posing as a porno film dealer.

Sanders: Oh, yeah, one time I posed as a pornography dealer for rich Eastern clients. I wanted to get some films. More than that, I wanted to verify their existence. Another time I went around as an occultist who was interested in purchasing human skulls.

Now I realize how hard it is to reconstruct years of people's lives. Especially when no one wants to talk about it. Reality is really difficult to construct. I asked someone what they were doing in November of 1967, and about all they can remember is that they were alive. Then you get liars, guys who say no, I don't know anything about that.

Stambler: Why do you say your life is endangered for writing this book?

Sanders: I didn't say that. There was a minimum amount of danger. Just here and there you step on people's toes. There's no danger now—it's all over. I did my thing, wrote my book, and the facts stand. I didn't make anything up, I didn't hallucinate. It's just stuff people told me that seems to check out.

Stambler: What impact do you think the book is going to have?

Sanders: Nothing. There is no reality. It doesn't draw conclusions, makes no claims. The only claim it makes is to encourage people to be anarchists. For people not to follow leaders, to challenge every directive. Because if people did that, they wouldn't end up stabbing people for no reason. Just ultimately never to take orders. Always make sure you know the motives of people who try to tell you what to do, whether it's the President or some guru sitting in a lotus position mumbling about good and evil.

Stambler: What's not in the book is all the reports I read in earlier articles about Manson's hypnotic personality. You just get the feeling that Manson is this little greasy punk who likes to fuck all the time.

Sanders: I presented the facts. I don't believe in the supernatural, in reincarnation, in ghosts, in magic. I know that hypnosis is possible. I think there's been research on criminal behavior under hypnosis, and it's possible to get people who are submissive to commit criminal acts. And anybody who's desperate enough can get people, followers, to commit crimes. My book just presented the facts. I don't think Manson was a super-human raving Rasputin who had an aura of supernatural powers whose mere gaze got people to commit felonious acts.

Stambler: Why do you think Manson was a murderer?

Sanders: Well, he got more and more frustrated. First of all, when he got out of jail after having spent many years in prison, he became everything from a pimp to a bartender. His MO, his modus operandi, was that of a pimp. Why, you see those guys standing around in Times Square every day issuing sharp, hostile directives to these females. That's his thing. I just wanted to present him in a non-magical, non-religious, non-superstitious aura and do it as dryly as possible, and one way to do it is to deliberately create boredom. I love it when people say my book is boring. That's the greatest compliment. Because that is exactly what I wanted to do. They should have seen what the publishers took out. I was printing social security numbers. There couldn't have been enough trivia. I was ready to put in fingerprint indexes. I was ready to put in everything, just complete data. I got a lot of it pushed out because I guess they wanted to sell the book.

Stambler: Why did you do this?

Sanders: Because it creates this tedious boredom, and that's what it really was. Even though they killed them, everything they did was unaesthetic. There was nothing about them or the series of events that was aesthetic. At the Spahn Ranch all you see are horse flies swarming above this huge pile of manure and the sway-backed horses and the filthy buildings and just how pathetic it all was. And even the way they killed and everything they did was just sleazy, icky, junky—you'd have to go back to the words children use. Mushy and uck. And one way of doing it was to bore people to death—to life, to bore people to life.

Stambler: Does that mean you were bored when you were trying to write it?

Sanders: No, but I felt the events were. See, my book isn't about Manson. It's about criminal behavior under patterns of suggestion. It's about fascism. It's about blind obedience, about people wandering around not knowing what they're doing, without having plans and just willing to obey. It doesn't dig into their minds. It's purely existential: it's just what they did. It's a travelogue. See, I wanted to get that slow drive toward snuff. That slow, twisted path that led them from the counter culture to the crazy culture.

Stambler: Was there anyone connected to the murders whom you think hasn't been prosecuted?

Sanders: Yeah, I think so. But I think most of the stuff that I depicted in the book is pretty much curtailed.

Stambler: While they were at the Barker Ranch, how did they connect the murders to Manson? Was it because Susan Atkins talked in jail?

Sanders: No, it was very complicated. Manson burned a huge earth-moving device in Death Valley. Thought the Death Valley rangers had dug a hole just to trap him. He was really paranoid. So he had his people burn it. So that really made the park rangers angry. Death Valley is still gold mining country, so the people are very individualistic. They'll let you do whatever you want—the only thing is, you have to obey a few rules. Number one is if somebody is stopped in the desert, then you have to stop and help them. Two, you don't steal under any circumstances. It's just a code of the West: you steal, you die. Everybody kind of respects everybody else. And the Manson gang is out there and committed some robberies like breaking into cars. One guy complained to me that he was stopped by the side of the road and these people whizzed by and wouldn't stop. And people started to get suspicious minds about him, and then they found out that he was running around with stolen stuff.

After he burned the Michigan loader, they followed his tire tracks for twenty and thirty miles and found out where he was staying, and found out it was a bunch of hippies with stolen cars. And slowly they built up a case against him. He then became a suspect in the other murders, the Tate-LaBianca murders, because of a couple of informers who told the police. They couldn't get a case, though, until Susan Atkins started babbling to her cellmates. And when the cellmates reported to the police, they had sufficient evidence to go against everybody. So it took them about a month to get them after they thought it was Manson. It took time to get enough evidence to hold up in court. The rules of evidence are very strict.

Stambler: I know there was a list of future victims. Do you think they would have gone on killing people?

Sanders: I think he dug the media. He was a media freak. I think they wanted to raid and snuff, and they thought they could get away with it. They thought they could raid out of Death Valley with their dune buggies. They were really shooting big, everybody from Bing Crosby to Tom Jones. They wanted to snuff and then go back up into Death Valley, and create confusion as they would call it.

Stambler: By going to Death Valley?

Sanders: No, by killing. You know the three assassinations of King and the Kennedys killed a lot of sensitivity in the country, for types of change.

Stambler: What were the Manson women like?

Sanders: Well, they were varying types. They all had memorized this set of long, incredible lectures about any subject, just name a subject from astral projection to what they called sex paranoia.

Stambler: What was that?

Sanders: That's what they encountered when the so-called straight people observed them doing their thing sexually. It's a form of incredible chauvinism, where women have to instantly obey. Those girls were trained to obey anything a man said.

Stambler: Is it true that Manson used to fuck three times a day?

Sanders: Seven. He had a prison prostate, some abnormal condition. I think he used sex for control and that was part of the legend. It was really pathetic that his indoctrination of some of these young women, teenagers, and some in their late twenties, should have left their minds so completely restructured. He used females as a kind of tool. If he wanted to impress somebody, he just said "send four of them in" as a kind of masseuse squad. I heard he had them gobbling dogs, just every form of hideous kind of submission.

Stambler: Did you ever see any of those movies you talk about?

Sanders: I can't go into it—I can't even talk about it. Those people who are paranoid about it can rest at ease. I do not know where any of them are.

Stambler: Were there any motives to the Tate murder?

Sanders: Yeah, I think I did go into them in the book. The essence of the motive was that there was a hostile confrontation between Manson's group and one or more of the individuals killed. It happened just prior to the murders. I feel they just didn't realize who they were dealing with. I think there's a little drug angle there, and another angle is that they wanted to get Bobby Beausoleil out of jail, so they thought they'd commit some murders similar to the one he was charged with. And another thing they thought they could do was to have a continuity of violence, of snuffing people.

Stambler: What's happened to Tex Watson?

Sanders: Well, he turned into a vegetable. His IQ is now down to 80 or 90 and he's the first vegetable to be sent to death row. I mean he's really out to lunch. He can't even think or remember.

Stambler: That happened from his taking telache?

Sanders: They say that such a drastic drop in IQ comes from brain disease or certain drugs, possibly certain types of belladonna. Telache—I've seen the plant—and it doesn't really appear to be belladonna, although everybody says it's belladonna. It may be a form of belladonna. It grows out in creek beds. I saw it in Death Valley. It's a small dark green plant, and it's supposed to send you completely out to lunch. Just completely paralytic. They were interested in pouring it in the water supply. They evidently hijacked some frozen food truck on telache.

Stambler: Why did the defendants shave off all their hair?

Sanders: Because he told them to. I think he's still shaved. There aren't too many of the family left outside. They all got arrested after a machine gun shootout with the police while trying to raid an arms shop. Then recently some of them got picked up for prostitution.

Stambler: How long did it take you to write the book?

Sanders: I started writing in March of '71 almost fifteen hours a day, straight, until July. I almost abandoned it at one point.

Stambler: Why?

Sanders: Because I couldn't handle the facts. I'm a pacifist and I don't believe in violence, transgression, fascism, so it was getting too heavy for me. So I wrote up the data I had accrued to that time and handed in the book.

Stambler: What made you want to do the book?

Sanders: I thought it would be a quick book, not that I wanted to do a quickie. I don't know; I shouldn't have gotten involved. If I had to do it over again, I wouldn't have done it. I had this recording contract and I had a band to do left-wing songs with happy endings and I was just going to travel around with that but I had to abandon it. I haven't done any music in a long time. If I had to do it over again, I'd have a band.

Interview with Ed Sanders

Jennie Skerl

Originally published by Pace University Press in the Journal of Beat Studies, *6 (2018): 111–24. Reprinted by permission of the* Journal of Beat Studies.

The interview below took place in my home at the time in Schenectady, New York, on May 14, 1983. Sanders had received a Guggenheim and was temporarily living in the Albany area. I was primarily focused on Sanders as a poet and his connections with Burroughs and Ginsberg, since I was then researching Burroughs (for my book, *William S. Burroughs*, 1985). Publications by Sanders referred to in this interview include *Poem from Jail* (1963), *Fuck You/A Magazine of the Arts* (1962-65), *Egyptian Hieroglyphs* (1973), *Tales of Beatnik Glory*, volume 1 (1975), *Investigative Poetry* (1976), *The Z-D Generation* (1980), "Holy Was Demeter Walking the Corn Furrow," (first published in *20,000 A.D.*, 1976), and "Sappho on East Seventh," a long narrative poem which was published several years after this interview in *Tales of Beatnik Glory*, volume 2 (1990).

The interview summarizes many of Sanders's activities in the 1960s and his later commitment to investigative poetry. Since there were no other interviews with Sanders published in the 1980s, this conversation is informative about his perspective on his activities twenty years before and his published poetry to date. It wasn't until the publication of *Fug You* in 2011 that he provided full details on his life in the 1960s. Also, it wasn't until the publication of *Thirsting for Peace in a Raging Century* in 1987 that he began receiving attention for the body of his poetry. In this interview, he assesses his achievement as a poet. He also talks about continued work on *Tales of Beatnik Glory*, referring to volume 2, which would not be published until 1990, and which would evolve into four volumes published in 2004. In volume 2, as he describes, he developed long narrative poems—"short story poems" of which "Sappho on East Seventh" is one—which provided an important transition to his later historical and biographical book-length poems. Sanders speaks as he writes: informal, slangy, humorous language combined with impressive erudition on the modern and ancient Greek poetic traditions.

Jennie Skerl: I was just reading through *Tales of Beatnik Glory* [volume 1]. I don't think anyone could live in New York City like that anymore. It's too expensive.

Ed Sanders: Frankly, the civilization was brought about by two factors: one factor in the Lower East Side, or even the beatnik, ability to live in New York City was that the Lower East Side had been a slum for about 200 years plus, and so it had a karma, a tradition, of being cheap. Also the rent controls of World War II were still in place in 1958, '59, '60, '61—all the way up to the end of the '60s. So there were really cheap apartments, and, at the same time, cheap food. That was all that was necessary.

Skerl: What about your friendship with Ginsberg?

Sanders: Yeah, well, I met all these people through *Fuck You/A Magazine of the Arts.*

Skerl: You didn't know them before?

Sanders: No. Well, I came to New York City as a trembling little guy who had read "Howl." And I had read a lot of Ezra Pound, and Dylan Thomas, and E. E. Cummings.

Skerl: So it is true what George Butterick said in his essay about you [in the *Dictionary of Literary Biography*, volume 16]—you read "Howl" on campus in Kansas, and decided to go to New York City?

Sanders: You had a double choice: either you went to California or New York City. I got accepted by NYU [New York University], and Berkeley's acceptance came late, so I went to New York. Yeah, I read "Howl." I bought *Howl* at the [Missouri] university bookstore. I had it totally memorized, driving around, screaming it out there in the prairie. So, when I came to New York, I was very young. I thought I'd do a few years of research and studying language. I studied Latin, Greek, Egyptian.

Skerl: Oh, you actually studied Egyptian?

Sanders: Yeah, the state of my Egyptian has sort of dropped off in the last twenty years—but at one point I was able to read a sarcophagus. I was fairly adept. But Greek and Latin were my biggest subjects. Anyway, I wouldn't have approached these people in a million years back then. I used to go to all the Beat poetry readings, when I was nineteen or so. I saw Kerouac and all those people. I saw Frank O'Hara and Ginsberg at the Living Theatre, say in '58. But it was all, you know, I'd see Ginsberg one year and see him the next year at another poetry reading, and he still had the same shirt on or something like that. I'd get some cultural inputs, but I wasn't prepared to approach any of these people for years. I didn't want to go the Rimbaud route.

So, I just sat around there. Then when '62 hit and I started putting out *Fuck You/A Magazine of the Arts*, I thought I was ready. I'd written a poem while I was in jail (I had tried to board a Polaris submarine on a peace demonstration: I swam out and tried to get on the submarine, and was arrested.) I thought I had written a poem in jail that was as good as most of the poems that had been written by the Beat generation. Ferlinghetti printed it, *Poem from Jail*.

Skerl: So you had been writing and writing, and this was the first thing you had written that you thought was really good.

Sanders: Oh yeah, I had written lots of juvenilia—a thick stack of rewrites of Samuel Beckett, and rewrites of this and that, some good, some bad, crawling through the void puking and being young. So, in February, we got drunk one night after a Jonas Mekas movie, and I said I'm going to start a magazine called *Fuck You/A Magazine of the Arts*, and everybody was saying, "Sure, Ed, sure, yeah." So then I went the next day and bought a $30 mimeo and went down to the Catholic Worker where I used to eat (it was cheap) and went up on the second floor and typed it out on stencils, and they graciously gave me some of their paper, and I printed it. And then I thought of a great title, *Fuck You/A Magazine of the Arts*, a state of the art title. Everybody thought I could go to jail. In '62, it was handcuff city. But I had been in jail for sit-ins, down South in civil rights demonstrations. I was getting arrested all over. No big deal. So I decided that I believed in what I was doing.

I believed in my poetry at that time, *Poem from Jail*, because Ferlinghetti was going to print it. I thought, "Ferlinghetti is going to print my book! Hot stuff—this is it—big time—Ferlinghetti's Pocket Poets—City Lights!" It was a big thing because they printed William Carlos Williams, Corso, Ginsy—all my heroes. I was a 21-year-old ectomorph form the Midwest. It was like heaven. Like now getting a Guggenheim. If anybody had said to me in '58 I would ever get a Guggenheim, I would have laughed. So anyway at that time, to me, getting published by City Lights was the equivalent of a Guggenheim. [Sanders received a Guggenheim for poetry in in 1983.] So I had a lot of confidence from being published by City Lights. I knew I had a good title: *Fuck You/A Magazine of the Arts.*

Skerl: Definitely, everybody loves that title.

Sanders: Here I was, trembling and shy and afraid, I'd go to these open poetry readings, and they'd say, "Lets' put that skinny punk from the Midwest on at two in the morning." So everybody'd be reading, you know, "the green saliva of time," and I'd go on and read my poems. And then I put out *Fuck You/A Magazine of the Arts*, and they'd say, "Oh, when do you want to read, Ed? Just pick your time." So I learned corruption immediately. So everybody's groveling, wanting to get in: "Oh, here's some poems, Ed." They wanted to get in *Fuck You* because it became hot—all these people gave me articles to put in.

Skerl: How did you get all those really famous people to be contributors?

Sanders: I believed in what I did. I had a couple of semi-religious revelations, you know, from studying Egyptian and stuff. It was all happening right at the same time. So, I went into the 8th Street book shop and I got some addresses. I made this list of people I would send *Fuck You/A Magazine of the Arts:* I sent it to Fidel Castro, Pablo Picasso, Samuel Beckett, Jean-Paul Sartre, Allen Ginsberg, Philip Whalen,

Lawrence Ferlinghetti, Jack Kerouac. Of course, I would give it out, too. I had this endless list of people I respected, and I'd send it out to people just for the heck of it. Always first class, because I was afraid of getting arrested, because it took a radical stance for its time. For instance, I wrote the first editorial advocating the legalization of marijuana, and everybody was saying, "Oh Ed (this was in late '62, early sixties), you can't. It's gotta be handcuff city."

Skerl: That was pretty early for that stuff.

Sanders: I was very honest. I was trying to live an open life. So, if my friend wrote poems for *Fuck You Magazine* and was also a drug dealer, I'd put it in the contributor's notes. So, anyway, I sent it to Ginsberg (I got his address in India) and he was apparently in a big depression, so he wrote back. Charles Olson wrote back, Philip Whalen wrote back, Gary Snyder—they all started writing letters back. And I was just a trembling, little … So I said to myself, "you made your moves—you better get to know these people. Learn the language, get accepted as another beatnik schmo, just like a member of the club." So basically that's how it happened … that's how I met all those people. I did my apprenticeship, and I decided I was ready.

Skerl: But you were, I gather, really good friends with Ginsberg. He was involved with the Fugs.

Sanders: Yeah, well Ginsy and I got real close because I lived on the Lower East Side.

Skerl: So did he.

Sanders: Yeah. He always traveled a lot, but our apartments were pretty near, so I'd hang out. He's the one I got to know best of all of them, because he was on the set. Allen's the one with whom I had the greatest rapport because he got me out of the Midwest. I still think he's a great poet. Some of his poems are American treasures. And poetry was always my greatest interest, too.

Skerl: What do you think is his greatest significance as a poet?

Sanders: He's got a really good ear. He's brilliant. He's one of the most intelligent people I know, and able to cope with insanity. He's a guy who has on occasion had full Blakean visions. Usually when you meet a writer or somebody and you know them for twenty or thirty years, you develop a kind of a standoff, sort of begrudging friendship—but I feel very close to him still.

Skerl: When did you first meet William Burroughs?

Sanders: I remember a party at Grove Press in '65...I have various memories...I remember seeing him around the campus [NYU] a lot... He was more of an influence to me, frankly, in the books. A piece that was a big influence was in a little magazine called *The Outsider* [published in New Orleans in the 1960s], and also the books like *Exterminator* and *Nova Express*. Mainly, you got out of the early Burroughs things like you got from Sartre, from existentialism—"Existence precedes essence" and "Hell is other people"—apothegms. Burroughs was always interesting to me as a writer who was a distiller of apothegms—brilliant shards or fragments. We would all memorize stuff like that, or talk about Dr. Benway when *Naked Lunch* started coming out. So you picked up things then in segments when it came out in magazines. I couldn't afford to buy the book. Grove Press put it out for $5. In 1964 that was my weekly food bill.

Skerl: Did you know Burroughs's son?

Sanders: Yes.

Skerl: As I was reading *Tales of Beatnik Glory*, I kept comparing it to *Speed* [an autobiographical novel] by William Burroughs, Jr., because he portrayed the Lower East Side of the same era, around 1961, and there are a lot of parallels between your book and the amphetamine scene he described.

Sanders: Yeah, I had a lot of information about amphetamines. I made a documentary called *Amphetamine Head*.

Skerl: Yes, it's mentioned in *Tales of Beatnik Glory*.

Sanders: So I actually did it. The police took it. But I did do this film.

Skerl: They took the film?

Sanders: Yeah, they raided me. I had this little back building—one of those Lower East Side back buildings in the dark back courtyards, and they raided one night in 1965 in the summer and wiped out my film career. Some of it was pretty smutty. I did this film called *Mongolian Cluster*

Fuck. I used to get all my friends—we'd drink, and I'd have them come over, and film. In *Amphetamine Head* I think I had some footage of Corso, and some of Joel Oppenheimer. Yeah so, I rented this apartment on Allen Street, on the Lower East Side, a famous street in Lower East Side history. I bought a few ounces of amphetamines, and I strung lights all around, and I put this bag of amphetamines in the middle of the room, and put out the word. The only rule was that, whatever happened, I would be able to film it. It pretty much happened exactly as I wrote it in *Tales of Beatnik Glory.*

There were a couple of sordid things that I didn't write about, but mainly it's all there. People drew murals all over the wall, and they took off the front door and put up a curtain. That's what the landlord really freaked about—what did they do with the front door? They probably used as a staging area for art. They ripped the plumbing out to make plumbing flutes ... These were hardcore A-heads. These guys were the ones that said, "Hell man, wow, I was up three weeks, wow, thirteen visions," you know. These guys that had stayed up for a couple of weeks had sleep-death, a terrible sleep-death...They would put India Ink into hypodermic needles and squirt these arabesques. One or two of them were actually interesting artists. Most of the rest were just dopers—just burn-outs.

Skerl: Were they really young kids?

Sanders: There were old ones and young ones. Of course, with an A-head, you can't tell. If you go on amphetamines for a few weeks, you go kind of grey, and trembling, and skinny, and you don't know how old they are. They look like something casting called for cryptic movies [i.e., "from the crypt" horror movies]...

Skerl: What do you think is your most important work?

Sanders: I think it's a group of poems that will last...I guess I would say I'm a poet. I wrote a twenty-three-page poem about the ghost of Sappho. ["Sappho on East Seventh" was published in volume 2 of *Tales of Beatnik Glory* in 1990.] I spent six months writing it last year. I would say there is a group of poems, beginning with *Poem from Jail*, and including a group of poems I wrote based on my studies of Egyptology, a series called *Egyptian Hieroglyphs.* I think those will last. And there are various other poems in my sex mania period that I think will probably last, at least they will always be of interest to collectors of erotica. So, I think, in an aggregate, I've written and important group of maybe

100-150 pages of poetry that I'm very interested in having survive. I think I'm a pretty good short-story writer, too. *Tales of Beatnik Glory* were my first short stories, and since then I've written a whole bunch.

In fact, I'm just now finishing volume two of *Tales of Beatnik Glory*, where I mix narrative poetry with prose—poetry that's really narrative—I call them "sho-sto-poes"—short story poems that mix prose with the poetry sections. There's no slack, no vague imagery—it's very direct. I'm kind of proud of those. I studied a lot of Yiddish-speaking socialists in the Lower East Side and compared those people that lived in the same buildings in 1895 with those of us who lived there in 1963, '64, '65, sixty years later, switching back and forth, comparing two years. So I think those will last. It's interesting; I've never had anybody ask that question before. I guess that's the answer. There's about 150 pages of poetry and some short stories. It's like the Dadaists in 1916, sitting in the Cabaret Voltaire in Zurich and spewing out some manifesto in five minutes and that's what survives. And the rest of his life or her life they might have done fifty-nine volumes of work, but, this is it, the manifesto. So, I don't know, maybe something I scratched on a tablecloth at Le Metro Cafe in 1964 in the middle of a poetry reading will be anthologized. It's like Robert Graves says, all he wants is two poems in *The Oxford Book of English Verse*…

Skerl: I like that poem about Demeter ["Holy Was Demeter Walking the Corn Furrow"]. Is that one you would save?

Sanders: That's one of the sex maniac ones. I wrote the first version in '67, when Joel Oppenheimer and I were reading at the Folklore Center, and I had to have something hot for that. So I just wrote it off one morning. Then I kind of rewrote it after I met Robert Bly. Yeah, that's not bad. That's a very metrical poem. I got interested in Greek meters.

Skerl: Well, that was a question that I wanted to ask you, about your concept of poetic form. Ginsberg always talks about breath as the basis for his line, I wondered if you were working within that concept. But you also seem to have a lot of visual elements in your poems, too, which is an entirely different thing.

Sanders: Well, it's a question of left brain and right brain. I think it's important to develop your right brain, and I think visual and spatial perception in poetry is a right brain phenomenon. It developed in the twentieth century by using the typewriter as a typesetting process, with guys like Pound, William Carlos Williams in his tercets, Paul Blackburn, Gary Snyder, Phil Whalen. Allen's not too much into that.

Skerl: So you think it's all related to the typewriter. For some reason I never thought of that before.

Sanders: Well, and calligraphy. Those guys—Whalen, Lew Welch, and Snyder—all studied calligraphy at Reed College. So, that's why when you get a letter from Gary Snyder, it's a work of art. Ditto for Phil Whalen. Whalen's a master of the calligraphic poem. Apollinaire was. Some of those other French guys experimented with the way a poem looks. And Robert Duncan, for example. To him it's all a very serious matter. When Olson said poem is field, the way it looks is part of the field. So I have never hesitated to used glyphs; it comes out of my study of Egyptian.

Skerl: Are those drawings in your poems actually Egyptian? Or are they your own?

Sanders: It depends on what poems…I'm going full color now. I've decided to go full color type. I think that typeface is going to go full color now, and therefore, since colors seem to relate to emotions, why not program the reading public to become sensitive to the mode and nuances of color typography? So that will come into poetry. Like color serifs. Serifs on a type font are a little hook, eye hooks that hook into a text. It's proven that that's an easier way to read, these hooks, so why not have color serif hooks?

Skerl: Are you using color symbolism?

Sanders: You can relate colors primitively, like red with blood, blue with water, but it's more sophisticated than that because you perceive more than 1,500 color nuances, so you can relate them to emotions. Anyway, to me, it just goes to ability of your right brain in poetry, for your right brain to feed on as well as your linguistic half.

Skerl: So you're really putting the two things together—the visual and linguistic?

Sanders: That's why I want full color…to go the Blake route…

Skerl: Related to that, I wanted to ask you if you participated in the printing of your books, because the visual part is so important.

Sanders: Oh, sure, my attitude about publishers is torture them until they respect you, especially if you have a visual sense. I have a very well-defined right brain. So I know to the micro-inch where I'd like to see these things go. And you have get a little older and bolder to feel pushy enough to deal with the publishers. The best thing to do is to establish a cordial relationship and then force your will as much as possible on them, especially in spatial matters.

Skerl: I noticed you've been working with Open Studio. [Open Studio was a design, production, and training facility for writers, artists, and independent publishers in Rhinebeck, New York.]

Sanders: They did the little manifesto of mine about the secret police, *The Z-D Generation*. It's great to work with them.

Skerl: So what is your concept of investigative poetry which seems to be *The Z-D Generation*? It seems to me that's a whole new idea in your work.

Sanders: Basically, as a Newspeak précis, it's to keep poetry from becoming like Japanese flower arranging—not to trash Japanese flower arranging—but most people would rather be tortured than go to a poetry reading. I mean, if you go out there in the streets, people would maybe let you punch them in the face in lieu of going to a poetry reading, you know. At the same time, it's poetry's fault—it's a lot of gibberish. A lot of people are writing stuff that's just off the top of their heads—gibberish—without trying to take a step toward making it understandable.

And it's really the fault of these brilliant guys like Apollinaire and Mallarmé. Or, to go way back in time, the Greek dithyrambs—like Pindar—dithyrambs were just gibberish poems. But they were *sung*, you know, they had a chorus, so you can listen to the gibberish. It's like you don't really understand Wagner—most people don't—when it's sung, but it's beautiful and you don't mind. Same way in the dithyramb and just have somebody stand there—it's nod city…But that doesn't say much about investigative poetry. It's just a method, it's practical.

Skerl: You're saying it's a part of wanting to reach a larger audience, though.

Sanders: Well, another factor besides the gibberish factor, is that poetry used to be the six o'clock news, it used to tell the frustrations and hopes and desires and myths and inner meanings and secrets of the civilization. That's the *Iliad* and the *Odyssey*. They used to recite poems at the Olympics. If you trashed the emperor, it was a big deal. Catullus trashed Caesar, and they wondered if he was going to get killed for it. Poetry had an intimacy with the civilization. Probably only because of numbers, I suppose, because poetry and rhythm and singing and recitations were the most apt way mnemonically to store the information. That was the tape recorder of ancient times—metrics. But when 2,000 years go by, poetry is what? It's lost its relationship to civilization. So how would you, in a non-hokey, non-sellout, non-commercial, but in a socially and historically relevant way, bring poetry back to the position it had in ancient times? I thought one way would be by having poets write history and conduct investigations, using all the techniques from the last 200 years of French, German, and American poetry to write real time stuff—to do investigations to tell stories, to thrill a reader again, or the listener.

Skerl: In *The Z-D Generation* you're talking about investigating political issues.

Sanders: Yeah, another principle about investigative poetry is you don't have to drink the hemlock anymore. You throw the hemlock back in their faces. You say, "You drink the hemlock." It's like the Ginsberg line [from "Death to Van Gogh's Ear"], "Now is the time for prophecy without death as a consequence," which is another principle of investigative poetry: that you can prophesy in a democracy. American democracy *does* remind me of Athens. Inside Athens is a great zone of freedom, while Athens would send out its triremes to kill: "let's kill everybody in Lesbos because they didn't give us enough oil." So they would row off—to off the people of Lesbos. But within the walls of Athens there was a great freedom. If you wanted, you could be a drag queen, anything, whatever you wanted to do. As Aristophanes you could write *Lysistrata* in the middle of the war. It reminds me of America. So, "it's time for prophecy without death" is valid. So, why not have a Z-D generation—after Zola and Diderot—where you do the equivalent of the encyclopedia—which changed France for the better?

Skerl: Were you really interested in war criminals? [*The Z-D Generation* proposes to expose war criminals in the U.S. government.]

Sanders: Yeah, I thought, what would shake America to the core just like the encyclopedia did? In my judgement, the way you do it is to go up to the war caste, which I devoted a lot of time to. There's this group of people hooked into the machinations of power that come right out of World War II and Korea and Vietnam and are down there in El Salvador right now. I want to investigate the bombing practices of Curtis LeMay and the building of the bomb, and go right back to find the scientist who invented the fragmentation bomb, and locate the people that were responsible for Napalm, and just put them on the pickle fork of reality—write about them—poetry. So I thought that would be one project that would be equivalent [to the encyclopedia] because it would shake American civilization to the roots if you did it accurately.

An Interview with Ed Sanders

Tandy Sturgeon

Originally published in Contemporary Literature *31, no. 3 (1990): 263-80.*

Born in Kansas City on August 17, 1939, Ed Sanders migrated to New York's Greenwich Village as a young man. From this point on, as a voracious reader and tireless literary *artiste*, he became a full-fledged writer (of poetry, fiction, and investigative journalism), editor, Peace Eye Bookstore owner, musician (founding member of the Fugs), and antiwar activist. The appearance of *Poem from Jail* from City Lights Books in 1963 was followed by a steady stream of poetry collections, many of which are excerpted in Sanders's collected poems, *Thirsting for Peace in a Raging Century* (Coffee House Press, 1987). Sanders's work, despite its variety of intonations, has always remained committed to the idea promulgated by his *Investigative Poetry* (City Lights Books, 1975): "that poetry should again assume responsibility for the description of history."

As Charles Olson once noted, Sanders's work "advances in a direction of production which probably isn't even guessed at." In the 1975 edition of *Contemporary Poets*, Don Byrd remarked that in Sanders's poetry "the raw energy of a 1960s-style peace march, a rock concert, and an orgy impels a fine intelligence. Many of his poems can be read as political protest; some may be read, by a reader intent on it, as pornography." This last possibility may explain why Sanders's work, soundly planted in his enthusiastic, scholarly study of the classics, Egyptology, political philosophy, and the English romantics, is not as widely circulated as it should be.

In 1979, in an essay introducing John Clarke's *The End of This Side*, "The Clarke-Boat, the O-Boat, and the Bard-Boat," Sanders described the modern poet's role as a perpetuation of Noah's task. He argues that "the establishment of mythic poetry and National Epic, in the 'God-is-Dead' mythless bureaucratic era of money-grubbers operating mines in the asteroid belt, will be difficult." Despite this difficulty, Sanders sails on, as exemplified by a recent project, a touring opera production entitled *Star Peace*.

This interview began in June 1986 at Sanders's home in Woodstock, New York, where he lives with his wife, Miriam, and his daughter, Deirdre. It was completed in April 1988 during a visit by Sanders to the Woodland Pattern Book Center in Milwaukee.

Tandy Sturgeon: Can you tell me a little bit about your young adulthood?

Ed Sanders: I was raised a regular American by Stevensonian Democrats in the Midwest. I come from a family of engineers. My grandfather was an engineer; my brothers are both engineers. But in the roots of the family were agricultural. My father's family were farmers for a number of generations in Kentucky, Tennessee, Alabama, Missouri. My maternal grandfather was very creative, an inventor. He invented a machine to automatically lay down ballast and straighten railroad tracks. He was a mad inventor. My mother was also very creative. She would do things like buy a piano and take it apart all over the floor and put it back, or she would fix her own sewing machine. She was very intelligent and extremely gifted in art and restoration and using her hands. I was raised a regular American. I was in the Boy Scouts, and I was president of my high school student council.

I played football and basketball, went on overnight hikes, and was a regular American kid, but I discovered poetry when I was fifteen and was encouraged by a high school English teacher who, although being of very puritanical, perfect American stock, could tolerate a wild, confused-and-trembling kid of fifteen who wrote poetry that did not jibe entirely with the life of Plymouth Rock.

Sturgeon: What kind of poetry were you reading?

Sanders: My main heroes were, of course, those to whom I was supposed to be exposed. They were all from the middle of the nineteenth century. Hawthorne, Poe, Melville, maybe a little bit of William Cullen Bryant, and perhaps Robert Frost—all the ones in the pantheon of the golden age of American literature.

Sturgeon: So it was all American. They didn't give you any Keats or Shelley?

Sanders: No Shelley, nothing. Just America was where it was at. Manifest Destiny applied to writing also. You were forced to read in Endymion or maybe a little bit of "To a Skylark" for a little "furrin" vice. The main thing was Poe and a little Whitman, but not much. Mainly Poe—and John Greenleaf Whittier, who was thought of highly in the Midwest in my generation.

Sturgeon: Yes. You can find dozens of editions of Whittier in any used bookstore today.

Sanders: Right! So I was raised on that, and then I began writing my own poetry. And although I was a regular American guy, I would walk around high school with my clipboard full of poetry. I had really no one, no soulmate other than my schoolteacher with whom to share this poetry. The next person I could share it with would be three years later when I met my future wife Miriam in Greek class at NYU.

Sturgeon: How did you get from Missouri to NYU?

Sanders: I was a kid in the Midwest in a suburb of Kansas City and going to Blue Springs High School. Then, in the spring of '57, the worst thing that could befall a young man happened: my mother died suddenly, causing a lot of family turmoil—you know, here we go rebellious-teenage-boy-not-getting-along-with-his-parents, and one of them dies tragically and way before her time—that was the worst thing. I figured nothing could be worse than that. It just tore my mind apart. It's reflected in the poem "Cemetery Hill" [*Thirsting for Peace*, 29-36]. That was March 1957; I graduated from high school shortly thereafter, and I went for a year to Missouri University. My family demanded that I become an engineer, or a chemist, or a biologist. I thought I might want to be a physicist because at that time I was interested in the space program that was beginning the following year—the Mercury program. I thought I might become one of these macho guys with a Ph.D. that actually get to go into orbit.

Sturgeon: So you took classes in physics.

Sanders: I studied physics and I studied a lot of math. I took a few semesters of calculus and functions and complex variables and differential equations.

Sturgeon: Tell me about your transformation into a poet.

Sanders: I was at Missouri University for a year and I did not like it.

I was nobody—there was no literary scene that I felt I could cooperate with, nor were their simpatico brothers and sisters with whom I could share my interest in literature, so I got out of there. I hitchhiked to New York in the summer of 1958 with thirty-five dollars and got into Manhattan and went immediately to the Gotham Book Mart which I had been reading about a lot. I had in my knapsack my Dylan Thomas, my Ezra Pound, my William Carlos Williams, early issues of *Evergreen Review* (which I had purchased at the University of Missouri Bookstore), and Ginsberg's *Howl.* I had my little packet of sacred books. You know, I had *Waiting for Godot*, et cetera.

Sturgeon: D. H. Lawrence maybe? In *Tales of Beatnik Glory* the central character is carrying Lawrence's poems in a backpack.

Sanders: Kenneth Rexroth wrote a tremendous essay, as a preface to D. H. Lawrence's *Selected Poems*, that set me on Lawrence for all time.

Sturgeon: You also had the *Cantos* in your Book Boat, didn't you?

Sanders: I had my Book Boat. I had all that stuff. As I said, I had *Howl*, I had *Being and Nothingness* by Sartre…I don't know. I think I must have had a New Directions William Carlos Williams, one of them.

I used to go out with these drinking buddies from my high school when I'd go home weekends from the University of Missouri, and the mode of operation was to circle around the county courthouse drinking beer and throw the cans into the Methodist Church front yard, and I had *Howl* memorized, and I would recite it to these guys. It's an embarrassing thing, like being Monk in a jazz club or something and having everybody talk while you play.

I was memorizing a lot of poetry. I went to New York City, spent all my money in the Gotham Book Mart, and decided to stay. I went to NYU, and out of deference to my mother who had just died—she had said that a gentleman always knows Greek or Latin—I decided to pick up Latin again and also to take Greek. I wandered into room 901 in the main building at NYU in the fall of '58, and there were about nine other people, and I met Miriam there, who was also taking Greek because she, at that time, intended to be an archaeologist. She was someone with whom I felt confident enough to show my poetry.

Sturgeon: What was the New York literary scene like at that time?

Sanders: I was too shy to meet many people. We would go out and go to all the bookstores and the poetry readings. I actually heard Jack Kerouac read in the Gaslight, and also Edward Dahlberg and Corso. I went to the Living Theatre and met Paul Goodman, who became a friend, and heard Frank O'Hara and Allen Ginsberg. I was just a guy on the edge of learning what was going on. At the same time, I became intensely interested in languages. I was reading as much as I could, traveling around being a beatnik, hitchhiking in the summer across the country. Once I dropped out to go on a peace walk across America. After that I went to jail.

The first little book, the one Ferlinghetti printed, was the result of a peace demonstration where I tried to board a Polaris Submarine at New London, Connecticut; we kept swimming out and trying to get on these submarines. I finally got arrested and spent a couple of weeks in jail. That was in August of '61, and I wrote a little book-length poem, a thirty-pager, which I thought was state of the art. I thought I had finally written something that was equal in quality to what was going on.

Sturgeon: Is that *Poem from Jail*?

Sanders: Yes. I wrote *Poem from Jail* on toilet paper in my jail cell in specific Greek meters. I had taken a course at New York University in Greek lyric poetry, and I had memorized, and still do have memorized, all the little Greek meters, *ionic a minore*, *a majore*, et cetera. I'd elucidate a meter, like *ionic a minore*, say, which is two shorts followed by two longs, di-di, da, da, or I would think of a specific meter and then think of a line. All of the lines, basically, are written in little Greek paradigms. I don't think I ever told anybody that; it's not obvious. I wrote this in my jail cell and smuggled it out in my shoe and read it, along with Ginsberg's *Kaddish* and parts of Homer I had memorized, to the people at the peace camp. I was the mad poet who would shriek out Ginsberg's *Kaddish* and other poems. I'd have all these trapped pacifists in their sleeping bags around the campfire and I would cry, "O mother, what have I left out, o mother, what have I forgotten, farewell with your torn black … " Then the final thing: "Caw caw caw crow shriek in the white sun over the grave-stones in Long Island Lord Lord."[1]

I sent a copy of the poem to Lawrence Ferlinghetti, and to my lasting gratitude, he wrote a very enthusiastic letter back, liked it, agreed to publish it. I was ecstatic. But it became one of those horrible situations for a person just beginning a career, where a reputable publisher says, "I'm going to do the book," and you go out like an ape, beating your chest, blowing smoke in coffee houses, saying, "Well, my book is going to be good, and I'm very important," you know. But then umpteen years go by, and it's, "Sure, Ed, where's your book?"

Sturgeon: Did years go by?

Sanders: Yeah. Finally, I stopped telling people, and by the time the book came out, I no longer cared.

Sturgeon: That was in 1963?

Sanders: Yeah. Two years went by. But the fact is, this all led to *Fuck You* magazine. I had an apartment at 509 East Eleventh. I describe it in the editorial conference in *Tales of Beatnik Glory*. And that's where I formed *Fuck You/A Magazine of the Arts*. I was drinking all the time. I was hanging out at the Catholic Worker. I wasn't a Catholic, but I was very sympathetic to their peace cause. A number of the people at Polaris Action and in the various peace rallies were hard-living

1 The correct lines from *Kaddish* are "O mother/ what have I left out/ O mother/ what have I forgotten/ O mother/ farewell/ with a long black shoe" and "Caw caw caw crows shriek in the white sun over grave stones in Long Island/ Lord Lord. . ."

Catholics. They were young people who felt very sympathetic to the Catholic vision as interpreted by Dorothy Day: voluntary poverty, helping others, antiwar.

Sturgeon: Had you met the poet Jean Morton then? She's in your first issue in 1962.

Sanders: Jean Morton was a friend of mine. She had been in the Air Force and then dopped out, and I met her at the soup kitchen at the Catholic Worker. I'd go get my clothing there; I'd go get a free lunch. I was totally broke. I had no money—zilch, nothing. They helped me and later, when I first put out *Fuck You*, they let me type my stencils on the second floor. I used their paper, that green, grainy-textured Catholic Worker protest-leaflet paper. When Dorothy Day found about that, she went totally crazy. But I could understand her position. Even though I never imposed my beliefs on anyone there, they were given the choice: either sever connections with me or leave the Catholic Worker. A number of people associated with the Worker left out of protest; others stayed.

Sturgeon: So were people generally sympathetic to *Fuck You*?

Sanders: Sure, because I was totally in the pacifist, direct-action, nonviolent, peace-walk group of people. One night in February of '62 I said, "I'm gonna start a magazine called *Fuck You/A Magazine the Arts*, and I need some poetry." And everybody said, "Sure." I collected poetry and I added a lot of my own poetry—featured myself in the first issue, in fact. But I had Jean Morton's stuff, and I sucked some various verses out of people. There were some things about the magazine that I now regret emphasizing, such as heroin and some male chauvinism, but at the time I felt like it was free and good and pure and that I was doing something that was wonderful. I was having such a great time giving out these values, giving the magazine away for free; through all its faults, I thought I was promulgating something that made sense: pacifism and disarmament.

Sturgeon: Did anybody help you with the magazine?

Sanders: No. I did it all, and I gave it away free except I was making up little book catalogues to earn money. I did sell it to university libraries such as the one in Madison, Wisconsin, and other places, but I mostly gave it all away. I'd walk around the Lower East Side and just give this stuff away, and I got kind of instantly famous. From friends I developed a mailing list of people I wanted to send *Fuck You/A Magazine of the Arts* to. I sent it to Pablo Picasso; I sent it to Samuel Beckett at Ussy-sur-Marne.

Sturgeon: Did he ever answer?

Sanders: He didn't, but I heard he read it. I heard rumors. I'd know people that he gave copies to. I also sent it to Fidel Castro, Allen Ginsberg in India, Gary Snyder, Philip Whalen, and Marianne Moore. I sent it to Ferlinghetti, of course. Allen sent poems and so did Charles Olson. I started a fairly extensive correspondence with Olson that lasted until he died—we must have exchanged fifty or sixty letters.

Sturgeon: Tell me about this connection to Olson.

Sanders: He and I intersected on Hesiod. One of the first things I sent him,after reading "Maximus from Dogtown 1," was a copy of Hesiod in the original Greek. He knew enough Greek that he could get into it a little bit. I had a lot of Hesiod's *Theogony* memorized—it's the only thing I like of his. *Poem from Jail* comes out of Hesiod. All the myth is from Hesiod and from certain Egyptian myths, and Olson loved that. We exchanged letters, and I visited him in Boston, saw him here and there. But the first time I sent him something I couldn't write directly—I just sent him a copy of *Fuck You.*

Sturgeon: So you did the magazine alone. Would you do it all in one run, all night long?

Sanders: I would work—I've always been a workaholic, and I worked real hard. I just never slept, I guess. I had a terrific amount of energy, and I would stay up all night drinking and smoking pot and turning it out.

Sturgeon: You never had any collators?

Sanders: I don't know if I have ever written about the yoga of doing this. I developed a system of sitting in lotus posture on my black floor surrounded by concentric semicircles of pages, and I have long arms like a gibbon and could reach about six feet out from a lotus posture and suck up these concentric semicircles of pagination. Later on when the issues got real thick, Peter Orlovsky, who was in his manic amphetamine phase, and his brother Julius, who was a little slower but could function, used to help me collate, sometimes. Like the

"God" issue—the one with the Tibetan Martian Mantra cover [5:7, September 1964]. That was the cover that Robert Levine did. That was a giant issue and those two helped, but mainly I did it myself.

Sturgeon: And you drew the covers?

Sanders: Yes. Except for—well, Warhol did a cover [5:8, February 1965] and Robert Levine did the one I just mentioned. Most of them were done by me. I didn't have any electricity in my apartment, so I became quite skilled at drawing with a thin stylus and engraver's tools on stencils. All those *Fuck You*s except for the very last few issues were hand drawn on stencils, and it took me forever because I'd use a flash-light—no lights on, so I'd have to have a flashlight shining up through the back of the stencil. I remember late at night drawing those fairly complicated drawings. It was like a Sumi painting—make a mistake with a stencil and you've got to do it again.

Sturgeon: And then you used a stapler to bind it.

Sanders: Right. I'd stack and staple it. I loved the physical labor of stapling and squashing with the heel of my hand on a good stapler. It became a healthy, holistic thing to do. What wasn't healthy and holistic were the ink cutters, the benzine. I discovered after trial and error that benzine was great at cleaning off ink. Then to my horror I learned—after having bathed my knuckles in this damned substance for five years in the sixties and breathing it—that it's leukogenic. It's a carcinogen.

Sturgeon: Tell me about the erotic Auden poem you published in *Fuck You* [5:8, February 1965], "Platonic Blow." That must have caused something of a furor. Where did you obtain the manuscript?

Sanders: I got the poem from two sources. One was a friend of mine, a poet who had a relationship with this librarian at the Morgan Library. The other source was another acquaintance, another poet, who somehow had his own copy and sent it to me from the islands, Trinidad or St. Thomas. The poem describes the male oral experience. I've never had a homosexual experience, but I'm very sympathetic to gays. It was a good poem, and it didn't seem to me to be out of bounds to have been written by Auden, whom everybody knew was gay. And I'd heard that there are other erotic poems of Auden's out there. So I went ahead and printed it—all by itself to begin with, and later in *Fuck You*. Ted Berrigan helped me with the first version, and we made a couple hundred dollars, enough to pay rent and expenses, and of course gave a lot of them away, too.

Sturgeon: You had met Berrigan around that time?

Sanders: Yes, I met him at the mimeograph machine in Bob Wilson's Phoenix Bookshop. I was printing *Fuck You* and he was doing *C* magazine. He and I really hit it off. We had unique language systems. Together, our verbal styles created a kind of universe—people would copy the way we spoke. Berrigan was one of those wall-to-wall poets. He was the guy who made up the dictum that there are no weekends for poets. Anyway, we distributed the Auden booklet together.

Sturgeon: And the reaction?

Sanders: Well, I remember having the third anniversary party for *Fuck You/A Magazine of the Arts* in February 1965 at my bookstore. Burroughs and Warhol were there; Warhol had put up big banners for the party. Jason Epstein and James Michener and some other friends of Auden came in, and they were really bent out of shape. They felt that the author of "The Age of Anxiety" could never have written "The Platonic Blow," but it seemed to me the same verse line, for one thing. Somebody told me that whoever's done the bibliography on Auden has accepted it as a legitimate Auden poem. So I don't feel bad about it.

Sturgeon: That was 1965, and you mention your Peace Eye Bookstore. When did you start that?

Sanders: The bookstore began in late '64. I had been putting out book catalogues to help put myself through college, and I'd get telegrams from university libraries fighting for this material. I'd go around to parties and collect things and get people to sign them. I'd sell Allen Ginsberg's cold cream jar, but also books and pamphlets.

Sturgeon: Allen didn't care?

Sanders: Allen couldn't find his cold cream. I'd go over to his house and get his cold cream. All that stuff was getting snuffed right up, and I was making money, so I figured, why not open a bookstore rather than go to graduate school? I found an old kosher meat market, left up the Hebrew sign, "strictly kosher," cleaned all the chicken feathers and rendered fat off the floor, painted it, and opened it up. It went on for approximately four and a half years, and it was something of a gold mine; people would rush in from all over the country to go to Peace Eye. I stopped it in early 1970. Miriam and I flew out to L.A., and I began the Manson book a week later [*The Family*, Dutton 1971]. I just opened the doors and said, "Who wants this stuff?" Boy, they came and got it.

Sturgeon: During the bookstore period, you were arrested for publishing your "lewd" magazine. Can you tell me about that?

Sanders: I guess I'll never know precisely what was going on. Since I have an FBI file, I guess the government became aware of me somehow. I was getting the ink. I was getting some articles written so I was getting a fair amount of renown, and, beginning with late '65, it looks [according to my FBI files] like they're trying to figure out what to do. I had formed the Fugs. We had gone on a cross-country caravan against the Vietnam War. We had records out. Somebody was writing to the FBI in the fall of '65 about this scurrilous, creepy group named the Fugs and please do something about them. Right at the time the Justice Department actually did mount an investigation. That's in my FBI files. It made me proud to be an American when I read in the FBI document that we weren't indictable. We were using the freedoms of expression found in the Constitution.

Sturgeon: Go on.

Sanders: Anyway, strange things were happening. We gave a Fugs show in 1966 in New York, on New Year's night, and late that night a junkie apparently broke into my bookstore, smashed the window, and stole stuff. Tuli Kupferburg came to my house at four in the morning, waking Miriam and me. He said, "Ed, these police are in your store, and there's this guy in there really upset." So I took a cab down, and there was a sergeant there named Fetta who was so upset by *Fuck You* that he was trembling. He said, "Did you do this, is this yours?" I said, "Yeah." They were boxing up my stuff—the *Fuck You* press, including *The Toe-Queen: Poems* [Fuck You Press, 1964], and the poem I printed of Auden's, and all my copies of *Fuck You*. In fact, for years, they kept a box of *Fuck You*s at the ninth precinct to show to visiting dignitaries—local smut, definitely "actionable" smut, even though I later won the case.

I was arrested and taken to the ninth precinct. There was one cover of *Fuck You* [5:4, Fall 1963] with a picture of a boy with a lizard on his leg and an Egyptian hawk with a phallus in its claw. So Fetta is coming up to me, saying, "What about this bird with this penis? It's going to attack this boy, right?" And I said, "No, it's just a lizard spurting things out of its mouth." I told him I copied the boy off a Danish tobacco pouch, and the hawk represents a sound in ancient Egyptian and not to get bent out of shape about it—it's satirical, don't worry about it. Later, while I'm waiting with one of the arresting officers, who's pecking out my name and social security number on an old Underwood typewriter, Fetta rushes in. He's totally upset. He says, "Do you have any tattoos?" I said no. Then I see he's clutching a copy of *Fuck You* magazine, and he says, "You said you had no tattoos. Go in the other room and take off your clothes." Well, it turns out that in my editorial notes I had said, "Ed Sanders has the first twenty-five hieroglyphs of Akhenaton's 'Hymn to the Sun Disk' tattooed on his genitals."

Sturgeon: This Fetta was one of your most careful readers!

Sanders: Yeah. So I go in this little room and I take off my clothes and I've got these two heads of these two cops down, you know, they don't want to touch; they couldn't lift up my balls and look. They're in there like a couple of boys about three feet from my naked body, looking at me. I said, "Hey, take a look. It was a joke!" Anyway, I went before the judge the first time after being all night in the wino tank with all the puke and drunks.

Sturgeon: How long did you actually spend in jail?

Sanders: About a day, but you see the idea was to keep me coming to court to humiliate me. I think I went seventeen times before I finally won the case, and I'd have to go in at nine o'clock in the morning, feeling like a criminal. Especially that first morning—I felt like mucus. I didn't have any sleep. I had just given a concert. But I knew my Bill of Rights, and I told Fetta as we were waiting to go in to court, "Someday I'm going to win this case because I'm in the right and I represent freedom and I'm not doing anything wrong. And I'm going to invite you to the party."

I'm a night person, and in those days I'd go to bed at five in the morning and get up at three. But I could never tell when the trial would happen and it just went on and on. I got a lot of support from the ACLU and letters from Frank O'Hara, John Ashbery, Ed Dorn. Stephanie Harrington wrote a nice article in the *Village Voice*. Meanwhile I'm on the cover of *Life*—I'm getting terribly famous for a young guy from the Midwest. I tour, I play off Broadway for nine hundred performances. I've got Peter O'Toole and Richard Burton coming backstage, yet I have to trudge down regularly every month or so to this courtroom.

One day I showed up totally dressed in white—white suit, white tie, white shoes; I'm in my Beau Brummell phase of fluff, beatnik foppery. Then at the next court date I come dressed in red, everything red—red tie, red scarf, red shoes, red socks, red pants, red sweater, red coat. And the judge said, "Young man, this is not a ski lodge. I want you to come to my court dressed properly." I'm brought to this point—I'm playing games. It was that very same judge who got me off when the case finally went to trial a year and a half after the arrest, in 1967. That was Judge Ringel, and I'm forever in his debt because he realized that what I was doing was protected by the Constitution.

So I'm planning the party and I turn around to find Sergeant Fetta and he's gone because he knows I'm going to invite him to the party. I have a party and the prosecutor comes to the party. It's really weird.

Sturgeon: Sergeant Fetta didn't come?

Sanders: Fetta didn't show. I had a great party. I polished my bookstore up and had champagne, and I had all the court exhibits all over the wall, my jail photos—I had the whole thing. I was so happy and proud of my country. I was thinking, by that time, gee, I can do the magazine again, but I couldn't pick it up again. I was too busy.

Sturgeon: So actually Sergeant Fetta and his tribe only managed to stop the magazine by default. As far as the trial's outcome—one can't help but think of D. H. Lawrence, of Joyce, and of course Burroughs's and Ginsberg's pornography trials. In all of those instances, society needed to be taught a lesson regarding the definition of literature. The kernel of knowledge you seem to have imparted, as a result of this experience, has to do with the fact that much of what was on trial was not the product of a single author. As a small magazine, *Fuck You* was a time capsule, as you might call it, containing various "literatures."

Sanders: That's very true, especially since I was preparing a prose issue on poetics when I was arrested. I had some really interesting stuff from Olson that I had received, some from Gary Snyder and others. I could detect that there wasn't a lot of poetics being discussed in free form. I was trained in classical Greek and Latin and knew Egyptian and Mycenaean and some other languages, as well as being trained as a mathematician and a scientist, so I had a really cold, analytical mind, despite my being a space cadet. I felt I could get a really interesting discussion going on poetics that utilized my anarchic-pacifist perspective—I thought I would surprise my audience a little. I guess it all ended up in the part of my archives that I've turned over to the University of Connecticut [Storrs]—that included my correspondence with Olson as well. Anyway, the ACLU, specifically Rosenberg, my lawyer, who's now Judge Rosenberg, convinced me not to run any more issues.

Sturgeon: Why?

Sanders: They felt that it would just add more fuel, or that the judges could interpret it that way. Basically, it probably was just to make their time easier. Anyway, when you're young and hot and you drop something, you tend not to pick it up again.

Sturgeon: So the magazine went the way of the bookstore by the end of the sixties.

Sanders: Right.

Sturgeon: Yet *Fuck You* is a repository of early, often first appearances of so many writers. I went through its thirteen-issue run, 1962 to 1965, and found all these names ... Tuli Kupferberg, Carol Berge, John Weiners, Michael McClure, Jackson MacLow, Ray Bremser, Duncan, Robert Creeley, William Burroughs, Joel Oppenheimer, Barbara Moraff, Charles Olson, Paul Blackburn, Lenore Kandel, Rochelle Owens, Diane Wakoski, Ted Berrigan, Frank O'Hara, Allen Ginsberg—

Sanders: All these stars—and more! You might call it my pre-saturation phase. Olson said if you want to prepare yourself as a historian or a writer who uses history or real events you need one giant saturation job. He said it doesn't matter whether you study pemmican or whatever. The idea is that you immerse yourself in it.

The Family was my first big saturation job. That prepared me as a novice. People think I did too good a job. I've got a giant map of every bloodstain in that house that I questioned all the defendants with; I sent them lists of questions asking how they killed these people. I got a lot of inside information. But if I had to do the book over again, I probably wouldn't have described the murder so well. I would be a little less intense in that murder description, and I think I would have been—the criticism that I got was that the book was not analytical or sociological enough. Because the information that's in there was known by everybody at the time. But a few years go by and people forget or a new generation comes up and so it becomes more sociological because the information is not fresh and known. I did my best. I worked hard for eighteen months and haven't read it in many years. I haven't looked at it in a long time.

Sturgeon: You explain in the introduction that you took on a persona to secure data: "I posed as a Satanic guru-maniac and dope-trapped psychopath."

Sanders: If you're talking to people to whom killing doesn't matter, you also have to act like it doesn't matter. That's probably a bit overstated; I never engaged in any weird activity. But if you're talking to people who would kill you for a candy bar, you have to talk their language. It's like any reporting on the beat: if you're covering the CIA, you've got to talk that lingo, if you're covering the State Department, you talk their lingo; if you're covering the street crimes in the Bronx, you're talking street language. Whatever you're covering, you've got to have an exchange of minds. You've got to be able to talk to them in order to get more information. That's what I meant by that.

Sturgeon: *The Family* has been touted as the story of the other side of the sixties, a dream about the idea of a commune of gentle hippies whose wills combine in such a way that it turns into something quite other than what might have been intended. So isn't *The Family* a critique of a certain time as well as of specific people?

Sanders: No. It doesn't have *my* politics and beliefs in it. I was a little too old to be a hippie, but I was sympathetic to them. I used to go out to California during the sixties all the time to perform, give poetry readings, hang out, goof off, so I was very sympathetic to the communal movement. But the problem was that there were no institutions set up to support that world view. If you have a world view that's shared by a lot of people, you have to set up institutions that support that world view. And the hippies, of course—and they're not to be judged for it—could not easily set up hippiedom. There's the question of who cooks while everybody's dancing and making love or playing the tambourine. That surfaced as the woman's movement. There are other questions that surfaced that grew out of that time. How do you have non-rat-race, free-time oriented society where you still have dental care? What do you do about cancer? All the issues that were latent are still working themselves through. The institutions to solve these many problems are still growing.

Sturgeon: I sense that you're expressing a lack of interest in this part of your career, that you've turned in other directions.

Sanders: Basically I've worked through the necessary interest I once had in the Manson case. Eventually you come to a determination about evil—that you can't do anything about it. What you can do something about is the overt, public aspects of evil. Now I'd rather work for cleaning up the environment than cleaning up cults. For example, my poetic manifesto *The Z-D Generation* [Station Hill, 1981] is a call for new reform of the secret side of the American military apparatus.

Sturgeon: Yes. It's a realization of the quotation you use in its epigraph, as well as in Investigative Poetry, Olson's "know the new facts early." Your work has a very broad range, and I was wondering whether you think of it as being divided into poetry and prose, or along some other lines. Do you have a particular division in mind?

Sanders: I don't know. I don't really think of it like that. Most of my writing nobody knows about. Obviously it's a simple division—poetry and prose. Most things I write are done in poetic lines, including my book on the Manson family. Almost everything I do has a version in poetry. *The Z-D Generation* is prose, but it's broken up. It's a manifesto—it's the kind of prose that has line breaks that's still prose, not poetry, and why not?

Sturgeon: Yes, and that's a form you've already established in *Investigative Poetry*. There you make your claims like this:

> when practicing
> writing up Morality Lists or data-grids
> you will feel the lines break—
> you will automatically break
> your data torrent on
> the lines.

Is that the sort of thing you're talking about?

Sanders: I do that naturally because I think prose is trapped in the Gutenberg Bible. The guy who printed the Gutenberg Bible in two columns locked everybody forever into that concept. It's convenient. Your eye moves back and forth and picks up the page as a gestalt so you're really reading the whole page while you're reading each line. It can be useful, but there's no reason theoretically that one couldn't—especially now that everybody's going digital—make line breaks for prose at will.

There are two or three guiding lights for this kind of thinking. There's Olson's metaphor of a high energy grid in which one line instantly leads to another. That's from *Projective Verse*. There's an "energy warp" going on between the page and the mind, and your eyes are drawn down the page by the energy of the poem. The Pound metaphor is "distillation." There you have data clusters. He was really good at line arrangement. He would distill, out of his information, all these lyrics that would appear in his *Cantos*, these little four or five lines and all of a sudden bring out the essence, or part of the essence—and they're found all through the *Cantos*.

And then there's Blackburn, the guy who was always bending down putting reel-to-reel tape on the spool at poetry readings. He was an inspiration and a proto-archivist. What made the biggest impression on me was watching him read. The guy was the first besides Ginsberg who really knew what he was doing with cadence. At the end of a line he would drop a tone—it wasn't a quarter tone, but an eighth of a tone drop—so his lines were like layers of bluestone because each one was separate, and he was great. He knew how to end a line so beautifully and how to use his voice as an instrument.

Sturgeon: What attracts you, then, is the idea of having some lyric passages set in a "grid"?

Sanders: Right. The problem is that things change so much that you can't be guaranteed that the basic information that supplies the poem will be understood ten years from now. So the poet has an obligation. It's like a court record. You can assume facts, not evidence. You can't be overly didactic.

Sturgeon: One of your attributes is that you have a mania for facts and information, and yet I'm puzzled at a paradox in your work. It's that you record so much factually, and at the same time there's this whole other you, this sort of Irish songbird quality. Do you find any kind of contradiction in that?

Sanders: I'm a poet! I'm supposed to be a difficult individual and full of contradictions. Seriously, though, a poet is a person who has poetic skills. But not all poets partake equally of all poetic skills. I have certain skills that I know to a moral certainty are good, and so therefore I array those poetic skills on a page. I have a gift for telling a story, for nature poetry, for certain types of image structures. I have an ear, a sense of sequence of vowels which carry the melody and consonants which are the guts of things. I have, through long practice and probably through inherited genetics, the gift of the skill to present these vowels and consonants in interesting patterns, and then I have a further skill of observation.

The thing about this is that you work very hard and that you isolate your poetic skills. Know what you can do and try to do that. Also there are more than nine muses. There are maybe a couple hundred, and you have to know from which of those couple hundred muses your skills are derived.

Sturgeon: Do you have names for any of these muses?

Sanders: Yes. I would say one is Retentia—the use of the retained image, so that in an age of data retention poets use more typesetting and graphic images. I use her in my long ghost poem "Sappho on East Seventh" [*Thirsting for Peace*, 169-96]. A good example is Robert Duncan—or Charles Olson. One could think of, if one really wanted to, linking two parts of the brain. For instance, the muse of intense visual images might be in your hippocampus, which is where your primal fear/non-fear image-sorting system is. You could go to modern brain taxonomy and isolate all kinds of muses. There are many different skills.

Sturgeon: You've definitely got the lyric skill. Could you tell me how you came to write your ode about the "pondic lun' flash" ("The Plane," *Thirsting for Peace* 218)?

Sanders: I did that one while flying back from reading at the Chicago Art Institute in 1984. I was flying to Albany at night, during the full moon, and I went over these little lakes. They're not the Finger Lakes. They're smaller. They're just gouged-out-of-gravel glacial lakes. They're very beautiful. "Pond 'pon pond." That's a twenty thousand dollar line. It's a transmission poem, a shamanistic transmission poem, as I wrote it. In the instant—two minutes, three minutes, five minutes—just before the terror: Are we going to crash? The plane's getting a lot lower. Landing in Albany is always iffy. Before the final terror-tremor, you go over these lakes, and the moon's out, and you actually see—it's a quick thing. And I'm saying, "Wait, that's fun. Let's have more of that."

Sturgeon: So you've practiced many trades, yet maintain you're basically a poet. Do you see yourself as a policy maker, artistically as well as politically?

Sanders: Yeah. I'm in the left wing of the Democratic party, believing that anything's possible.

Sturgeon: You mean you're really democratic with a small d?

Sanders: *Demos*, "people," *kratos*, "rule"—people ruling. People ruling people. It requires a kind of faith that human nature may be capable of, after all.

Ed Sanders Interview

Sean Thomas Dougherty

Originally published in Long Shot *13 (1992): 87–90. Reprinted by permission of Danny Shot.*

Poet, writer, political activist, founder of the satirical-protest-rock band, the Fugs, the once famous Peace Eye Bookstore, and the seminal lit mag *Fuck You/A Magazine of the Arts*, Ed Sanders was one of the fathers of the sixties counterculture renaissance. His contributions to American counterculture continue to this day. His *Thirsting for Peace in a Raging Century: Selected Poems 1961-1985* won the 1988 American Book Award, and his investigation of the Charles Manson group, *The Family*, was recently reissued to great acclaim. Citadel Underground publications has just released an expanded version of his *Tales of Beatnik Glory*.

This interview was conducted by Sean Thomas Dougherty in Spring 1991 by phone to Ed's home in upstate New York where he lives with his wife and family. The interview centered on *Tales of Beatnik Glory*, and the book's dominant setting, the Lower East Side.

Sean Dougherty: Why did you write the first series of stories?

Ed Sanders: Well, I wrote a book on the Manson Family that came out in '71. Then '72 went by, and it was kind of a bad time—'72, '73—what with Watergate and all. That's when I began writing the first volume. I finished it in '75. I wanted to return to a time I had known when I knew I could write about it well, a time that I lived through and that I felt really good about.

Dougherty: That feeling comes through when you write about the Lower East Side. It seems as though you have a real spiritual connection to the neighborhood, and to the events that happened in the ten years you lived there.

Sanders: That's true, as I say in the introduction and also in some of the stories, such as "Farbrente Rose" and "A Night at the Cafe Perf-Po;" I go into the history of the Lower East Side—kind of a rebel zone for over a hundred years. It always attracted the avant-garde of its time. And it always attracted a vast variety of immigrants, from the Eastern European immigrants—Czechoslovakia, Poland, the Ukraine—to the Jewish immigrants escaping the pogroms, to the Spanish speaking immigrants, the Puerto Ricans. They were all there and the more I studied it the more I realized it was kind of a sacred zone.

Dougherty: Where did the idea for the sho-sto-poem "Farbrente Rose" come from?

Sanders: In '81 I was doing research on the early twentieth-century radical women and union activists for a song. I studied these powerful women. I also knew a couple of older women who were active in the environmental and consumer movement up here in the Catskills. I incorporated what I knew about them onto the research from the various books I had studied and came up with a sort of composite fiery red-haired woman. I showed Rose Snyder coming back to her earliest roots—sort of like Matisse—who came back at the end of his life after a lot of despair to create some incredibly brilliant collage work.

Dougherty: One thing I liked about the stories was your concern for the women of the Lower East Side community in those ten years.

Sanders: Well, there were some very interesting women and I want to bring in more of them in the third volume. I want to show a more four-dimensional view of the plight of all the women, and I want to fair and accurate.

Dougherty: Why don't you live in the Lower East Side anymore?

Sanders: My wife and I talked about it. The school wasn't very good. Well, it was all right, but there were some incidents where they cut the hair of a couple kids. And they didn't have the open school policy they have now where you can send your kid to any school you want. And we'd seen some murders. There were a couple of people murdered outside our house. And I'd gotten mugged. I don't know. It was getting a little weird at the end of the sixties. It was getting a little more violent.

Dougherty: Was the whole character of the city changing?

Sanders: There was a lot more heroin around. There seemed to be more muggings, more violence. Those were the first two years of the Nixon regime. So we moved to the West Village for a couple of years. And then off to Woodstock in '74.

Dougherty: What do you think of the Lower East Side now, and what's going on there?

Sanders: Oh, there's a lot of interesting stuff, all the galleries. It seems to be as perky as ever, though it's a different kind of scene. The rents are certainly a lot higher than when I lived there. And we didn't have the homeless problem—there weren't any homeless when I lived around New York City in the sixties. Even through the middle-seventies there were very few homeless people. Now, of course, Tompkins Square Park has been the scene of riots and squatters. Then the gentrification, and people trying to control their own blocks It's quite a brew now, but it's still very full of life, still carrying on some of those traditions.

Dougherty: What made you first come to the Lower East Side? One story, "A Book of Verse," touches on this. I wondered how autobiographical it was.

Sanders: That was pure fiction. But it does contain some elements of truth. I lived in the Midwest. I did read "Howl" when I was in high school. I did memorize it. And I did recite it to my friends while drinking beer. But most of it is fiction. I came to New York to study engineering. I had in mind joining the Mercury Program, or going into orbit, or becoming a rocket scientist. NYU had a good graduate program in that kind of thing. But then I started studying Greek and Latin and became interested in poetry, and changed my college major from mathematics to Greek and Latin. But that's why I came to new York.

Dougherty: Was it originally just to go to school?

Sanders: I had been there while I was in high school—in 1956, and it was romantic. I mean Dylan Thomas, the Beats, the Village. It was very magnetic.

Dougherty: It must have been, especially coming from the Midwest.

Sanders: You either went to California or you came to New York.

Dougherty: Do you see any place today that has that same homogeneity of art and politics the way the Lower East Side did in the sixties?

Sanders: I think it's more a state of mind now. I think you could do it anywhere you could link up. Things are much more regional. You could probably live someplace else besides NYC—Berkeley is pretty interesting. I was just in Berkeley for a few days. The level of political discourse in Berkeley and San Francisco is very high. There are a lot of very good poets living out there. Or Colorado. You could live in Boulder. Or you could live in Taos, or Albuquerque, New Mexico, Santa Fe. There are a lot of interesting places, New Orleans, Baltimore. Most big cities. And the country is very alluring, too. Vermont. But it doesn't matter where you live. It's almost better to find a piece of land that you love, or a village, a road, a street, a mountain, a cave, a cliff—someplace that rhymes with your spirit.

Dougherty: But isn't that tough to do and keep a sense of community?

Sanders: It is. You can get isolated. But writers and painters and poets and musicians tend to be kind of loners when they create. You need a lot of personal time. But it is true that in a rural place or in a cave or up on a mountain you can become pretty remote, removed, isolated.

Dougherty: You have to find that balance between political involvement and what you need for yourself as an artist?

Sanders: Yeah, you put it right.

Dougherty: I'm intrigued by the story, "I Have a Dream," which opens up the second sequence. In the story, Sam Thomas goes to the Library of Congress to hear Ezra Pound's war archives—just before Martin

Luther King is to give his most famous speech. Is that based on any real experience?

Sanders: I did go from reading those horrible transcripts to hear King's speech. The rest is made up.

Dougherty: What a transition.

Sanders: Well, I was close to Pound, and it made me realize that just because you like somebody or like their art doesn't mean you shouldn't examine more than that to come to an accurate assessment. But Sam Thomas—that's not me. He's just a character. I think of these characters and just sort of let them do things.

Dougherty: Is that how you write? Through character?

Sanders: I have some skill at creating these people, these archetypes: Uncle Thrills, Sam Thomas, the Catholic woman Claudia Pruitt, the dancer Louise Adams, Barton McIntyre the jealous painter, John Barrett the proto-academic poet. I invent these people and the character just takes over.

Dougherty: Where do you think you'll take them up to?

Sanders: If I have the strength, I'll end it in the early seventies or late sixties and have them go their own way. I'm working on volume three now. And a book on organized crime and illegal dumping of hazardous waste in New York State. And a new book of poems. And a play. But I am taking notes and preparing volume three. The end of the sixties was really wild, fertile. I'm going to take some of the stories out to Los Angeles and into the rock and roll world. And to a rural hippie commune in the woods somewhere, maybe Woodstock. I've got a lot of things to work with. I can spread it out across the country. It doesn't have to be strictly in New York. I want to have On the Road Mulligan (five-year-old novelist who chronicles his parents turbulent beatnik relationship) around, and I want to have Johnnie Ray Slage the Klan kid come up to New York City to be a guitarist. He's going to bring Dylan's guitar to the Lower East Side and become a teenage club star struggling musician.

Dougherty: What do you think of all the sixties retrospection going on now? What with a re-examination of the Vietnam War, the Oliver Stone movies, and all the other hype?

Sanders: It was a very interesting ten years. People can trash it, put it down, and say that it was horrible. Or they can look at it from another perspective and try to accentuate the good things. I intend to end volume three on an upbeat note. The sixties asked hard questions. It may have failed. But it did try to raise standards of human behavior. And it helped to spread freedom: freedom of expression—to speak and sing and say whatever you want.

Thirsting for Peace
An Interview with Ed Sanders

Kevin Ring

Originally published in Beat Scene, *no. 17 (Autumn 1993): 28–32. Reprinted by permission of* Beat Scene.

He's one of America's bravest and most outspoken writers. He crosses into so many areas of living it's hard to keep pace. Environmental concerns, Charles Manson, investigative journalism, classic poetry, raging novels, and also the life of a musician in The Fugs. A direct descendant of the Beats, he teaches at Naropa in Colorado and continues the same hectic pace as ever. A new book of poems and the reissuing of those outrageous Fugs albums on compact disc has brought Ed Sanders out from the seclusion of rural life in New York state. Through the post, where he wrote answers at Gary Snyder's home in Northern California, and on the phone, Ed Sanders spoke to *Beat Scene* recently.

Ed Sanders: Did you get my letter? I did it at Gary Snyder's. Is that where I sent it from? I finally had a moment—it was right in the middle of eighty acres of forest, it was really beautiful to sit there on a rainy day. Me and my wife had just spent three days with Carol and Gary at their house. It was quite beautiful. It's outside of Nevada City. There's a big environmental fight there over a huge goldmine they're trying to revive from a hundred years ago where they're trying to scoop a million gallons of water a day to blast this gold out of the ground. They're fighting it. Otherwise it's a beautiful Ponderosa Pine and Black Oak forest. Manzanita bushes, dark, wine-colored bush. Very beautiful, just paradise. He makes his electricity with solar panels, quite rural. He's been there about twenty years. It's a whole complex, outbuildings, he's got an old barn. He and his wife use it as their studio. They have a beautiful rounded house with all the accoutrements of modern civilization. All solar powered. And then various outbuildings, pond, wash house. It's quite lovely. Nevada City, it's northwest of Sacramento, San Francisco, couple of hundred miles. Gold country, nuggets washed down in the creek beds, stuff like that. But there's the spirit of greed there—that's always a problem. You're supposed to leave the gold in Mother Gaia.

Kevin Ring: Apparently there's no phone there?

Sanders: Yeah, he has a phone. He has a phone, fax, modems. He's high tech. He's got a Macintosh computer. He's got all the accoutrements. I'm sure you can reach him automatically because he's quite internationally renowned, as you know. In order to write and be part of your, what you call your bioregion, or your drainage area, you need to have solitude in order to be there with it. But he's in good spirits. He's sharp as ever, witty and full of life. It's always a thrill to be around him.

Ring: You've been friends for a long time?

Sanders: Oh, yes. Since around the Berkeley Poetry Festival in 1965. We've corresponded, I guess, since the early sixties. I used to print stuff of his, poems. He was always a friend. He sent me, from Japan, very early in the sixties, an Egyptian eye, carved in one of those Japanese stamps. He's been a friend a long time.

Ring: Apparently you're working on a screenplay?

Sanders: No, a play. I was working this spring right up until when we left for California, every day for ten hours a day, on *Cassandra*, which is a musical drama I wrote, tracing the life of the Trojan prophetess and princess Cassandra, from ancient sources—so I was working very hard all year getting that ready. There's a full professional production. The other thing is there's a movie of *Tales of Beatnik Glory*, which is supposed to start filming this month, in New York City. I don't have anything to do with it. I did not write the screenplay. Philip Hartman and Mark Jacobsen wrote the screenplay. I guess I'm not allowed to say who's in it. Quite a prestigious lineup of people apparently in the film. I have nothing to do with it. I hope they'll let me on the set; I think they will. But they often don't let the author of the book on the set so they don't go jumping up and down. [Note: This film was not made.]

Ring: I heard a rumor that Willem Defoe is in it.

Sanders: I have no idea—that's a rumor I heard too. Defoe has got a... he'll be in Europe in August. He may be in it. It's what the producer told me, that Defoe was gonna be in it. I have no idea. I'm only relying on what I'm told from the producer and the director.

Ring: What are your feelings on this?

Sanders: I'm honored. I never thought a book of mine would be made into a movie. I think it's perfectly adaptable to a film, *Tales of Beatnik Glory*. They used stories from volume one and volume two. They've woven together a very interesting storyline; it combines some of the women characters and other characters...which is all right. So I think they came up with a good storyline, they use the kid, "On the Road Mulligan" ... [as] a character. They use various stories. I think the weave is pretty good.

Ring: Are you optimistic they'll do a reasonable version?

Sanders: I don't know. Yes, of course I am. I'm optimistic and I'm sure it'll be an interesting film. I think some of it has to do with the kind of music they put together for it. I think they're gonna kind of put together a kind of all-star neo-beatnik band maybe for the music, which would be a smart move. I think it'll get general release, I have no idea. I don't know how much that I know is secret or how much I can say. Basically they have a good distribution deal with it, fairly large distributor. I expect it to be released. I'd like to go over to Cannes and hang out there and drink coffee at dawn. [*Laughs*]

Ring: The play is being put on by the Woodstock Guild. Tell us a little about that.

Sanders: Yes. Cassandra was the daughter of the King and Queen of Troy. It's set at the time of the Trojan War, which is around 1184 BC. I take material from Euripides, from *Trojan Women*, and from the

Odyssey, books ten and eleven. That's the major amount of ancient material on Cassandra. There's also material on Cassandra in Virgil and Ovid [mentions other ancient sources here]. So I take all this information and I stitched it all together in a kind of rhapsody storyline and left some of the Greek choruses from Euripides and Homer—not much, but a little bit. Then wrote a kind of poetic treatment to her life. No one has ever done it. It's a kind of modern thing. It's as old as the Bosnian/Croatian/Serbian battle, or the Trojan battle. The ancient struggle between Asia Minor and Greece is reflected forward into the Greek/Turkish struggles now, or the Bosnian situation.

It's very ancient, this idea of cyclical violence, multi-generational vengeance. Multi-century ire and anger is a continuing problem. It's also about the plight of women in ancient times, as reflected in the modern era. Cassandra nowadays would be a woman who is very intelligent, has a lot of energy, a certain amount of aggression. Demanding to have her place in society. So I interpret Cassandra as being a princess of a royal family, privy to state secrets, always demanding to know things, pushy, aggressive and very witty. She's fluent with words and she gets into trouble. That's her psychological situation. In the spiritual or religious areas, she offends the god Apollo. A kind of schizophrenic god. Apollo, the god of mathematics, beauty, statues, pleasing paintings, order, form, healing—but he's also the god of male rage, of violence, of violence of men. He's the god of plagues, tuberculosis, and AIDS. He has a down side to him. He offers her a deal, that if she will make love with him he will give her the gift of prophecy, and she takes the gift of prophecy and tells him to come back later for the love, and when he comes … she … like many a young girl … changes her mind, and he curses her. That's the spiritual side of it.

So when she wants her parents not to let the Trojan horse into Troy, they laugh at her. Or when she wants her country to send Helen back to the Greeks … You see, this Trojan War thing, it's as if Boris Yeltsin ran off with Margaret Thatcher when Margaret Thatcher was head of England. Then the English would bomb Moscow and send over cruise missiles or whatever, nuclear weapons. It was that level of conflict. Cassandra warned against it. Her tragedy is that she's the woman to whom no one will listen. So basically that's the whole plot line. It traces it from ancient sources and then she's murdered by Clytemnestra. Cassandra is also raped in the fall of Troy by a surly Greek soldier named Ajax, which is a modern paradigm for all the rape and plunder which goes on during any war. So we have that in there. So I think it's an interesting story. Little bit of a modern twist at the ending. I have Cassandra and Hades join forces with Persephone. I add a little Sanders fillip at the end.

Ring: Does Tolstoy know about this—it sounds like one heck of a play?

Sanders: Maybe on the astral plane. It tells a good story. It has thirty-one musical sections. The Cassandra role is very demanding—it's a soprano role, the songs are fairly demanding. We have a very good Cassandra named Amy Fraden; she's quite skilled. Leslie Ritter sings the part of Persephone. Those two voices are just terrific, very beautiful voices and they sing very well together. So it's going to be real good. It's in Woodstock, New York, at the Woodstock Guild, from August 24th through September 5th.

Ring: What sort of place is Woodstock?

Sanders: It's 6,000 people when it's ten below zero, and in the summertime it swells up to 20,000 people. It's beautiful. The mountains are up to thirty-eight hundred feet—it's very hilly and quite beautiful. We keep it quite rural—we don't let McDonald's in there, don't let malls in, and we keep it pretty. We had a production last summer which sold out, there were huge waiting lines. We feel that probably, though you never know, it will do well. Our goal is to take it to Broadway if we can. Or to make a movie out of it, that's my real goal. If there are any readers of your magazine [who] want to produce a movie of *Cassandra*, I'm in the Woodstock telephone directory. Woodstock is extremely beautiful in August! We don't want to see a house every three feet in Woodstock; the animals have a right to live there too. These deer and these chipmunks, raccoons, and groundhogs have been here millions of years—they have a right to live here too. There's a whole group of jazz musicians and experimental composers, a whole variety of different…Carla Bley lives here, Jack DeJohnette lives there, lots of musicians. I've been there since '74. We moved up there to get clean air. A woman can walk in the streets in the middle of the night in Woodstock and nothing will happen. There's never been a woman attacked in twenty years, that I know of. Safety, that's good. A woman has a right, if she wants to go walk out and look at the moon at three in the morning. She should be allowed. There's that kind of safety and that's good.

We moved to Woodstock in 1974, in part to escape the geeky, confusion rife, quasi-violent world of 1970s New York leftist factionalism. Plus, there was more and more street hostility from muggers. Miriam was held up by a young addict brandishing a butcher's knife, so we "headed for the hills" 100 miles north of NYC. Living in the country is not that much less hectic. "There are no weekends for poets." It's the era of faxes at midnight, crickets at dawn.

Ring: What's happened to the other guys in the Fugs?

Sanders: Well, Tuli Kupferberg and I founded the band; we continue the legacy. We own the master tapes and we are making arrangements to have them put out. We have hundreds of hours of performances and stuff. Tuli's okay, he lives in New York. He's doing quite well, he has a son that has just graduated from Harvard, which is unusual for an anarcho-syndicalist! He raised a couple of wonderful children, he and his wife Sylvia. Ken Weaver is in Tucson, I talked to him a couple of weeks ago, he's ok. Steve Weber, he's in Portland. Quite a folk hero and still having fun I heard, playing music. Peter Stampfel, I met a couple of weeks ago at a Poets Cafe down on the Lower East Side; I went down there for a reading. He's doing quite well. I think he does gigs, still writing his razor sharp witty tunes I believe. Jake Jacobs, he's okay and doing a record, I understand. Danny Kootch is of course Don Henley's co-songwriter and plays in Don Henley's band. Charlie Larkie, I dunno, he married Carol King. Carol King came to a Fugs concert and squirreled off our bass player! He left the band soon thereafter. Should never have gone to L.A. I guess! I don't know, they trickle on. There's one or two Fugs, I think, are dead. Lee Crabtree died in the early '70s and I believe Pete Carney, who was on our second record, may be dead. John Anderson, who played bass on our first two albums, is now a lawyer in Portland, Maine. He's done quite well, he went to Harvard Law School, I guess. He lives on an island off Portland. Bob Mason, one of our drummers, was out in Venice, California. I think he's a session man. I know where they are. All that is from basically keeping in touch. Not close, but enough to cover a certain amount of cordiality.

Certainly with Tuli—Tuli's my brother. We work very close together. We're gonna do one more rock and roll record, by the way. We're gonna do our final rock album. It's our last one. Tuli's 69 and we decided to do one more and then fade it. One more rock record. That's no sentimental throb tunes, no ballads, just rock. We'll do that this fall. Then cap our career. I wanted to do a career that lasted a little. Actually, a career should be like fifty years. Our career, beginning with our first jumping up and down and screaming studio thing in '65 will now have its final moments twenty-eight years later in a high tech environment. We'll use the latest recording techniques, do it on a big Mac with a 5,000 meg hard disc. We're there.

Ring: You've lasted longer than the Beatles, the Who …

Sanders: That's right! I wouldn't call us the Who or the Beatles! We're the Fugs. We're bards. We're in the tradition of Coleridge singing "Christabel" to Wordsworth. William Blake intoning and singing from *The Songs of Experience*, or the tradition of Walt Whitman singsonging "When Lilacs Last in the Dooryard Bloomed" to a large crowd in New York City after the Civil War. Or in the tradition of Sappho on a Greek island singing to her students. We're in that tradition, singing poets. Not singers who use poetry.

Ring: Besides all the noise the Fugs made, you are obviously people who are concerned. Do you feel your generation and the prevailing spirit of the '60s has been allowed to slip, as regards the environment and a generally better society?

Sanders: I think there's a lot more work now on the environment. Nobody really knew … We didn't ask questions. Where does our water come from? Where does our waste go? Everybody I know now looks into that, even casually. So I think things are a little better in the environment. There's more personal freedom now. I think some battles have been won—there's a better deal for women. So I think it's a little better for that struggle. It's true, you gotta try and reach every young generation and get them to pay attention to some of the good things of the past. Don't just totally ignore the past. Some good things that we did then and the young people now should be made aware of so that they can use some of those things and do their own things. They have to mix a little bit of the past with a lot of the present. That's exactly what my generation did—we mixed in some stuff we learned when we were kids with a sense of newness. That's what this generation has to do. I'm sure it'll do okay.

Ring: Your early years ... you talk about your literary influences, your parents.

Sanders: Oh, yeah. My dad making up spontaneous poem songs. My mother read us Charles Dickens for bedside reading. There was a certain exposure to literature. I had a [high] school English teacher who encouraged me to write poetry. Her name was Mrs. Hall, she encouraged me to write anything I wanted. In the Midwest I was allowed to write weird Poe-like threnodies and she didn't try to censor them. This was in Missouri, Blue Springs High School. She's still alive. She uses some of my early religious poetry for her Sunday School classes. She sort of ignores some of my more randy...

Ring: How do you know this?

Sanders: I always go visit her. I go clip the hedges on my parents' grave every summer, when I go to Naropa. I often stop off and tidy up my parents' grave. My English teacher lives about a mile away, so I always stop by and say hello to her. So she forgives me for some of my weird books. She has them all. I send her all my books; she just glides over some of the more randy sections!

I received a "regular" high school education in poetry, the Romantics, a dash of Shakespeare, Poe, Tennyson, Longfellow, Sandburg, Frost, and as a teenager in the '50s discovered by chance Dylan Thomas, Ezra Pound, Sappho, Charles Olson, the Beats—it wasn't easy. I had to travel hundreds of miles sometimes to encounter in the Midwest "Howl" and William Carlos Williams. It was studying Greek, Latin, and languages that truly opened the world of poetry for me. My mother and father helped—my mother by reading to us at night.

Ring: You teach at Naropa?

Sanders: Often. Every year I teach there, I'm on the guest faculty. It's a wonderful place. It brings a confluence of American poetics into the same place. It's not just beatnik stuff, it's a wide variety of poets and thinkers who go there. Of course Colorado is extremely beautiful in July: it's when all the Rocky Mountain flowers are out. You can drive up to about ten thousand feet above sea level, see ten miles off columbines and Indian paintbrushes, Colorado flowers up to the glaciers. Beautiful visually, the air is very nice. It has a kind of sense of the ancient academy. All the poets and students are housed in these complexes with courtyards—it encourages communication. Then there's always a lot of partying. So there's partying, teaching, intermingling of faculty and students in a way that allows for direct transmission of mind. It's pretty good. They're not parochial, in the sense they don't ... the type of poetry that's taught ... they bring in every kind of American and international strain of verse, from performance poetry to rhymed poetry, to story poetry, to beatnik poetry, to language school poetry, to Black Mountain poetry, to the tradition of George Oppen and Chinese and Japanese poetry, French poetry. Many different streams that run together in one nice tributary there.

Ring: Do you still feel the same way about things you had strong convictions about in the 1960s?

Sanders: There were many good things about the 1960s and some bad. I liked the twin paths of partying, aimless frenzy, good times and wildness, mixed with the demand for a more sharing world. There was too much male chauvinism, and we did not factor in enough ... the impact of jealousy, envy, greed, obsession, fanaticism, lying. All in all, the era was good to me.

Ring: What are you doing now?

Sanders: My career's over, baby! [*Laughs*] We're gonna do one more rock album. I've got a television show called *The Sanders Report*. I'm going to experiment in song and chanted news stories, using the latest musical equipment. Singing news stories. I've done two—one with Gary Snyder in California and I just did one from Sweden. Analyzing the Swedish methods of supporting artists and the arts. Just overwhelmingly amazing.

Ring: Where do they broadcast?

Sanders: In Woodstock and stations in California I'm sending them out to. I just began. This is my fifth show. In the fall I'll begin the song and chanted news shows. I have a book I've been working on for about three and a half years on organized crime, or the Mafia and illegal waste dumping in New York State. I've been working on that for three or four years.

Ring: Does that worry you?

Sanders: Nah … after Manson. Once you've been threatened by Manson everything else seems pretty easy to take. And I'm very happy with my new book *Hymn to the Rebel Cafe* that Black Sparrow has just put out. I've been out on the road doing book parties around California and the East Coast. It represents about all my most complete statement, my social and economic philosophies mixed in with my storytelling ability, my researches into ancient civilizations and my environmental concerns. It contains the best poems I had written from 1986 through 1991, following *Thirsting for Peace in a Raging Century: Poems 1961–1985,* which came out in '87. *Hymn* has my work in site specific nature poetry and environmental concerns ("Some Poems from Mead's Mountain Road," "At Century's End," and "For the Waterworkers"), politics and economics, plus a long humorous poem in the tradition of Cowper's "John Gilpin" called "An East Village Hippie in King Arthur's Court."

Ring: How did Black Sparrow come to publish the book?

Sanders: Black Sparrow is one of America's premier publishers and the poet Tom Clark facilitated the placing of the manuscript of *Hymn to the Rebel Cafe* in the hands of John Martin, who, to my gratitude, wanted to publish it.

Ring: You've always been recognized as a writer who has shown ecological and political concern and expressed that in your writing. Where does this spring from?

Sanders: I was very much part of the "rising tide of expectation" in the late 1950s and 1960s [and] into the 1970s, when we wanted a sharing, war-free society that promoted freedom and at the same time restructured the banking and money system to banish poverty. I grew up feeling close to the wilderness of the American outdoors. Some of the perfect haunts of my youth, ice skating ponds, meadows, farmland, river banks, have long been seized by malls, tract housing and the bulldozer. So I have vowed to "go out in a blaze of leaflets" and to my last breath speak up for Gaia's wild ways and a democratic socialist economy.

Ring: Your writing has crossed from poetry, to journalism, investigative journalism, political writing, fiction, novels, a very broad span. Do you think this stops you reaching a wider audience?

Sanders: If you write in one field, you tend to be able to focus on others. I don't believe that working in a number of fields limits the results, but it might in some cases limit public renown, but so what? The examples of William Blake, Yeats, and others are too strong not to be indifferent to the same wave of renown and fame-lack.

An Interview with Ed Sanders

Steve Luttrell
Transcribed by Robert Dutton

Originally published in The Cafe Review *6 (Fall 1995): 23–35. Reprinted by permission of* The Cafe Review.

Steve Luttrell: What was it that first attracted your interest in ancient languages?

Ed Sanders: I took Latin in high school and always enjoyed studying Latin. My mother said a gentleman should know Greek, and when she died and when I was in high school, I decided to study Greek in her honor. So, when I went to New York University, in 1958, I took a course in Greek and kept taking courses. After the initial Greek course, I took a course in Homer and studied the *Iliad* and then I took a course in the *Odyssey* and I took a course in Herodotus and I took Greek lyric poetry. I took a course in Mycenaean language. I took a course in Hesiod and studied his *Theogony*. I took a lot of Greek courses and gradually developed a major and so changed my major from mathematics to Greek. I took a lot of Latin courses, too. And then I took Egyptian at the New School for Social Research, studied a little French, and a little German. I felt that you had to know languages.

Luttrell: Well, of course, studying Greek and having started off as a math major, you must have come across the Pythagoreans at that point, where they, I think, believed that true language was mathematically rooted.

Sanders: That's right. Yes, there did seem to be some relationship between certain elegant types of mathematics and poetry. I guess that's true. So, that's how I got into Greek, and then I decided that I would, now and then, translate things just to stay involved and keep my mind refreshed as to the language.

Luttrell: Do you enjoy translation?

Sanders: Yeah, I do. I have fun. I, now and then, translate poetry. I did a recording project a few years ago of Greek text set to music, so I had an opportunity, then, to do some translating. And then, when I wrote my musical drama, *Cassandra*, a couple years ago, I translated from Aeschylus, Euripides, and Homer to use in that drama.

Luttrell: Do you think that translating poetry, being a poet yourself, is an advantage or a handicap?

Sanders: It's added because it forces you to really use your brain. You can't be lazy and do a good translation. It requires a lot of work and a lot of thought—transforming a nuance from another language to nuance in your own language—and it's not that easy. It forces you to focus on the correlatives between one spirit zone and another spirit zone—and that transformation is an act of art. It's not easy to do, but it's great discipline. It forces you to really think about your own writing, and really carefully place the words side by side. Good discipline.

Luttrell: I would call your new book, *Chekhov*, a long biographical poem. Is this a relatively new literary genre?

Sanders: I think once the professors discover this genre, it could be very popular because academic presses could easily print thousands of this kind of thing. Professors could transform their research into verse clusters as easily as they could form it into other things, I think—other things like prose paragraphs.

Luttrell: It's a lot more musical.

Sanders: You've got to use your ear, yeah, right. And you have to pick a pleasing flow of vowels and consonants. As Charles Olson says, it's difficult to be both an historian and a poet. So, you have all this raw material and it's difficult, sometimes, to transform a list of things you want to include in a section of a poem that's based in real life. It's difficult to transform that list of information, sometimes, into a sequence of poetic language. Because not everything sounds so poetic. If you just place names of people, the names of streets, boulevards, rivers, and lakes, the names of mountains, the names of parts of the city—not poetic sounding—so it's difficult. Then, there's someone like Chekhov, who wrote four thousand letters.

And I was, in *Chekhov*, determined to give a sense of life in Russia during Chekhov's era, and I put all kinds of information about the radicals, about the rise of the Bolsheviks, about Lenin, about Maxim Gorky, about the literary scene, about all the censorship that was going on, about the Russian police state in the nineteenth century. That's a giant wealth of material. So, my book is 225 pages long. And, as I say on the first page, the biography of a genius can swerve to 10,000 pages. So, the biggest problem was the negative capability thing, where I had to say "no" to so many things before I said "yes" to anything. I said "no" to thousands of pages of possible material, while I said "yes" to 225 pages. So, it was difficult. But, it's an interesting genre. I worked very hard on it—did a lot of library research.

Luttrell: How did you come to settle on Chekhov as a subject?

Sanders: I don't know. I had this production of my play, *Cassandra*, in Woodstock two years ago and I was going to do a play about the life of Sappho. I thought, after Cassandra, I would do Sappho. but there's not a lot of material about Sappho. I would have had to speculate a lot. Then as I was driving to the play, the production, the word "Chekhov" entered my mind, and I said "yeah." I'd known quite a bit about Chekhov. I'd read, of course, virtually all his stories over the course of my life and really admired him. Then in '87 there was biography by Henri Troyat called *Chekhov*, which many people read. It was really an amazing biography. Having read that and read all his short stories over the years, I knew something about his life. I knew that he was a compulsive do-gooder. I knew that he had built schools and built hospitals, built clinics, built a tubercular sanatorium, and libraries—while at the same time, being a writer, a playwright, a doctor. He had fantastic energy. So, I was interested in his metabolism, and how, in only forty-four years, he managed to do what he did. So one thing led to another. I had a publishing arrangement with Black

Sparrow Press. They did *Hymn to the Rebel Cafe*. So, I wrote a draft and sent it to Black Sparrow, John Martin, and he, to my great and lasting gratitude, agreed to publish it.

Luttrell: You mentioned, in talking about Chekhov, now and in the performance of it, the idea of censorship. How do you see the new censorship and what are your general feelings on that subject?

Sanders: Well, I think the right wing and conservatives in America, particularly, try to limit the social discourse and what's allowed in "proper company." In America, it's true, you can pretty well publish everything but images of children making love. You're pretty well free to write about everything, but there's a lot of self-censorship in America. For instance, when I got my NEA [National Endowment for the Arts] grant a couple years ago, I think I had to promise not to write pornography or excessively erotic material during the time I was getting that $20,000 grant. So, the first thing I did was write an extremely erotic poem. And part of the poem was a photocopy of my check from the NEA. I said, I have just received a check for $20,000 from the United States government to write poetry and here is a photocopy of the check, but first I am going to lie down with a beautiful woman and lick her clitoris like a postage stamp and mail it to paradise.

So, anyway, censorship is pretty bad on certain levels, but there's certainly a lot more freedom to write than there was in the '60s because, you see, the libertarian conservatives would love to censor, but they can't because their thing is personal freedom—freedom to own guns, freedom to do this, freedom to do that. So, there's a funny right-wing libertarian streak now in the country that is for the legalization of pot, who say you can do what you want with your own body and time as long as it doesn't harm or encroach on other people. So, in that milieu, between the liberals and the right-wing libertarian freedom lovers, you have kind of coalition that wants to protect personal expression. It's not so bad. But, I think in literary circles there is a lot of self-censorship. Let's say you want to get a grant, or people, they want to get a prize or something, or they want to get tenure, they'll calm down what they write, in order to get what they want.

Luttrell: On that subject, how do you feel your experience as a social activist is important to your poetry?

Sanders: It has [been important]. There are many great poets who don't bring much of their social activism into their poetry. There are some poets who are quite active socially, in social causes, yet keep a lot of it out of their poetry. I find myself doing that, somewhat. I write my poetry for a civilization, really, that doesn't exist—a peaceful civilization—a civilization that's more sharing, where men and women are more equal, where no one has to work that much, where there's a lot of free time, where children are raised in a noncompetitive way, where there are no wars. And so, I try to bring that sense of peace and harmony to my public performance, realizing that the world's often quite cruel. But, I do bring a lot of my own world view and politics into my work, obviously. My poem, "Yiddish-Speaking Socialists of the Lower East Side," is sort of a manifesto of my own social democratic beliefs. I guess I'm a European style or Swedish style social democrat.

Luttrell: I know that some poets immediately come to mind. Amiri Baraka, for example, I think, from having heard him, believes that it's almost incumbent upon the poet to take some sort of social stand.

Sanders: It's difficult. The problem is if you do a big manifesto against somebody or something in poetry form—you want to write poetry that stays around and can be of interest, at least during your own lifetime. And if you write poetry that is like a broadside it can become "dated" in a way that is quite bewildering. So, you just have to be careful about writing bumper sticker poetry. You don't want bumper sticker poetry, yet there's a lot of interesting phrases on bumper stickers. So, you want to rise beyond bumper sticker poetry toward a poetry that's beautiful and refreshing, and yet offers hope and is a paradigm for a better world, obviously. There's no easy answer. It's a lot of work. It's the same amount of work whether it's protest poetry, verse plays, sonnets, or Chekhov. It's just a lot of work. And you've got to polish them. You wait for those beautiful moments of inspiration and you write that stuff down, but then there's a lot of times when the dictation from the sky doesn't come and you are there as a kind of desperate mammal roaming around your word processor seeking those beautiful stretches of words that you can stitch together to form a rhapsody of glory. And that can be a lot of work. Writing poetry has glorious moments of inspiration, then a lot of hard work, glorious moments of inspiration, then a lot of hard work, contained within a larger field of glorious inspirations—I guess that's what I'm trying to say.

Luttrell: Speaking of work, as we were talking earlier, you're on the verge of leaving for the West Coast and over to Europe. Do you still enjoy traveling as much as you did when you first began?

Sanders: I like to travel with my family, my wife. She likes to travel, and it's fun. As I get a little older, I see more and more the value of museums and art galleries. I love to visit the great treasures of the past and the present in museums. And I like the visual Gestalt: the beauty that is preserved everywhere you go. A lot of people preserve forests and beautiful vistas. And there are so many cliffs, valleys, and mountains. So, nature is there, Gaia. So, it's fun to travel over Gaia. I feel bad in a jet plane knowing that I am polluting the atmosphere with exhausts. And I feel bad sitting here at this fine little motel squeezing a Styrofoam cup, knowing that every time I do, I release gases that end up in the stratosphere and cause skin cancer.

Luttrell: I know that you have been environmentally concerned for a long time—both in your work and in your own life. Do you feel environmental concerns are in danger of cutbacks down the road with the present politics?

Sanders: Oh, yeah! These rats want to do away with the EPA. There's this hideous right-wing land use movement—the "wise use" movement that's seeking to assert that anybody can do anything they want with their own property. What it is, is that, in America the economy is based, basically, on the taking of open space and that's been the "banking and loan" paradigm for American culture. And it worked for a couple hundred years because there were so many open spaces. The banks issue loans to someone who's going to take a piece of open space and convert it into something. Now, in the east, the farmland is being divided up so that you have a mall being built every twenty miles and then subdividers and developers will fill in the twenty miles between the two sets of malls with tract houses. And that's the paradigm for the ruination of American water and the ruination of the air through auto exhausts.

When I was in Gloucester the other day, Robert Creeley pointed out something that I'd forgotten about, perhaps never knew, how there used to be a trolley service between Worcester and Gloucester and between

Gloucester and Boston. We're not talking trains, we're talking trolleys. Yeah, I'm worried about the environment because once the water is gone—it's underneath the earth—once the water is gone, it's gone for centuries. The air, we could clean up the air pretty quickly, but not the water. So, what you have is a civilization spreading out all over the land in the east. All the land is being taken. So, yeah, I'm really worried. But, basically, humans like whatever they were born into. So, if everything is full of houses, they'll like it, too.

Luttrell: Things are still okay in Woodstock?

Sanders: Things are all right in Woodstock. There's a certain amount of land preservation and we make it difficult for them to build malls or McDonald's.

Luttrell: How did you first come to Woodstock?

Sanders: Oh, sort of washed up there, you know, like a beached poet. Things were tough for me after I wrote my book on the Manson family because I sold like a million copies, it made me famous, and I was drinking too much. So, basically, we decided to move to Woodstock for a while, just for the summer really, and then we decided to stay there. Our daughter was in grade school. So, I figure it was for the lungs as much as anything. The air was a lot cleaner—and the water—so, we decided to stay there. And then, once you wash ashore somewhere, and you're getting close to middle age, the years just sorta tick by. It's like those movie things where the calendar suddenly speeds up. That's the way it is. You know, you turn your back on a year and all of a sudden it's gone.

Luttrell: You came from the East Village to Woodstock. That's quite a move.

Sanders: Well, I moved from the East Village to the West Village, to a loft for a few years so my daughter could go to P.S. 41, and then it just got too heavy. My wife got mugged on New Year's day in 1974 by a kid holding a butcher knife. There were a lot of murders on the streets. It just got a little too weird, so we decided to move to the country. We moved to a farmhouse that was 200 years old and never had any locks—we were street-wise and I had been investigating a lot of cults and stuff—so we were quite decompressed into the country life style, which is quite lonely. You've gotta drive twenty miles to get a piece of office equipment sometimes. It's quite spread out. Your day can be spent, as you can guess, your day can be spent driving around doing errands. You have to manage your time a lot better in the country than in the city because it's so spread out.

Luttrell: I'd like to talk about your new project with your newspaper and maybe get you to tell us why you decided to take on the project and how it got started and what you hoped it would turn into.

Sanders: The reason we really decided to do it was because of the elections last fall when the right wing, through really a sham set of arguments and proposals and through really not a majority vote, grabbed power in the United States. And so, we figure, if they are going to play an elitist game and grab power, then everybody's got to do a little share of confronting them. So, a friend and I formed a corporation and decided to put out a very progressive newspaper—progressive as we could get away with in our bio-region. And we've put out six issues. It comes out every other week, features a lot of poetry and local investigations. It's not meant to be a gigantic thing. It is meant to focus on our area and try to make a difference there. We have no illusions about anything. We'll do the best we can to be a progressive environmental investigative force in our region. We'll cover culture as much as we can, but our focus is not really culture. Our focus is going to be on medical care, on the environment, on protecting the water, on education, and on making sure the right wing doesn't come in and make too many incursions, and if they do, confront them.

Like I went to my local militia meeting and wrote a long article about it. I just paid my twenty-five bucks and went right in there and took notes and then published it. That's the kind of thing we do. We go right to the militia. If the Klan shows up, if the skinheads show up, whoever shows up—we will deal with them and write about it—having some basic belief in words and images as a way of keeping civilization from swinging too far to the right. We're playing, in America, a kind of holding action against the right wing and hoping that progressive forces in the country will be able to gather again and make another move to create a kind of different economy. A slightly different economy, a more European style, planned economy.

Luttrell: I was looking at it yesterday and it's an interesting mix of bio-regional environmental issues and poetics.

Sanders: Well, I mix myths. Like when I did the piece on bovine growth hormone. I combined it with ancient Egyptian imagery of Hathor, the cow goddess. I tried to give a broader perspective. The thing is, on the masthead, we are local and global news, and you can't urge people to think globally and act locally unless they have some sense of the global—and the global, to me, means also the mythic and the sense of culture in its broadest sense, like poetry. I intend to do investigative poems—that is, research pieces are done in poetry form. I think the next militia meeting I will write up as a poem. They've got some things happening, and I'll go there, and maybe write it up as a long poem.

Luttrell: Since you are interested in the myths, I would ask where you see the new myths coming from? Where can we find the new myths?

Sanders: I don't know. You got any? Listen, I'll give you thirty thousand dollars for a new myth.

Luttrell: It seems like myth would be a dynamic process, but probably hard to pinpoint—maybe in space?

Sanders: Yeah, some space myth—like the new cosmic books. Out of those probably some myths could be derived. This multidimensional universe they're proposing—the seven dimensional universes are pretty interesting.

Luttrell: The Fugs. I can't do an interview without making some reference to the Fugs. Your work with the Fugs has been such an ongoing experience. Is there still more to come?

Sanders: I think it's over. I wanted to get the band together in the '80s—because of Reagan more than anything—to make some statements. Then, it occurred to me that—what is a band, really, ultimately? A band is however long you take the time to hold it together. And you may not be as popular, in terms of audience, during some part of your history. But, if you feel like it, why not? In other words, history is going to look at all these tapes and photos and text and they don't care—history won't care that, at a certain point, not that many people were interested in it. Whereas, at another time it was wildly popular. All our reunions, though, have been sellouts. We don't play big venues, but where we play, a lot of people come. Anyway, we wanted to continue our story and our concerns in a longer context. Our first gigs were in early '65 and our last concerts were in the summer of '94. That's almost thirty years.

Luttrell: This is probably a cliché question for any poet in an interview, but I'm always interested in knowing what poets got you interested early on and what poets still remain influential to you?

Sanders: Well, I join Allen Ginsberg and Baudelaire and others whose prime poetic influence is Edgar Allan Poe. Every young man, at least, reads Poe and his throbbing works of desire and doom are always thrilling to sensitive young men. And it was to me. It changed my life just reading Poe.

Luttrell: Poe is considered, by many, to be the first truly American poet, in terms of writing in the American vernacular. So many of the poets in his generation were sort of the apes of the British style.

Sanders: I was surprised, once, talking with Allen Ginsberg, that Poe was his guy, too. And I told him that Poe had been the one to focus me in on poetry. And he said it was the same with him. So, Poe was the original guy, and then I read something about Dylan Thomas in a woman's magazine my mother had and became determined to find out who Dylan Thomas was. Then I was reading about this guy, Ezra Pound, and his being in a lot of trouble for treason—and I didn't know much about him. I wanted to find out about him, so I ordered some books in Kansas city about Ezra Pound from the Catholic bookstore—from the local bookstore—they ordered Pound's poetry for me and I began reading it. And then I bought Dylan Thomas' book. And then the San Francisco literary magazines were in the Missouri University bookstore. I went there for a fraternity weekend—you know, these fraternities would bring you in as a high school student and you would go to parties and they might ask you to pledge when you went to school there—and I went to the university bookstore and bought *Howl* and *The Evergreen Review*, and so Ginsberg joined Poe and Pound. But, Poe was my big influence, then Pound, then Ginsberg. And I also liked Edna St. Vincent Millay a lot, and Sandburg, too, when I was a kid. And then I discovered Robinson Jeffers when I was very young and I loved his long poems. "Roan Stallion" and the translation of *Medea*. In fact, he was an influence to me on how to write longer poems, I think.

Luttrell: Sort of like America's only epic poet.

Sanders: Yes, and I liked his tough-edged take on nature—he had a toughness I liked. And then I found Olson in the beginning of 1959 or '60 and he became an influence. By then I was reading Gary Snyder—and then, of course. I began studying Greek and Latin—I was reading a lot of Greek and Latin Poets like Homer and Hesiod—Sappho was a real big influence early in my poetic development.

Luttrell: I got the feeling, hearing you read at the Olson Festival, that Charles Olson was not only quite a good friend, but there was a lot of mutual respect.

Sanders: Yeah, we had a good time. He accepted me as a 23-year-old poet. He just accepted me as a valid thing. I was amazed because I was very insecure. There were years I was afraid to try to meet any of these poets. I used to go to see Ginsberg, and Frank O'Hara, and Jack Kerouac, and Edward Dahlberg, and Gregory Corso, and Lawrence Ferlinghetti. I went to see these people read for years before I introduced myself. I was too shy. I would tell myself I would at least have to write a poem that I wouldn't be embarrassed for them to read. So, finally that happened and they became my friends. I put out *Fuck You/A Magazine of the Arts*, and all of a sudden I was publishing all my heroes and writing letters back and forth and was accepted. It was the most amazing experience.

Luttrell: Would you say that your interest in investigative poetry directly stems back to what you got from Olson?

Sanders: Yes, partly. He had this thing about "saturation job" where you have to do one giant research project, where you saturate an issue. And in learning how to do that one big investigative work, or scholarly work, or research work, where you have to deal with the real world and really find out what happened and translate it into writing—that, that "saturation job," if it's done correctly, will prepare you for almost anything you have to do for the rest of your life. My "saturation job" was writing about the Manson family. It wasn't poetry, but gave me some techniques I was able to transform, using Olson as an example. Also,

Allen Ginsberg's researches into the CIA connection to heroin dealing, for instance, were emblematic to me and a beacon of how things could be done. In other words, you can investigate evil, while surviving. That's the issue: to investigate a kind of a poison world, a world that has palpable evil, and yet, survive. So, the birth of investigative poetry was just getting to know Allen, looking at the way he lived, looking at Olson and the way he wrote and collected information, and my own experience in writing a book on the Manson family—plus some journalism I was doing, and my own research techniques of hanging out with a lot of private investigators and getting to know police officers. I developed this theory, that I still haven't been able to carry out adequately yet—but Chekhov is a kind of example of investigative poetry in the past—so I hope in my newspaper, *The Woodstock Journal*, to do some investigations in the present that are in poetry form. I'm going to spring that on my readers. I hope they still read it.

Luttrell: Final question. Does each morning bring Ed Sanders a crack of grace?

Sanders: This morning did, waking up in Portland, Maine. Yeah, I felt good. You go to bed, you feel like there's a giant minus sign pulsing inside your frontal lobes, you look in the mirror and you say, yi, yi, yi—you look in the mirror of your career and you say, is this a career? You think about old age in a wheelchair with no pain killers in the golden bard retirement home and nobody reading your books any more. But, when you wake up on such a morning in Portland, Maine. It's such a beautiful sea town, and you know you'll get to go to a lot of good bookstores, like Pat Murphy's book store and Harding's bookstore, and there's the coast of Maine awaiting you—and that's called *crack of grace*.

Transcriber's note: *Cracks of Grace* is the title of Ed's book of poems published earlier this year. The final line of the final poem reads, "and morn brings a crack of grace again."

An Interview with Ed Sanders

Jason Gross

Originally published in Perfect Sound Forever, *June 1997, http://www.furious.com/perfect/sanders.html. Reprinted by permission of Perfect Sound Forever.*

Jason Gross: Could you talk about your writing and work before the Fugs?

Ed Sanders: I had a small book out from City Lights in '63. I had written it in jail in Connecticut, having tried to board a Polaris submarine at its commissioning in August of '61. So I wrote this poem I smuggled out, written on toilet paper (because we weren't allowed to write) and copied it onto bits of foil and cigarette packs. I sent it to [Lawrence] Ferlinghetti, and to my everlasting gratitude, he published it. It was a long poem based on an ancient legend. Then I had a small book of poetry published from Renegade Press in Cleveland. There were also various pamphlets that I had published.

Gross: What kind of things were you listening to then that got you interested in music?

Sanders: The Fugs musically grew out of the Civil Rights area when we all used to go out to marches in the South. We would sing all of these Civil Rights songs that had their basis in three chord, rural folk music: "Down by the Riverside" and "We Shall Overcome" and Pete Seeger's songs.

But also, I grew up in Kansas City and was exposed to a lot of jazz. I used to go as a kid and to see Jay McShann and others. We didn't realize it was jazz. It was just this beautiful music we used to go see. And then, of course, there was a country and western strain in the mid-West, like Roy Acuff. I also studied drums for a while with the drummer for the Kansas City Philharmonic—this gave me exposure to classical music. Then I took piano [lessons]—my mother bought one when I was a kid. Like most American boys of that era, I took piano for four or five years. Tchaikovsky's and Beethoven's piano concertos were a big influence on me. I also sang in my high school choir and I belonged to the society of Barbershop Quartet Singers. I used to sing a lot of stuff when I was in high school, like the Cleftones—it was a Queens teenage band and we used to sing their songs in Missouri. There was also various arrangements of show tunes that we did. I got a lot of singing done as a kid and listened to a lot of music.

Of course, there was rock'n'roll with Elvis Presley. I used to go to Kansas City Municipal Auditorium where I used to see Chuck Berry, Bo Didley and Bill Haley. I used to come to New York as a kid and I would come to ABC Studios and see rock'n'roll shows. Then there was the happening movement. There was a lot of jazz and poetry. I went to see Sonny Rollins and others at the clubs in the Lower East Side.

It was a whole hodgepodge of music for me. As pacifists, we used to listen to Stravinsky's *Rite of Spring* before we would go out to commit civil disobedience. Early Joan Baez records were really influential, too. Then of course, there was Dylan. There was this thing called the Worldwide General Strike for Peace, and this kid played there in the fall of '61 named Dylan. Then I later knew Phil Ochs and the folk singers. So everyone was influencing everyone else. that was kind of the way it was.

Gross: What kind of influence was the Beat movement for you?

Sanders: When I was in high school, I first became exposed to Beat literature. I didn't know what it was. The story's told in *Tales of Beatnik Glory*, my book of short stories. In particular, I bought *Howl* when I was 17 at the University of Missouri bookstore. It changed my life. I memorized it. I went to New York a few months later and I immediately went to all the poetry readings I could. I loved the Beats.

The poems in *Howl* struck a note that reverberated across the entire culture of America. It had an impact on a number of generations right then. It had a long threnodic line that took quite a breath to read. It had interesting metrics and it had a brilliant analysis of America in a kind of Blake/Whitman/cabalistic, doom-tinged Poe-like line that also had a lot of populism that grew out of William Carlos Williams and Carl Sandburg. At one point, Ginsberg had wanted to be a labor lawyer. His mother was a communist and his father was a social democrat so he had a radical "let's make a big change" upbringing that was reflected in "Howl." He called upon a new America to be formed really. He dared to be overtly sexual. It was quite a brave document. It changed my life.

Gross: How did things change for you when you came to New York?

Sanders: There wasn't a tradition of coffee house poetry in the Midwest, although there is now. I travel all over America and there's coffee shop poetry and magazines in every city and college. It was quite different to come to New York because it had a lot of theaters. One of the first things I did was to see Anton Chekhov's *Ivanov* and *Playboy of the Western World* and Beckett's *Waiting for Godot* all in a short time. There were also a lot more bookstores in New York in those days. The rents were cheaper. Then there was the whole wonderful Beat culture, which was combative and controversial at the time. There were a lot of interesting gallery things happening—abstract expressionism like Franz Kline and William DeKooning who I'd see in the Cedar Bar where I used to drink. I met people like Larry Rivers and Andy Warhol.

I was finding the best minds of my generation. In those days, if you were a poet, you went to San Francisco, Berkeley, or New York. It was just packed and full of life. There weren't that many people doing it, but you knew where they were. There weren't that many publications where you got data on where to meet people and where the shows were. That's where you went and hung out.

Gross: How did you meet up with Tuli?

Sanders: Tuli was a Beat hero. He was in all these books. I saw him selling things on the street. He had Birth Press and a magazine called *Yeah*. I read these and I saw his picture around in various anthologies. Then I was publishing a magazine, *Fuck You/A Magazine of the Arts*. He gave me some poetry for that in '62. In late '64, when I opened a bookstore on East 10th called Peace Eye, his pad was next door above Lescer's Wholesale Egg Market. I took over an old Kosher meat market with Hebrew on the window and kept the words "strictly kosher" up there.

This was the time of Roy Orbison's "Pretty Woman," and the Beatles's "I Wanna Hold Your Hand," and Wilson Pickett's "Mustang Sally." There was a lot of interesting music being created. Folk rock was a year away. Dylan hadn't gone electric yet. We decided to form a band and do some poetry and music. We didn't have any grandiose scheme in mind—we just wanted to have some fun. I had a bookstore where we could practice. I had met this guy who played drums for his high school marching band named [Ken] Weaver so we asked him to come aboard. These guys from the Holy Modal Rounders were around for three years on their own so they came aboard. We did some gigs at some theaters at the Lower East Side and a bunch of little art galleries. One thing led to another and all of a sudden, these places began to get packed. People would line up outside. Right away we wrote about 50 or 60 songs. Some of them were written right there in the bookstore—I had a little tape recorder. Junkies kept stealing our equipment though. We had our first gig at Izzy Young's Folk Center, and a day or two before, the junkies broke into my store and stole our equipment. Ken had to use a cardboard peach box as a drum. I had a pair of maracas so that might have been the whole sum of our music right then.

We had pretty humble beginnings and we stayed that way although we ultimately, after a few years, wound up on a major recording label. It was a *long* jump to make from such a primitive beginning.

Gross: Tuli thought the Fugs were kind of a punk band before its time because the band went ahead without any great technical skills.

Sanders: It was the era of happenings. You could fill up a bathtub with cherry Jell-O, get a strobe light and some paintings, and have a happening in a gallery. We played in all these galleries. We sang and shouted our songs, but we had good timing. If you listen to those early tapes, one thing about them is they weren't tuned perfectly to a tuning fork, but the timing is good. Tuli, Weaver, and I and the others had a good time. We sang together. You could hear the words and they were quite clear. Our tunes seem to have some literary merit because they keep reissuing CDs of this stuff 30-35 years later.

We had an attitude to use our youthful energy to surge ahead and present our music, no matter what. But there has to be some level of talent somewhere to pull it off.

Gross: Another thing [that] made the Fugs different were the lyrics. At that time a lot of rock lyrics were love songs, but your group was using poetry for your music.

Sanders: I would love to say that this was a deliberate plot and we had a vast scheme to change American civilization, but part of it was just to have fun. We were all "literate." Our whole life, in part, was books. Kupferberg, the whole time I've known him, always goes out to look for books. When we travel in Europe, he's in the bookstores. He's always reading. I remember being in a van in Italy a few weeks ago. I look over my shoulder and he's reading a dictionary of obscure philosophical terms. But it's true that we did bring poetry to our songs, but that's just the way we wrote. I had a bunch of books out, Kupferberg had a bunch of books out. I knew Greek and Latin, and I had just graduated from college. I was corresponding with all these poets like Gary Snyder and Charles Olson. I was writing these learned letters to Ginsberg and then hanging out with him when he got back from India in '63. I was friends with all these guys. I was invited to the Berkeley Poetry Conference where I gave a reading in '65.

I was a poet and I thought that this [the Fugs] was a joke and a game that would be over in a few months. But then it went on and on. Here we are 30–35 years later, still surging onward.

Gross: Tuli was also saying that and important part of the band was dope and fucking.

Sanders: That's a little bit simplistic. We were a pot band more than anything else. I certainly never take heroin for instance. When my friend Janis Joplin died, I vowed to tell people as much as I could about the dangers of heroin. I wouldn't throw the word "dope" around. If you mean pot or magic mushrooms, you could certainly say we were in favor of the legalization of the stuff and took our share of it. You can look at the songs we put out. "Tune in Drop Out" was a satire on rock lyrics. "I Couldn't Get High" was a satire too. Everybody has a right to have had a wild youth and we guess I did. But I would say our main thing was satire and antiwar. We were randy young men.

Gross: Did you think that the Fugs fit in with other bands at the time?

Sanders: We got along with everybody. What upset me most is that we were promised to get invited to the Monterey festival in '67—Derek Taylor promised me over the phone. Then they didn't invite us. But we knew Jimi Hendrix, we knew Frank Zappa—I just wrote the liner notes for this record of his that came out. At one time or another, I guess I met almost everybody. I don't think we were outcasts. But once we played a big hall, we had a hard time playing it again. It would be our lyrics like "River of Shit" or other tunes we did. The concert managers tend to be pretty conservative.

Gross: You were talking about how politics were an important part of the Fugs.

Sanders: We put daisies in the rifle barrels at the Pentagon. We did the exorcism of the Pentagon with the San Francisco Diggers. In October of '67, Tuli and I paid for the flatbed truck and the sound system for this. We stood outside the Pentagon with the Diggers shouting "Out demons out" and it's on our record *Tenderness Junction*. We must have done 50 benefits to raise money for the Resistance.

Gross: How about when the Fugs moved to a major label?

Sanders: We did an album for Atlantic and they didn't like the cut of its jib. They bounced us off the label. We started the record in early '67 and we got bounced off in the early summer. We lost a year and that really screwed us up. I was on the cover of *Life* magazine and we were a very famous group. Fans camped outside our houses. It was right at the most optimal moment to do a record. Then we signed with Reprise, to their credit. We're very grateful to them. Mo Ostin and Reprise never censored us. They always put out what we released. They never told us to do anything at all. It was total freedom. But that record, *Tenderness Junction*, didn't come out until early '68.

Gross: What do you think changed for the band by that time?

Sanders: We had 700 to 800 performances by then. My judgment, as leader of the band, was that we had to have some musicians that were stable—who would show up for gigs, who were willing to rehearse and do harmony singing and who had good chops. By hook or by crook, I finally came up with some guys who could really play. We had Danny Kootch there for a while—he was really a talented musician. He wrote with Don Henley of the Eagles later, but he was just a boy from the East somewhere when he was with us. We finally wound up with Ken Pine on guitar and Bob Mason on second drums (we had two drum sets like the Mothers) and a bass player named Bill Wolf. They were really good, especially Pine. He was really an underrated, creative, and talented guitar player. I understand that one of Jimi Hendrix's jam sessions has just been released with Ken sitting in on guitar. [He appears on "My Friend" from *First Rays of the New Rising Sun.*] We used to jam with Jimi.

Gross: What was the band doing at that time?

Sanders: We went to Europe twice in '68 in the spring and the fall. Our opening band was Fleetwood Mac. We played constantly. We went to California twice. We played the Avalon Ballroom and psychedelic clubs up and down the coast. We went to Detroit, Chicago, Boston, all over the United States, and we also put out two records that year.

Gross: If the band was getting it together, why did it break up?

Sanders: I reopened the Peace Eye Bookstore. It had been closed for a while. I moved it to the old *East Village Other* office on Avenue A. I really didn't know what I wanted to do. I was very discouraged with what happened in '68 with all of the assassinations. In early '69, it came out about the My Lai massacre. Nixon was president and we didn't know what the hell he was going to do. So, these political things were very, very disturbing to me. '68 was a very good year and a very bad year. It should have been the best in American civilization.

By '69, I decided that I just wanted to be a beatnik and run my bookstore. So we did some touring and a gig with the Grateful Dead in Pennsylvania in the spring and that was it. I decided I had it. It was kind of dumb, too. We had an opportunity to tour that summer for what was good money for us, but I decided to turn that down. I did my own record for Warner Brothers called *Sanders's Truck Stop* during that spring and summer. In the fall, I got interested in the Manson case and I got a book contract. By then it was really too late to get the Fugs back together. I was busy day and night, writing my book on the Manson family.

Then 15 years went by until we had our reunion. We started having reunions quite regularly because I found this guy named Steve Taylor who sings really well. We got a guy also to do harmony parts named Coby Batty. We did reunions in '84, '85, '86, '89, '94, and now in '97. We've just been invited to Japan. We're going to do one more studio record. We decided to do *Fugs Final Record* just in case.

Gross: What do you see as the achievements or legacy of the Fugs?

Sanders: I think it has an honest legacy. It wasn't perfect—there are plenty of things I guess I wish I could re-record and fix up a little bit. But it's what it was. I'm honored that people are still interested. I thought that *nobody* would ever be interested or even think about it now. Because of these compact discs, I have more records out now than when I was in my twenties. I think I'll do what Zappa did—put out a record of guitar breaks. I listened to a lot of those [Fugs] records and we had some really brilliant guitar players—Pine, Kootch, John Kalb, Stefan Grossman.

Gross: Grossman once said that when you interviewed him for the band, you asked "are you crazy?"

Sanders: No, I might have said "you have to be a little crazy to join the band." We had things like "Kill for Peace" and "River of Shit." Anyway, he was a good player. So, Zappa did this guitar break album and I wanted to do G*reat Moments of Tuning*. You didn't have the electronic tuners then so tuning was quite an existential praxis back then.

So again, I'm honored that people are still interested. It was a little bit of poetry. It wasn't perfect. There was honesty, verve, energy, directness, a certain amount of skill, some timing in there. Tuli wrote some really good songs. You're rolling the dice when you leave art behind.

Gross: How did the reunions happen after all those years?

Sanders: The first one made sense as it was 1984, the era of Reagan. We were a little bit upset about Ronnie. Tuli and I got together. We had written some songs and we were involved in a film project. We started working together again and we decided "what the hell." The guys who ran the Bottom Line were really decent. So we got together and it was wildly successful. People really liked it. I had worked also with Steve Taylor. We went to Europe that fall. Then in '86 I wrote this antiwar Star Wars piece called "Star Peace" which we performed here and there. We did another reunion in '88. We'd done a bunch of them up here [Woodstock] because they really like us here, we have a huge crowd. We're thinking about doing a salute to Allen Ginsberg maybe later on this summer if I can get it together. We did reunions here in Woodstock in '88 ad '89. In '94 we did the Real Woodstock Festival with Allen Ginsberg and Country Joe McDonald. Out of that came a two CD set which Ace Records put out a couple of years ago.

The idea is to get together when it makes sense. It's wonderful to sing three-part harmony. It's thrilling to sing with guys who really know how to sing and how to do some really good music. The band's really good now. I've had the same band for 10 years.

Gross: How does this version of the band differ from the '60s band?

Sanders: I don't know but I think the music is better. Another reason that I wanted to do these reunions is because I realized that there were some aspects of us that we did not reveal in our crazy '60s persona. So now we have a 33-year history. You do change a little bit as you get older. We're not as radically wild as we were but we're as politically dedicated. I'm a democratic socialist and Tuli's an anarchist—between those poles an interesting tension derives. I fuels some of our songwriting. Comparing our songs from the '60s with our songs from the '80s, I think a lot of our best music ultimately in the long run will be from some of our stuff in the '80s and '90s.

Gross: Outside of the Fugs, what have you been doing?

Sanders: For the last two years, my wife and I have run a newspaper called the *Woodstock Journal.* We formed it directly to go up against the right wing after Newt Gingrich won in '94. In '95, I also finished my biography of Anton Chekov as a 240-page poem that traces his life. Just now a book is coming out called *1968, A History in Verse*, Black Sparrow Press, a poem tracing that year. I completed Volume 3 of *Tales of Beatnik Glory.* Volumes 1 and 2 came out in 1990 and they're still in print. They keep re-releasing my book on the Manson family all over, like in Czechoslovakia, Japan, and Poland. Then this record company in London keeps putting our Fugs records.

I have a very busy life. I'm going on a book tour for 1968 this summer and doing a bunch of book signings. I'm lecturing at Yale. I'm going to teach at a poetry school this fall. I have a whole recording studio here. I build musical instruments. I'm working on an instrument with bird calls—it plays different layered sounds of birds so I can write poetry to it.

So my life is, knock on wood, not so bad. I'm 57 and I'm facing a kind of right-wing laissez-faire America that I thought would not be quite as cruel as it is. But hey, it's not bad. I'm still having fun. I've been married 36 years now, and we have a daughter that's grown up. I have a lot to be thankful for, especially considering that I'm missing a lot of my brothers and sisters who are now dead. Like Allen Ginsberg, who we really, really miss.

An Interview with Ed Sanders

Lisa Jarnot

Originally published in Poetry Project Newsletter *166 (Oct./Nov. 1997): 5–9, 28–29. Reprinted by permission of the* Poetry Project Newsletter, *Lisa Jarnot, and Ed Sanders.*

Ed Sanders is a poet, musician, editor, historian, and activist. His most recent publication, *1968: A History in Verse*, was published this year by Black Sparrow Press. This interview was conducted at the Naropa Institute in Boulder, Colorado, on July 12, 1997, and at the Cedar Bar in New York City on July 23, 1997.

Jarnot: I want to talk to you about Allen Ginsberg. Partly, what was your relationship with Allen like?

Sanders: I was a senior in high school and read "Howl" and I bought *Howl* actually at the University of Missouri Bookstore on a fraternity weekend. And it seemed like, as a young man, about everything I'd been looking for in terms of a model for writing poetry and combining poetry with your personal life in a way I thought would be appropriate, although I was living in the Midwest, in a 50s type all-American environment. Then I moved to New York later and saw him from afar. I attended poetry readings at places like the Gaslight on MacDougal Street or the Living Theater on 14th Street. I saw him read as I did other poets—Edward Dahlberg, Kerouac, Corso; I saw Frank O'Hara read.

So wherever I could go to find poets that I admired to watch them read I went, but I never considered introducing myself or trying to be a part of it; I was just a witness. And I was going to New York University trying to study languages, so I didn't really meet Allen until 1963 when he came back from a long stay in India and Japan and Cambodia, Vietnam, and other places—he went to the Vancouver Poetry Festival—and then he came back. And before that I had corresponded with him, I sent him *Fuck You/A Magazine of the Arts* in India, and he liked it and sent me the really important poem, "The Change," where he kind of changed spiritual directions and came to terms with his body on a train in Japan after visiting Joanne Kyger and Gary Snyder on the way back to Vancouver.

So anyway, from 1963 on, when I formally met him, and he took me to a party at Robert and Mary Frank's house, I began hanging out with him any time we were around in the same area until he died 34 years later. We had many, many capers and adventures and he called all the time and we saw each other now and then. A number of people could say the same thing. He was part of the household. He gave us advice, a lot of advice. And you know, he'd give advice on what kind of furniture to have in your kitchen; we was very much a teacher.

Jarnot: What do you think his significance is historically?

Sanders: Well, I think he's left behind a body of a lot of wonderful poetry going back to his early days, like a Byron or an Emily Dickinson or a Shelley. There are poems that are quite on the Whitman/Poe level of skill. Another way is as an educator. Someone told me his Blake lectures alone are 3,000 typed pages—his analysis of Blake is quite bright and brilliant. And I think that's one of the reasons some of the academics were so hostile to him, because he was like a walking Encyclopedia Britannica of Western poetry, and also Eastern poetry and Chinese poetry, so he knew very much. He's a scholar is all I'm saying and this scholarliness is a legacy. And then his politics are a legacy. He was originally to be a labor lawyer. His mother was a Communist and his father was a Social Democrat and out of that came Allen, always hungering to celebrate the regular people, but with a sense that not that many poets are "great" or that there is winnowing out and judgment that occurs unfortunately among those people that create, as to a hierarchy of "value" or "genius" of their labors.

So he was very active in that and very capable of looking quite snooty and judgmental, and he had a lot of anger in him that he, like all men I guess, was trying to control by writing his own personal *Iliad* and *Odyssey*. His poems are like this epic of coming to terms with violence. But anyway, he has a lasting legacy. He was an American genius. They didn't put Lord Byron into Westminster Abbey until 1968, so it may take some decades. He may go through what I call a Poe job—they may savage him for a while before he can re-emerge.

Jarnot: Do you think that poets have to take on more responsibility now that Allen's gone?

Sanders: Allen had natural metabolism that was very, very elevated. He's such a difficult role model to emulate because of his enormous psychic and actual energy, and he was not, in ways that he would let on, having the cycles of manic depression that other famous poets did, going all the way back to William Cowper, and forward to Robert Lowell, or Anne Sexton, or other poets. His energy cycle was always above the Y axis, so it's difficult. In my own feeble way I try to emulate his political activity with my vow to go out in a blaze of leaflets. Not only do you have to tend to the current stages, you have to set the stage, the soil, the ground—to use an agricultural metaphor—for the future. Every thirty or forty years a big social attempt is made to make things better for working people. You can go back to 1825, 1848, 1870, 1905, 1917, the '30s and '40s, and then later the '60s. Personally, now that I'm middle aged, I think that part of my goal is to help set the soil for the next period of stress where there is an attempt to make an improvement for working people, a genre that I think includes poets.

Jarnot: Do you think there are particular things that poets need to know or to put forward into the world?

Sanders: Two different things, right? "Need to know" and "need to put forward." What was that Ezra Pound thing as to what a poet should do? It's like getting a dictionary and learn the meaning of words. And again, that's a metaphor for the curiosity that a poet a should have. And if you don't have the curiosity, you should train yourself to have that level of curiosity where you are always researching the world, and if we're talking about Allen, that's a great example of what he was like. He's the first Jack the Clipper I ever met—always handing me swatches of clippings, and making clippings and systematic filings on issues and subjects part of his life. In my own archives I have some of his files that he would give to me so I could do some work on them too. I have these manila folders with his handwriting and then the various subjects. So you have to prepare yourself and always study many different things. And therefore it makes the planning of personal time very important.

Poets tend to be Bacchic sometimes. They can don the fox skin masks of the Bassarids and go dancing off into partying. So the idea is—since poets tend to travel a lot—to travel with portable research systems. Gary Snyder does that. I'm always impressed with the way he studies while he travels, studies books and his ecological studies. And so, I think poets, without being preachy, without succumbing to doggerel, should present issues and opinions, revving up the culture of the next "cycle of improvement" I call it, or revolutionary period, hopefully without violence.

Jarnot: How much does research overlap what Allen did? I know he did a lot of research on the CIA.

Sanders: I'm not as overt. I do a lot of almost secret research into cases. I've done a lot of research helping elected officials in investigating things, such as illegal dumping by organized crime. And with respect to the CIA, I've done lot gathering of files and information for the last 27 years on certain cases, quietly, because I believe that there is a class of killers, and I would say serial killers, that were attracted to clandestine government work. These guys—many of them from the post-World War II era are retired and old—some of them I think may still be in place. Allen's thing began in 1965 when the federal narcotics agents tried to get a bunch of people to set Allen up, and get him busted, and Allen started looking into the connection between the CIA and the government and illegal drug dealing, and came to kind of realize that a portion of the people trying to control it and to make arrests were selling it. So it became like a scene out of Brecht's *Rise and Fall of the City of a Mahagonny*.

You know, it turned out that a portion of the CIA were selling drugs and doing illegal things to raise money. So Allen, with his "CIA Calypso Blues" and his speaking out in public, are emblems of deportment for a poet. I don't know if any of us can do it with his verve. That's why it's too bad on one level that he didn't become a labor lawyer. He knew how to work the bureaucracy to get something done. There are examples in his life that, hundreds of examples, where he used his uncanny ability to analyze a bureaucracy to find out whom to call. I've come to his house in the '60s and '70s and seen him on the phone, say, to somebody in the governor's office. You know most of us would say, well I better write a letter to the paper, but Allen would try to call Governor Rockefeller and speak to him directly. So he would try to call Clinton for instance, and maybe get right through. So the idea is to overcome shyness. You have to beg your psyche to emulate some of the better aspect of Ginsberg's public deportment.

Jarnot: When you were writing *1968: A History in Verse*, was there information that you left out of it because you felt like you shouldn't publish it?

Sanders: Well, if you write about a year and there are many, many things—there's not room. When you create a book-length poem and then you have files and boxes of things that possibly you could use, but you have to make choices. Sometimes you leave things out because they're too similar to other things you write about that are more emblematic. Mine is a kind of allegory for American civilization, the 1968 book: it speaks to the best aspects of America, of which there are plenty, but also horrible aspects, of which there are a number. It's almost an allegorical thing, archetypal, so I had to make some decisions. Yeah, but it's true, because I knew many things that I left out, and there were some things that I left out for reasons of privacy, but I didn't put in a lot of material that would be deemed controversial, but you know personal information about other people that would just be like trash. You know like the section "Greta Gabo's Mouth" where I was going to do this gossip sheet. Janis Joplin sometimes told me about her erotic life—she would fill me in, in great detail. I left that out of the book. Why tell all just because Tell tells you to tell? I did leave things out that didn't make sense to put in.

Jarnot: Do you think that you learned a lot about yourself from that project? I mean you learned what the FBI knew about you, right?

Sanders: Yes. I was always too shy to read my FBI file and I finally read through them. Well, you live your own life. You have your own time track and your little portable zone—your body and ten feet around your body that you travel in life with—and through that year you go interact with the people that come into that ten-foot zone by phone calls, by vision, by conversations, whatever—that's your experience of that year. So if you want to make a year more living—that's why I use the image of creating a living structure—if you start bringing in other things, and other strands of information about what other people were doing at the same time, it does help you to fill in to understand the broader picture. So doing that kind of research is like a three-dimensional sculpture. It's a sculptural thing where the year becomes like a living sculpture and the other aspects of the sculpture are outside your zone, and it helps you to understand. So, yes, if you're asking did it help me understand what I did or my own experiences, the answer is a resounding yes, for sure.

I tracked a bunch of people—I call them time tracks, where you track—the analogy would be like a multi-track recording studio where you have 24 tracks and each one is going along in time with an instrument or something happening on it, and for a whole book of poetry—a multi-track book—yeah, you have parallel tracking and every once in a while you bring information from these parallel tracks into the book, into the flow of the book where it makes sense. So then it's like a 24-track mix, and you bring some things to the foreground and you submerge other things at different points in the flow of time. So you're like a maestro, or to use that metaphor, you're like a recording engineer that's mixing and bringing some things out at one point and pulling them back at other points.

Jarnot: How much of that comes out of Olson?

Sanders: Well, Olson was kind of pre-electronic, but he had some good ideas. He was the first guy I knew that cared about wetlands. In the '60s there was this thing called urban renewal where they were determined to do away with poverty, and one of the things the anti-poverty program did was tear down buildings and build new buildings. And doing that does a couple of things. It gives jobs to the construction business, and to the paving business, and it creates jobs. But in the town where Olson lived, Gloucester, they were attempting to fill in some of these tidal wetlands which he would walk by—he was a walker. He loved to walk in the town he was writing about, so he didn't want these beautiful tidal oceanic wetlands to be destroyed, and the same way with the interesting old houses, the federal or Greek revival from the nineteenth century that they would tear down to put up a parking lot. And he would fight against that.

But his techniques I followed a lot, and some of his writing techniques such as the shamanic rev-up method of writing, where he would study things, study his files and get kind of revved up, and then a transmission occurs and you write this stuff down. That's a definite possible method for writing certain sections of a work that contains history—where you have a bunch of files and notes and you study them carefully, and then you get what Robert Duncan called your "body tones"—you get your muscularity and your bios revved up like a drag racer, and then out comes this poetry. That can be useful in historic poetry; it can distill the essence of a thing. So I owe something to him. And also all his observations in "Projective Verse," which is now a manifesto that's from 1950—so it's 47 years old—but like good writing it often has useful material for the present, and his perception that one insight must lead directly to another, and his metaphor of the poem as a high energy construct, where the mind receives energy, or it's like a high energy grid, so that the mind reading it receives this energy as it proceeds down the page. So what that's saying is to charge your language with energy, so work on it so that it doesn't have any points where it doesn't discharge that energy, or that élan, or dare we use the word beauty. It's kind of a macho image really. Why not have part of your poems without any energy at all and just sort of like a tidal pool? Of course a tidal pool's full of life forms—crustaceans and sea urchins and pieces of kelp, and eaten claws of lobsters.

Anyway, Olson wrote this poem called "Maximus from Dogtown 1" which completely revised my thinking on how poetry could be written because I'd been influenced a lot by the long-lined "Howl" and Olson was much more systematically mythological than Ginsberg. He had Egyptian elements and all kinds of mythic elements in his story about this guy who wrestles a bull in Dogtown Meadow and the bull's like this symbol of the universe. And finally the bull kills this guy because it grows up. Anyway, you'd have to read the poem. So, I read that, and then I started putting out *Fuck You/A Magazine of the Arts*, and I started writing to Olson, sending issues. And he wrote back. And he had read "Poem from Jail" which is a mythopoetic thing. The basic structure of it is a re-creation of the Demeter/Persephone myth in the nuclear era, against the background of a doomsday machine. Olson's the only one who ever picked up on that. He understood the mythology, that a lot of it was borrowed from Hesiod's *Theogony* which we both loved, and I knew by heart because I'd just taken a course at NYU in Hesiod's *Theogony*, so I had the thing memorized, almost. So Olson wrote me letters. He wrote me about 50 or 60 letters treating me like an equal. I was a 22-year-old kid. I didn't even know Ginsberg yet. I knew nobody. I was afraid of becoming intimate with these heroes.

Jarnot: How much does New York School writing influence your work? I mean we're talking about Olson and Ginsberg, but you were also a major part of the New York School, being on the Lower East Side, and hanging out with Ted Berrigan…

Sanders: And Frank O'Hara. I didn't see O'Hara very much, but he was very supportive. And Ashbery was very supportive when I was a young man. We would have some conversations. He wanted me to put together a book of poetry and he encouraged me, that he would help get it published under that foundation that was set up after Frank died. And when I was arrested for *Fuck You/A Magazine of the Arts*, Ashbery appeared in court, as did Kenneth Koch, to be expert witnesses. They weren't called on to testify, but they were there, Kenneth Koch holding a tennis racket and John Ashbery in the front row of the state supreme court in lower Manhattan in the summer of 1967.

So, how much was the influence? Quite a bit, O'Hara particularly—those city walking poems—of which Ron Padgett is also a master—of the gazing around while you're walking; it's a variety of the Buddhist pacing meditation type of thing that Gary Snyder picked up on in *Mountains and Rivers Without End*, the idea of walking through an environment and observing, and Apollinaire walking through Paris. And picking up information as you're walking and buying your Gauloises and checking out the new *Art Forum* and saying hello to a friend, that idea of using your body where your body and your heartbeat is part of it. That was an important lesson to me—that it wasn't just Zen monks that could pace their white sand gardens in Kyoto—but it was also Frank O'Hara on the way to work at the Museum of Modern Art. That was an incident where you could create poetry And then of course Ted Berrigan and I were close friends for a number of years, and his writing was an influence. I often thought I sounded just like Ted, I often emulated his speech patterns and the way he looked at things.

Jarnot: So how did you manage to end up on the Lower East Side, from the Midwest?

Sanders: Well, New York University was in Washington Square Park, and there were all these interesting types that hung out in Washington Square Park, especially early in the morning in the summertime. I was living at the Hotel Colburne off Washington Square in a little 17-dollar-a week room there in the summer of 1959. I'd go to Washington Square while all the street sweepers were there and all the bohemians were hanging out, guys with names like Billy Budd, stuff I've written about in Volume 1 of *Tales of Beatnik Glory*—"Vulture Egg Matsoh Brei" is the story that deals with that. But they kept talking about this thing called "the East Side." So, one day I took a walk with some people to get some peyote and there was the East Side and the West Side and there was this no man's/no woman's land there that they literally sprinted through, just between Broadway and 1st Avenue—and then you were at this other place called the East Side where I quickly learned there were all these cheap apartments, and all these painters with things in the storefronts.

Jarnot: So you were studying Classics at that point. Did you go to NYU to do that?

Sanders: No. I went there because it had a good graduate program in rocket science and I wanted to be a rocket scientist or physicist at one point because 1958, when I first went to NYU, was the time that Alan Shepard went overhead, the Mercury Program. For a lonely young insecure poet boy from the Midwest, it seemed like a kind of nice loner thing to do, go up in a rocket and orbit the earth. So that was the reason I went to NYU. But my mother had passed away in 1957 and my mother had always said that a gentleman knew Greek and Latin. So in high school I took Latin, and I wasn't very skilled at it, but it helped me. So in honor of my mother who passed away when I was in high school, I decided to take Greek.

I had thought I should take Russian, because obviously they were the competitors and they were going into space also, but anyway I decided to take Greek. It's a difficult language to get going in but I quickly started to study Greek poetry. Almost immediately they make you take an *Iliad* and *Odyssey* course, which really changed my life. And then I had some really good teachers at NYU—Dr. Bluma Trell was one of them. I took a Greek lyric poetry class with her where she was able to explain these meters. We're not talking iambic pentameter—but very complicated and variegated meters. So I was able to, through her, to jump right into Sappho and Simonides and Anacreon and Stesichorus—a lot of Greek poets that opened me up to the meter. So after a while I decided to change my major to Classics and that's what I graduated in ultimately in 1964. I took a lot of mathematics but I really wasn't cut out to be a rocket scientist.

Jarnot: What about the origins of your political consciousness?

Sanders: My parents were like Stevensonian Democrats in a very conservative area and they were always volunteering for things. Like in the 50s there was a big drive in America to do away with one-room schoolhouses and have consolidated school districts on the grounds you could get a better education. My parents were involved in that and reorganizing school districts When Roosevelt died, my parents went out on the front steps of our house and we all wept. So Roosevelt was like a hero to my parent's generation. My parents would sneer at Joseph McCarthy and the McCarthy hearings. I knew about people like Norman Thomas and I knew a little bit about the '30s, because even in the '40s where I was raised in a rural area of Missouri, hobos would come because we were a quarter mile from the train tracks. The rule was that they weren't allowed in the house, but we were to feed them. So it was a knowledge of the '30s and memories of the horror of the '30s [that] were very ingrained in the consciousness of my family.

So then when I got to New York, I picked up issues of a great publication of the time called *I.F. Stone's Weekly* which taught me that there's a sub-surface to everything; you can't believe what you see on television or what you hear on the radio or read in the newspaper. There's always a subtext, there's always a reason, there's always an underlying set of muscles and sinews that are really explaining what's going on. Then I got exposed to things like the *Monthly Review* which was a socialist publication and I began to follow the Cuban Revolution through the *Monthly Review*, and there were other left-wing publications I began to read and I slowly began to read and study things. Now I had no idea—they didn't talk about Buchenwald back in Missouri, so when in the late '50s the photographs from Buchenwald began to appear in books which I would look at in the 8th Street Bookshop. I really couldn't afford these books, but I would see the concentration camp pictures and I'd already started studying Ezra Pound and I didn't realize what the deal was. So finally I realized why people were so upset with Ezra Pound—I understood by seeing these wasted bodies in boxcars that I was not told at all about in the Midwest.

So I had the sense of what one country can do to another by looking at these horrible concentration camp pictures. So I began to evolve and to become a social democrat, and I point out in my book on 1968 that it took 1968 in all it moil and toil and boil to realize that that's really where I was. I believed in voting. Like Sweden in 1968 voted to have 25 percent of their economy controlled in the interests of the people, by the state, and I realized that I believed in that, and the nationalization of certain key industries, while allowing for some entrepreneurial activity, what they called a mixed economy. And I realized that's what I believed in when I was running though the tear gas of Chicago with Allen Ginsberg.

Jarnot: How did the Fugs fit into all of that?

Sanders: We really didn't. The Fugs were formed in 1964 out of my bookstore. And we didn't grow out of the political culture of the late '60s so much as out of the Civil Rights and Happening movements. And my bookstore was just a block away from where Claes Oldenburg had his storefront and those happenings and stuff. I had this little kosher meat market that I rented and left the "strictly kosher" sign up. It's gone now, it's a community garden. And Tuli Kupferberg lived above an egg store next door and we got talking, and one thing led to another and we decided to form a poetry group and he thought of the title the Fugs. The Peace Eye for a while was a very famous hang out place, like there'd be Nico or Donovan. People would, visiting poets would come by. Jerry Rothenberg, whoever was in town. And

Allen lived just down the street at 408 East 10th. It was half a block away. And there were all these bars on Avenue B, Mazur's, Stanley's, and then there was the Charles Theatre which had all the avant-garde films—Jonas Mekas, Ron Rice, the Taylor Mead movies.

So, there was a four block area of culture, and it was a hangout, and then we formed the Fugs there and I put out *Fuck You/A Magazine of the Arts* in the back room. The exact spot last summer was a zucchini barrel. They made a better use of the space probably. So anyway, the Fugs grew out of the labor union songs of the '30s and "We Shall Overcome" of Pete Seeger and out of the three-chord Protestant hymns that were transformed into civil rights songs. And out of jazz poetry and out of Bird and bebop and early rock and roll. 1964, when we formed, that was "Mustang Sally," Roy Orbison's "Pretty Woman" and the Beatles's "I Want to Hold Your Hand." Those were the things that were happening—early Beach Boys, Dylan hadn't gone folk-rock yet. That's how we came out. We came out of those concepts of a happening. You'd go to these galleries and there'd be people jumping up and down in barrels full of grapes and then somebody naked covering their head with pieces of ticker tape. And you could call that art. Easy rules—all you had to do was bring youthful genius and will. For all the flaws of the early Fugs, we had pretty good timing, and a lot of energy, and we were quite confident in ourselves. And we were all poets so we could whip out these songs that well—we're not talking Schumann here or Schubert. Because of the recording equipment, they were able to capture these things. These things we did one take only, as wild young men looking at each other. We didn't know that you were supposed to face the microphone. So these things we did had a certain life for 32 years.

Jarnot: Did you have training as a musician?

Sanders: Well, training, sure—in the '50s all young men and women took their five years of piano. My mother bought a piano at my aunt's auction when she died and brought it home, a baby grand, and took it apart in the living room. She was quite skilled with her hands, and she rebuilt it, fixed hammers, and got it all organized, and I remember that piano all over our living room rug and she put that piano back together, had it tuned so that we could take piano lessons. So I took piano lessons. Then I studied drums for while with the woman who was a drummer for the Kansas City Philharmonic.

I used to go to Kansas City for a lot of stuff. Kansas City was jazz, so we would go there to these clubs so that we could dance with black girls and Mexican girls. I didn't even know it was jazz. It was just wonderful music that you could be interracial and sneak liquor bottles into the club when you were a teenager. They never asked for identification in Kansas City. So I got exposed to a lot of jazz. And then we would go to the country-western shows in Kansas City. I would see Roy Acuff; I'd see country acts. And then there was the big arena shows in '55 at the Kansas City municipal auditorium where I saw great shows of Bill Haley. I saw Chuck Berry. I saw Bo Diddley. I saw Laverne Baker. And then of course the mating teenage lust game conducted to the Christian emblems of Elvis Presley and the Clovers. So we were exposed to this rock and roll tied to country and western, Hank Williams. And then as soon as I got to New York, I got exposed to the civil rights music, "We Shall Overcome" and "Down by the Riverside." I went on a lot of peace walks and took part in civil rights stuff. I didn't know about things like Eric Satie or Debussy at that stage. Oh yeah. And I left out the Christian church. My mother was very religious. She taught Sunday school classes for high school kids. And I went to church. I was exposed to all these Christian three-chord hymns; I knew all of them, still do. That was a big boon when we were starting writing popular songs and realizing that they were just fast versions of Christian hymn structures.

Jarnot: The Fugs were in Europe recently. What was your sense of the political scene there?

Sanders: We were in Italy for three weeks in the spring. The Center Left is in control of Italy. Berlusconi; the right-wing populist media magnate, was tossed from power and so the cutbacks in medical care and cutbacks in social programs are over for now. And it's true of a number of places in Europe where the right wing has begun to ebb, such as in England with the labor party winning. Sweden, of course, which has always been a social democracy. Denmark is the most left of all those advanced countries. Austria is still under the control of the Social Democrats, and even the Social Democrats in Germany could theoretically take over.

But anyway, the point is their politics were quite grand and I was impressed with the country; the economy was booming. Allen died while we were in Europe and that was a great, sad experience, a national time of mourning. It was all over the newspapers, and on the national television and radio networks. I broke down weeping on Italian national radio. And oddly enough just an hour before he died, we got back from a gig in Milan and we had heard that he was pretty ill and we toasted his soul, just about 45 minutes before he actually passed away. But Italy was glorious other than that great sadness. I recommend it to painters and poets.

Jarnot: What are you working on now?

Sanders: I'm preparing a lot of galleys and stuff for European publications. *Tales of Beatnik Glory*, volume 1, volume 2, and the new one, volume 3, are coming out in Italy and Austria. I've got to teach a course in Vienna in September called "the Poetry and Life of Allen Ginsberg," so I'm preparing for that. I've got to find something to do, another book. Maybe I'll finish *Tales of Beatnik Glory* Volume 4: I've sort of begun it. I thought about writing a novel, a short novel. And I have this play called *Cassandra*—I thought I would polish it up a little bit, change it, and try to get it produced somewhere. And I have to hang around to see that *1968: A History in Verse* gets a fair listen. It's designed to be read quietly in a room. It's not really designed to be performed.

Of all my books, it's the one most deliberately designed to be just sort of studied. My other book, the biography in verse of Chekhov is also designed to be read quietly in somebody's house or room. With Allen's passing I've decided to read more and not be so driven and calm down a little bit, and not to be so clingy to my possessions and boxes of files. You realize how impermanent—because here's a guy who because of his congestive heart condition and other reasons had to get this big fancy loft and a place to put his things up in, and he had just unpacked when he passed. So you really can't cling to anything. So that's my program at this point—do a little writing and do a lot of reading. And that's about it. Except for my little newspaper which eats up a lot of time. Just getting used to post-Ginsberg life.

Interview with Ed Sanders

Marian Mollin

This previously unpublished telephone interview (August 13, 1998) is used by permission from Marian Mollin. The transcript was edited by Jennie Skerl.

I conducted this interview with Ed Sanders as part of the research for my book, *Radical Pacifism in Modern America: Egalitarianism and Protest* (University of Pennsylvania Press, 2006).

My encounter with Ed Sanders is one of those wonderful stories of serendipitous discovery. Several of my book's chapters cover the history of the Committee for Nonviolent Action (CNVA) and its various radical pacifist direct action campaigns from the late 1950s through the 1960s. I had already done quite a bit of research and knew that many young people joined CNVA's protests. I considered these cultural and political rebels, many of whom hailed from New York's Lower East Side, the "activist wing" of the Beat Generation. Unfortunately, as much as I knew about their activism, I found it difficult to get inside their heads and figure out what really motivated them to risk arrest and imprisonment for their actions. There is a lot written by and about the Beats, but the material I encountered focused primarily on the famous male writers (Ginsberg, Kerouac, et al.) and women (such as Joyce Johnson) who defined this renegade cultural movement. None of these works gave me any sense of the *mentalité* of the anonymous young writers, artists, and activists who considered themselves part of this new and free-spirited milieu.

Then one day, while perusing the shelves of a local used bookstore, I encountered Ed Sanders's book of short stories, *Tales of Beatnik Glory*. I had no idea at the time who Sanders was, but the book looked promising. Indeed, when I opened it up, scanned the Table of Contents, and began reading the stories, I quickly realized I had hit a research jackpot. A number of the stories specifically chronicled what is was like to participate in CNVA's demonstrations and actions in the early 1960s, while others provided an inside, tongue-in-cheek view of life as a cultural rebel on the Lower East Side. It was clear that Sanders was an eyewitness to the history of the people I was writing about and that he could provide me with the insights I needed to understand CNVA's activist culture. I remain immensely grateful for Sanders's willingness to share his memories with me; his short stories and this interview served as invaluable resources for my book.

—Marian Mollin, June 2019

Marian Mollin: Just to start with what for me is the beginning of my story is: how you heard about Polaris Action and CNVA in the first place, and what attracted you to that?

Ed Sanders: There were some articles. There was one photo in *The New York Times* in the fall of '60, I think.

Mollin: Of Don Martin climbing on the sub?

Sanders: Yeah. And then there were a number printed in Greenwich Village, near New York University—a lot of leaflets and things down there. There were flyers. I remember they had this—I guess SANE sponsored a Peace Walk from McGuire to the UN.

Mollin: That Easter?

Sanders: Yes, it might have been. I heard of the San Francisco-to-Moscow Walk for Peace. And I also heard of Polaris Action, I guess probably through reading a CNVA newsletter. So I had been aware of them because they were quite good at printing things on mimeographs.

Mollin: So they got the word out pretty well?

Sanders: Well—there weren't that many people into it … but once you were exposed to it, you could figure out how to get more information.

A very circumscribed group of people, although actually in number only 20 or 30 full-time San Francisco-to-Moscow Peace Walkers. And Polaris Action—I don't know—that summer [1961] there was, off and on, 30. And there were the Catholic Worker people, who were always coming up to Voluntown [Connecticut] for special demonstrations and for commissionings and launchings.

Mollin: So you were an NYU student at that time?

Sanders: Yeah. I dropped out for a while. Yep.

Mollin: Did you actually live up in Norwich that summer of '61?

Sanders: Yes.

Mollin: What were some of your most outstanding memories from that summer?

Sanders: I remember … the first one was June 6th [really June 15]. We went out there. We went out to lakes to practice swimming. I was a very good swimmer. I was as fast as any of these Navy frogmen, except they had on flippers and could get me. So I was very fast. We practiced eluding Coast Guard frog-guys in a pond, a lake not far from Voluntown. Then, that June 6th it was …

I always listened to, before any civil disobedience I would listen to Joan Baez's first record and then, symbolically, Stravinsky's "Rite of Spring." I always liked to listen to that just before we were off to the demonstration. So I did, I listened.

Mollin: Is that the Joan Baez record with the black cover with the white drawing of her?

Sanders: Yes. "Hush little baby, don't you cry." ["All My Trials"] Nice record. Her voice was at its peak at that record. Anyway … I listened to that, and then headed off. What was her name? The wife of the guy who died of lung cancer? Neil?

Mollin: Margaret Windus?

Sanders: Yeah. She was my drive-in person. She took me to my point where I—we entered the water and our goal was to swim in. So she escorted me down to the dock. I think Gladney was filming, and I believe also Hillary Harris may have been filming. Those of us who were entering the water—we all wrote statements. I suppose you've seen mine.

Mollin: Yes.

Sanders: Well, I was a young man and I wrote this statement. I entered the water. I remember I had a dime—made sure I had a dime—to make a phone call. And I painted the Egyptian Eye of Horus on my light-colored swimming suit: a symbol of healing. And then I swam out there. But then these—it was the launching ... of the Thomas Edison, so all the boat workers were there. And they started throwing rivets at me.

Mollin: While you were swimming?

Sanders: Yes. Those plobbing [sic] sounds. I saw what they were and realized it was quite dangerous. I think I described it in my collected poems [*Thirsting for Peace in a Raging Century*], in the notes in the back. There were two incidents, see, so I have to separate them.

Mollin: Right. Because you did a couple of actions.

Sanders: Yeah, two. Anyway ... they sent this guy after me with a rope around him, and they got me. The two incidents are confusing my mind. This one we swam in. The other one we had a boat that had the words "Action for Life," and we jumped off the boat. I think the first one I was rounded up.

Mollin: I know that the second one you were all rounded up and arrested, [actually, they were released] and then you went to the main gate of the sub base.

Sanders: And what happened to me? I guess the first one—I know—I was rounded up. I was kept on the boat. And then we were released, without getting arrested.

The second time, we had this boat. Somebody had these oil-cloth signs—I guess it was white on black, "Action for Life"—on a boat. Six or eight of us. We jumped in the water when they sent the Coast Guard cutter. They sent a boat after us as we got close. That's where I almost got in. By then we had trained a lot. And, as I said, I was a very fast swimmer. I was raised in lake country in Missouri and I had swum my whole life. I had taken part in competitions. So I was fast, I was ready to go. I was almost there. It's like a double bind though. If you touch it [the submarine], you get a year in prison. But I almost was there, but they had a green barge that they wedged in between me and the dock.

Well, what happened is they picked me up in the Coast Guard boat and I said, "Okay. Where will I stand? I give up." And he let go of me and he said, "Stand over there." And so over there was on the other side of the boat! So I jumped off. Then I was even closer. That's when the barge cut me off. I was almost there—I was really fast. Then he cut me off and, all of the sudden, I had to go under this barge. And I didn't know—I knew from my experience in swimming a lot near boats is you didn't really want to get anywhere near the propellers. So I didn't know where the propellers were for this thing. I could have gone underneath it and I would have been right at the docks, and then I could have gotten up on [the submarine]. This one was a commissioning—so the boat did not leave the key and go out to sea, it was already at sea and was at rest.

I think that's the one that Jacqueline Kennedy had trouble breaking the champagne bottle over. [That was a commissioning later that fall.] She was bashing away. I think they finally had to smash it for her. Anyway, Jackie was there. Then they tied me up—took me up on the barge and tied me up.

Then they let us go, though. So we decided to go sit-in in front, and that's what we did, we went around in front.

Mollin: At the sub [base] gate?

Sanders: At the entrance.

Mollin: That was what you went to jail for, ultimately?

Sanders: Yes.

Mollin: I was wondering. It seemed like the summer started off with Bill Henry and Don Martin getting those really long jail sentences. Did that scare you guys, at all? Or scare you? Especially when you were thinking about doing these actions and knowing that these guys had gotten a year. Actually, Don Martin had gotten that really long sentence.

Sanders: Well ... you see, these devices were—I guess each had 16 missiles. I don't know if they had MIRVs at that time. I believe they did not, but they might have. Each missile was—the way we understood it—was able to kill a city. Each sub—let's assume they didn't have multiple-entry weapons and each one was singly-dedicated to a target. I mean, we're talking Kiev, and Moscow, and St. Petersburg, and Odessa, and Brest—with just one boat. So it seemed to me to be excessive and evil even. I still think they're evil. I don't like to be near them and I still think they're disgraceful and unworthy of a great nation like the United States. To me they represented something very evil. So … I tried to get on one—I did intend to sit up there—for a while, probably just a minute or two, as an act. I was a wild young man from the Midwest with a sense of daring.

Mollin: How about a sense of community among those of you who were living at Polaris Action?

Sanders: There was that—that was another thing. It was shared—it was a breakdown—What I liked about both the Peace Walks—I was on the Nashville-to-Washington and also the San Francisco-to-Moscow Walk, the portion I was on—was the breakdown of roles among men and women.

Mollin: Can you explain that?

Sanders: Well—guys were expected to cook and clean up—clean up not only after themselves but as part of clean-up crews. There did not seem to be so clearly-drawn roles for men and women. Or between old people and young people. There was inter-generational community, too, so that a younger person could assume a leadership role with respect to older people.

Mollin: And then there was also room for women to take on leadership roles?

Sanders: Usually there was this concept of consensus, which made meetings go on longer. But there wasn't a kind of fierce, street-level decision making that had to be made so that consensus broke down. There was consensus in it. It was the first time I had ever heard a critique from women over the way they were treated in society.

It was a way, also, of—boy, there were different political persuasions. On the San Francisco Walk there was a Trostkyite; there was one or two anarchists; there was what you would call now a kind of libertarian-type; there were regular Democrats; associated with the CNVA was a sort of a right-winger economically—I forget his name, he was a manufacturer, he was associated with the National Association of Manufacturers, he was a nonviolent-type person.

There were many points—there was percolation—there was room to talk of anarcho-syndicalism, Trotskyism, the various shades of the left—in the context of a commune-type circumstance. People were expected to participate, and cook, and clean up, and farm even. There was a Japanese guy, I think, running sort of a farm, a vegetable garden that summer.

Mollin: And then that summer you organized those big demonstrations. Did you do other stuff in New London and Groton?

Sanders: There was a big—for us—a torch-lit canoe parade from New London harbor up—from the docks. I remember writing something for it that I read about Hiroshima. Then we—to the song of "Volga Boatman"—we sang "Hiroshima" to the same tune. We had these flaming torches and rode up past the sailor barracks there, and back. That was one demonstration.

Then there was some sort of—what, I don't remember. September there was a big international day of some sort. Down in my files I have posters for the that.

Mollin: I know there was a big demonstration in Holy Loch, I guess.

Sanders: Right, that's true. I remember helping organize, get people out of New York to come up in buses. I think we rented buses—maybe a bus, or maybe two buses came right from Greenwich Village to go up to the … I think it was September 8 [September 16]. I haven't looked at that material in a long time. It was in September—maybe the 8th—because I can picture in my mind the poster. It was an international day—it might have coordinated also with Bertrand Russell's Committee of 100. Peacemakers was—there was a tissue-thin, tissue paper European-style publication—

Mollin: Oh—*Peace News*.

Sanders: *Peace News*—that came out. Everybody read that—that was all interesting stuff. We all read that. Basically, you know, no one had a television really. So we got our information out of these things that were mailed around and then printed, mimeographed. The CNVA headquarters on Grand Street, where I used to visit all the time, was an important source because they printed stuff there. And then there was a printing operation in a storefront also in New London. I remember trying to—there was the O'Neill house was nearby. I was always interested in how badly the town had treated Eugene O'Neill—it still had not given him any recognition. I think they finally have—very recently.

The harbor was quite pretty, quite beautiful. We had a boat …

Mollin: Right—the office was right near the docks, right? So you could look across and see EB [Electric Boat submarine production facility] and the subs.

Sanders: We would come out—I would go over there and sketch the … we would row … Once they tried to kill us—if it hadn't been for the Coast Guard, we would have been drowned. I was out with Hazleton—we were rowing out—because I wanted to draw the docks over there. I had a plan about where we might be able to get ashore and do a back path and actually get on the sub from the back end during a commissioning.

But it got rejected because of the openness and truth aspect, which was one of the good [rules] that Brad Lyttle and others brought to us young people: the concept of openness and truth, where you tell—you always tell the authorities what you're going to do so there's no surprises such as could create violence. We were always sending letters and calling the Commander. We would tell them exactly who was going to do what and when it was going to be done. So this concept of openness and truth—we used the word "satyagraha" and "ahimsa." It was my first experience with the word "ahimsa." So … those concepts. And then we all read Brad Lyttle's little book, *National Defense Through Nonviolent Resistance.*

Mollin: So that was widely read amongst adherents?

Sanders: Yeah, yeah. And then there was *Tyranny Could Not Quell Them* about the Danish resistance to the Nazis—that was good book. And then *Peace News*, and the CNVA newsletter.

Mollin: Did you guys read Camus also—*Neither Victims nor Executioners*?

Sanders: Yeah—it was around. I had a whole other literary life … Camus had died in that car wreck in 1960. Well, all of us—anybody literate had read Camus a long time ago: *The Myth of Sisyphus.* And had read a lot of Sartre, and—of course—the Beat literature. I was a young poet, so I was reading a lot of that stuff, and a lot of the current literature: *Evergreen Review*. But not everybody in that group was very literary. In fact, I would say many of them were *not* that hip to what was going on in American literature, which was all right.

Mollin: What about tensions? Especially, I know—in your story about the Nashville Walk—you joke about the Discipline. There's definitely, even in the archives, a lot of stuff about people complaining about the Discipline—particularly about monitoring sexuality.

Sanders: Well that was the beginning of the sexual revolution. Young women had birth control apparatii—mainly the pill, some had diaphragms. Even the young women associated with the Catholic Worker were quite sexual. So it wasn't just guys.

Mollin: I meant inter-generationally—between the younger group of people and the older people —like the Swanns.

Sanders: I remember playing chess with their kid, Judy. I don't know. It's not—what happened was that there were all these rules. But there's always rules. There'd be the difficulty of getting Peace Walks—churches were the motels for Peace Walks. So you had to assure the good reverend or the church board that there were all these rules. And in the case of the Nashville-to-Washington Walk for Peace, it was going through rural Tennessee, birthplace of the Klan—through counties and cities where no blacks had ever stayed—and we had a black leading the Walk, and blacks on the Walk. There were really frightening circumstances there. I remember they took us to the National Guard armory to stay overnight in one of the villages because the Klan had threatened to burn down the church. So it was good to have rules to hand out. Then if there were occasional breaches, it's sort of like life—occasional breaches.

But there was nothing overt. People groaned and moaned. I mean, I was a wild young man … they made me promise not to bring any of my magazines to the Walk, I remember that. It's like dealing with people with whom you disagree on certain things, and we have to sort of work it out. But to my memory, there were no vividly intense discussions about it. There were just these rules. You may have had to sign something—I don't know if you did or not, I can't remember. Or maybe they didn't force you to sign this pledge of how you wouldn't ball or smoke pot. Pot was a secret thing. All the young people were smoking pot—*all* of them, every one of them then, many of them. So, that was a secret, forbidden thing that was going on.

Mollin: What did you end up doing afterwards? Did you go back to school after that summer [1961]?

Sanders: Yeah. I graduated, finally, from New York University with a degree in Greek and Latin. I lumbered on. It began with a poem I wrote. I wrote this poem in jail there, which I smuggled out on toilet paper. I sat with it during the Peacemaker conference and borrowed a typewriter, I think, from Dave Dellinger. I borrowed Dave's typewriter and I typed up this big wad of toilet paper I had smuggled out, and it turned out to be, oh, 30–40 pages long. We had a campfire that night and I read a lot of it. And my friend, Allen Hoffman, who was on the San Francisco-to-Moscow Walk and was around at the Peacemaker conference, said I should try to get it published. I had never gotten anything published. It was a long poem that combined the threat of the doomsday machine with the ancient myth of Persephone and Hades and going underground and chewing the pomegranate and having the seeds in her mouth. So I sent that to Lawrence Ferlinghetti, who had City Lights Books, and to my surprise he agreed to publish it. I was really a nameless young waif in the cosmos. No one knew who I was, [but] he liked it and he wanted to publish it. So that was my first book out of that …

Mollin: That's a lovely story.

Sanders: … two weeks in jail. We were agitating so much in jail [that] they let us out.

Mollin: Is that why they let you out early?

Sanders: Oh, yeah. We had a $150 fine which we were working off [at] $2 a day. I don't know … I was in the middle of a poker game with a bunch of sailors—they were crooks—and they came and got us. Told us to get our things out of our cell. That's when I put my poem I had been working on in my tennis shoe, and sort of waddled out with it, and made it out. And Holley Cantine was playing the trombone.

It was because we were agitating. We had a prison newspaper on toilet paper. We were talking to the people about nonviolence. There were a number of sailors in the jail who had gotten caught for drunk brawling, shoplifting, whatever.

What happened after that? I got out. I used to go to CNVA meetings. I got a pad in the East Village and I started to put out my magazine, *Fuck You/A Magazine of the Arts*. Then I went on the Nashville-to-Washington Walk for Peace. And I was in the AEC [Atomic Energy Commission] Sit-in, which is another story.

Mollin: I read that.

Sanders: That's very true—that's almost totally true in the way that it happened. And right around there I sort of got banished from the Catholic Worker. I had my famous brouhaha with Ms. Day, in which—because I had used her—I typed my first issue of my magazine up above the soup kitchen—they had an office. She forbade members of the Worker to publish in it. And some of them wanted to resign. Jim Forest, Jean Forest, who later—I guess they got married afterwards.

So then I lumbered on. Finally I went to school. I formed a bookstore—the Peace Eye Bookstore. And my magazine. And I had a rock band, the Fugs, that were pretty well known.

Mollin: I vaguely remember them from my childhood.

Sanders: I got famous. I was on the cover of *Life* ...

Mollin: So you had an illustrious life.

Sanders: Yes. I did that for a while. I was fairly well-known. I had a bookstore for a number of years. I was involved in the peace wing of the group, the Yippies. Allen Ginsberg and I sort of formed the nonviolent part of that. And I was involved in the ... I did hundreds of benefits—my band. We raised—I don't know how much we raised—but we did, we raised a lot. Did hundreds of benefits for all kinds of causes: communes, and jail funds, and bail funds, community centers, the Digger free store. We did many. And toured a lot through the '60s. Then I gave it up and wrote a book on the Manson family called *The Family*, which was a fairly successful book. In fact, it's still in print in a lot of countries, it's out all over.

On the Nashville-to-Washington Walk for Peace I began to bond with cows, so I became a vegetarian around that time, and I've been one since. And I've sort of stayed a pacifist—I'm certainly a pacifist. I've not left that philosophy.

Now, my wife and I have a newspaper. I got married after Polaris Action, and I'm still married to the same person. We own a newspaper now, *The Woodstock Journal.* And I keep putting out books of poetry. I've won—I'm a peer, a respected poet. I've won a Guggenheim Fellowship, and a bunch of National Endowment for the Arts fellowships, and the American Book Award. I have a lot of books out. I started writing a book of poems on history. I wrote a biography of Anton Chekhov in poetry form called *Chekhov.* I wrote a history of 1968 in poetry form. I'm now working on a five-volume history of the United States in poetry form. The first volume is to come out in 1999.

Mollin: I look forward to reading it. As I said to you yesterday, I ran across your book of short stories by accident, and I've really enjoyed reading them.

Sanders: Well, they are what they are—a slice of life. They're anthropologically accurate.

Mollin: That's what I figured. I was looking for a book on that time period and yours was what I found.

Sanders: Well, there were World War II rent controls in place. So you could get a cheap pad for $20–25 a month.

Mollin: So you could live like that.

Sanders: And food was—you could run down to the Catholic Worker for lunch. And the Catholic Worker kids would sell issues of the Catholic Worker. People always gave more than a penny— and they could buy a couple of quarts of Rheingold beer and listen to records at night and talk about pacifism and the world.

There was a lot of singing. The big difference that I find is there was a lot of singing. Everybody sang all the time. I mean, that's where I met Pete Seeger, on one of those little peace jaunts. This guy showed up playing the banjo. He could sing songs that made you cry because they were so new: "We Shall Overcome," and the thing he wrote with Lee Hays— "If I Had a Hammer"—that's a great Seeger tune. All the gospel tunes that we all sang. Everybody sang. And then if you add a few anarchist tunes that we learned, and a few folk tunes going around—there were a lot of songs sung. There were a lot of guitars and singing. Much more than now among the young people.

Mollin: Yeah—there's no comparison.

Sanders: So that's something a new generation might work on. Make sure that the young people sing a lot together.

Edward Sanders on His Fiction
An Interview

Brooke Horvath

Originally published in Review of Contemporary Fiction *19, no. 1 (Spring 1999): 23–30. Reprinted by permission of the* Review of Contemporary Fiction.

The following conversation was taped on 18 November 1997. Ed was visiting Cleveland to deliver a talk at the Rock and Roll Hall of Fame as part of its special exhibit "I Want to Take You Higher: The Psychedelic Era 1965–1969." On the 19th, Ed spoke on New York City's psychedelic scene and performed some poems. The previous evening over room-service pasta and coffee we talked about his fiction.

Brooke Horvath: Why don't people talk more about your fiction?

Ed Sanders: That's probably because when I travel, I travel as a poet. I perform as a poet, and my choice of life is as a poet, although I've been experimenting with long poems that tell stories. In *Tales* there are the long poems—"Farbrente Rose" and "Sappho on East Seventh"—and in Hymn to the Rebel Cafe there's "An East Village Hippie in King Arthur's Court"—another sho-sto-po [short story poem].

If I had the unfortunate task of selecting my own gravestone text, I'd probably say something like "Ed Sanders, American Bard." I'd rather be known as a bard, which is a poet who takes public stances. But I don't know why I'm not thought of as a fiction writer. Maybe I need to get a little older so I look more like Mark Twain; then the prose will get more attention.

Horvath: You'll have to wait until Vonnegut is through looking like Twain.

Sanders: I already look more like Twain than Vonnegut does. Vonnegut looks too unhappy, and Twain tried to dress well.

Horvath: Is it unproductive to focus here on the fiction apart from your other work?

Sanders: I have no problem with that. Right now I'm writing volume four of *Tales of Beatnik Glory*, so I've had a career as a short-story writer. Writing is a big sphere, and on that sphere are diaries, poems, plays, journalism, dialogues, stories, epics, epigrams, haiku, rhymed quatrains, projective verse … and I'm there on that sphere: have pen, will write.

Horvath: You said a second ago that you see yourself as a bard, one who speaks on public issues. Is that what holds your work together, that particular sense of purpose?

Sanders: I feel obligated to speak out because of my parents, who were Stevensonian Democrats, and because of my generation, that strange zone between Beat and postmodern where I grew up as a writer. I was trained by Allen Ginsberg, Kenneth Rexroth … Samuel Beckett talking about clawing through the wall with your fingernails, then, when they break off, the pads of your fingers, then the bones …

But I don't have a broad take of myself, although that may be terribly improper to admit. I see myself as a member of the avant-garde, going into unexplored territory. I'm not over yet. Up to now I have this work I've done, that's all, and it's embarrassing to me to think of my life as a completed thing. I have many abandoned books, and when I kick the bucket someone is going to find a lot of manuscripts—novels, all sorts of things.

Horvath: In *1968: A History in Verse* you talk about the people who criticized you for having fun in the midst of crisis. What pleasure do you find in writing fiction besides satisfying that need to speak out?

Sanders: Writing … it can't be called erotic, but it has a kind of thrill. Writing is the skin of the world, and you can drum on it, dance on it, play it … it's a great fun thing to do every morning. As you know, it's not always fun; it's also an act of discipline. It's like a Russian short story about a horrible train trip followed by a lot of fun when you finally arrive at St. Petersburg.

But back to 1968 and the "trap" of hedonism: we have to be hedonistic in a good part of our lives; otherwise, why live? You can't be just a dreary robot slaving away. So there's that double life-track of having fun while working for a better world, which was the theme of 1968 on one level. How do you combine the two? Maybe you can't. But you can't let only the ferocious carry the political flag to fruition. Clinton has solved the problem by having very well-disciplined pockets where he lets the Other project; he's a kind of hillbilly Bacchus. Euripides would have had a good time with Clinton—he'd have written a play called "Dionysus in Hot Springs, Arkansas."

Horvath: You are routinely described as a Beat. Donald Allen and George Butterick included you in their anthology *The Postmoderns*, and Lance Olsen has called you an avant-popist. Do such labels mean anything to you? Do you identify your work with a movement?

Sanders: I've always been a scholar in my own pursuits, and I must say that I really didn't know what postmodernism was when I saw myself in that anthology. So I did research—I did some at your house and in subsequent years to clarify for myself what it was. Understanding postmodern thought has helped with character definition in my short stories. But I feel confused. When I call Tuli Kupferberg and ask how he is, he says "still above room temperature," and that's how I feel often: I don't know about labels, but I feel glad, honored, simply to be alive at the end of a weird century and still creating, still having books come out. I'm so pleased and honored that these things are happening and that as an independent writer not connected to any school—and who hasn't had a job since 1965—I can afford to put out a left-liberal newspaper, to travel. So apply those labels, I like those labels, because they help define an independent writer. But I'm just a confused, skin-covered mammal at the end of a strange century beset by all my friends' health problems.

Horvath: A lot of reviewers of your books talk about an ambivalence they perceive on your part, an uncertainty regarding your attitude toward your subjects: for instance, in *Tales of Beatnik Glory*, whether you mean *glory* straight or satirically.

Sanders: Well, as far as *Tales* is concerned, there is a shift in tone from volume 1 to volume 2. Volume 1 is more deliberately upbeat and defiant because it seemed to me a period—the early sixties—when the people I was writing about were just that: partisans of beatnik glory. There are some stories in volume 1—for instance, "Mindscape Gallery"—where betrayal plays a factor, as it does in every scene, whether it's a straight, ultra-right scene or a left-wing or middle-wing scene. Betrayal is a threat, so I brought in betrayal. But my attitude in volume 1 is ebullience. As I said in my introduction [to the Citadel Underground edition], I had come through some very bad years, had written that book on the Manson family that had left me with what we used to call in the Fugs "metaphysical distress." So I wanted to write about an era I knew and loved—when I was young and came to Greenwich Village in 1958 through the Cuban Missile Crisis and Kennedy's assassination. I loved those years and knew I had met many, many interesting people I could combine and weave into stories about the past with each character morphed from ten or fifteen people I knew—things they might have said, clothes they might have worn, situations they could have gotten into. Once I had these characters, I let them do their thing and wrote it down. That's how I wrote that book, not quickly, but very precisely.

But when I got to volume 2, I faced some issues such as the way the Beat generation tended to treat women. So in a story such as "It's Like Living with a Mongol," I focused on the question of how women were sometimes treated like hookers, lookers, and cookers, entities that were supposed to drop everything and start cooking spaghetti. But I meant those stories seriously. I love those people, and I feel very sad now that I'm reaching the end of that decade. Volume 1, you see, went through 1962, volume 2 through '65, volume 3 from 1966 through 1967, and volume 4 will take me through 1969. Then it's over. To my horror, one of my characters, Uncle Thrills, gets leukemia and dies. And then there's the whole urban commune movement, and the question of Kerouac turning against his own generation late in his life, supporting William Buckley and voting for Nixon in 1968. I've got to deal with the politics of my people.

I take these stories very seriously and love those characters. I thought of them all, they all have careers, and they are all very alive in my mind, all the dancers and poets and thinkers. They're real to me still. As I finish volume 4, I've got to say goodbye to them unless I pick up on them later, but I don't know if I'll have time for that. I've got a list of books I want to write, and I'm already fifty-eight. So I'll have to start triaging off projects to get to the ones I really want to do.

Horvath: So when a reviewer writes of *Tales* as John Yohalem did in *The New York Times Book Review* (9 November 1975)—"Sanders can't decide whether he is glorying in decadence like a shopkeeper on a spree, or striking the poses of the self-righteously liberated, or putting the whole scene down"—that is simply missing the point, the intent.

Sanders: Yeah, that's missing the point. What I wanted to do was to be anthropologically exact, true to the times, nothing said by anyone that would be untrue to the era. For instance, they say that language as a whole changes every six hundred years, but the language of the cutting-edge counterculture, of bohemia, changes every couple years. So—in volume 3, for instance—I wanted to be true to that month in 1967 when "beatnik" was no longer used, and everybody was a "hippie."

But back to the review you quoted: that's why I don't read reviews, man. I was on the cover of *Life* magazine, but I've never read the story inside. I didn't want to get into one of those weird feedback loops. Oh, sometimes I read them because now there's this new generation of slash-and-burn types that attack, and I answer the overt attack. I learned from Clinton on that: if you are controversial and the attack is heavy, you've got to answer right away. But when someone totally misinterprets what I'm doing or just phones in the review, I forgive.

Horvath: *Tales* is an attempt to conjure through fiction the spirit of those times. When you write in the introduction to the Citadel edition that you have imagined places that "should have existed, but never did," you aren't saying, "it should have been like this but wasn't."

Sanders: No. Look, some of the stories in *Tales of Beatnik Glory* are broadly satirical but at the same time catch the essence of something. For instance, I think I very accurately capture the essence of the late fifties/early sixties open poetry readings in the story "The Poetry Reading" [*Tales* volume 1]. There are two theater groups out there right now doing plays about that time, and they're using that story as a way of putting people right there. On the other hand, when you use humor, when you satirize, you immediately point out how things might have been different. You make things slightly more grotesque than they were to point out the humor of it.

But again: that book was meant as an act of love. I talk about spiritual things in the book because although I'm not very spiritual; I know a lot of people are, so I talk about ghosts, other things. I'm not personally a believer, but a lot of people are and were.

Horvath: Satire seems a good word to use when talking about *Fame & Love in New York*. How did that book come about?

Sanders: It came in the same flow as volume 1 of *Tales*. I'd finished the Manson book in July 1971. I was totally devastated by that book, and my wife, daughter, and I went down to where her parents had had their honeymoon in rural Virginia, to an old southern mansion. I sat there for a week trying to decide what to do, wrote a long poem—"The VFW Crawling Contest"—then shortly thereafter a long piece about the entrapment of John Sinclair [former chairman of the White Panthers, jailed at the time on a marijuana charge] for the *L.A. Free Press*. John Lennon read that and made his decision to help.

Then I didn't know what to do. A year got blown—1972—but by 1973, I knew what I wanted to do. I worked on *Tales of Beatnik Glory*, and as I was finishing that, I noticed this thing called SoHo. There wasn't any SoHo then, just lofts—no boutiques, no fancy Guggenheims, no elegant places where you could spend $5 for a cup of coffee. It was illegal to live there then; the lofts still had oil stains from old machinery from fifty years earlier. It was funky, but I could see what was going to happen. I'd go into the Lion's Head and the same people buying beer were buying cocaine. I decided to study SoHo, do some research. I was reading Balzac, decided to read all of his novels, and then started to write this book called *Fame & Love in New York*. I knew a lot about rock 'n' roll, so I put a band in the book. It's a book about the problem of being an artist, a member of the avant-garde, and a democratic socialist. What are the problems associated with having a vision of a mixed economy where the government participates a lot in the economy, as in Sweden? And I had this idea of a deadline, like the year 2000. Creative people live with deadlines: deadline to get your record done, your book, you know? How many openings are there where the paintings are still wet and you can't touch them? So I had this idea of a "glorious deadline" for a real big future. But I had to predict SoHo because it hadn't even happened until right around the time the book was published in 1980.

The reason I'm babbling on is this: I wrote *Tales* as an act of auto/psychotherapy so I could feel better about my life and my generation. Then I wrote *Fame & Love* so I could get off my chest certain things I'd detected in the artistic left that I'd encountered in my experiences with the Yippies and also in 1972 during the Democratic convention. Some of what I was satirizing can be found in *1968: A History in Verse*.

So I wanted to have a good time and heal myself. I moved to the country and kept writing and writing. I finally got *Fame & Love* done, and to my everlasting gratitude Bob Callahan [of the Turtle Island Foundation], took it on, and George Mattingly did a genius design job. I wanted to write a humorous left-wing novel while I still had the chops and wasn't burned out. While I was writing it, we'd moved to Woodstock. I was removed by then, living in 1974 on a very beautiful farm. By the time the book came out, we'd already bought a house in Woodstock, and I'd become a country boy.

Horvath: You talk in *Fame & Love* of a "fear of the fate of Hipponax the Poet," a "bard of the gutter," and of the dangers of "smut and spew-spackled scandal."

Sanders: Yes, because Hipponax exists only as fragments, and the only reason those fragments exist is because he wrote in limping iambics, an interesting meter. He was a guy who would chase people around in public, a literary version of Don Rickles. But Rickles always smiled and shook the hand of the guy he lampooned in Vegas; Hipponax played for keeps. So his story shows that you're in trouble if you take on public figures when you don't have a support system-like Tom Paine taking on Washington. But the reference to Hipponax was also an in-joke for anyone who'd studied classics.

Horvath: You weren't warning writers against smut?

Sanders: No, it's not a warning. Just saying that if you pursue a certain life-track, you can get painted into corners as a writer.

Usually writers write all their erotic things up to about age thirty, then they harumph off and become quite proper, like Diderot. It's a tough gig to last thousands of years if your act is raillery and highly charged erotica. The only reason Catullus survived is because his home town saved his manuscripts. So there's a lesson: always put your erotic poems in your hometown library, where local patriotism and boosterism will keep them from being burnt.

Horvath: I thought maybe the Hipponax story explained why you've stopped listing *Shards of God* among your publications.

Sanders: Oh, no—I'm not ashamed of what's in *Shards of God*. I don't care about its erotic material—many of my books have lots of *eros* in them. It was my decision to omit it from the list of my publications in *Hymn to the Rebel Cafe* and so forth, but I've lots of booklets and other things I don't list; for instance, I don't often mention *Vote!*

But I don't think *Shards* is a very good book. I view it as a failure on my part. I had a perfect opportunity to write a book about Chicago in 1968 and the broader cultural issues that came into play in that police riot, which I've only thirty years later begun to discuss in things like *1968: A History in Verse*. I was afraid to look at that stuff for decades because I was horrified, shocked. What happened in Chicago made me weep for America and led, I think, to Phil Ochs's suicide. Such injustice.

Shards contains some interesting writing, and I certainly sign enough copies when I'm on the road. It has a certain pizzazz. But I'd never written a novel before, and as a whole it isn't constructed that well. It just didn't live up to what I intended, which is partly a critique of my own cowardice for not diving in and doing a real book on Chicago. I didn't know I could do it. I hadn't done my book on Manson yet. [Charles] Olson talks about a saturation job—one giant research project to prepare you for all the others—and I hadn't done mine yet, so I didn't know how. I was still, not a rock star, but very well known in those days, and I was caught in a weird warp I couldn't step out of.

Horvath: It seems to me that you must have had a very clear sense of what you didn't want *Shards* to be.

Sanders: I had had very little experience writing prose except for term papers in college. I had no models except that I knew microscopically a lot of prose—I knew Beckett's books backwards and forwards—-and was very influenced by my study of Greek culture, by the *Iliad*, the *Odyssey*, Hesiod, Diogenes. And Chekhov was a big influence, whom I read for pleasure as soon as I discovered him—when I opened the Peace Eye Bookstore and got his books from wholesalers. The first story I remember reading was "Rothschild's Fiddle," which completely changed my take on literature.

But I had done all the "proper" reading. Allen Ginsberg had told me to read Pierre, which was the Melville you were supposed to read if you were Beat. I read Edward Dahlberg, who became a friend. I liked his prose style; he was sort of an electronic Isaiah. I'd read all the Beat tomes, and my mother had read Dickens to us. So I had a primitive sense of narrative, although I'd never taken any literary classes, any workshops. I'd have rather stuck up a Seven-Eleven than take a workshop. In college I only took what I thought were useful courses: languages, mathematics, science.

And I never read the introductions to anything. I always thought that if the novel couldn't do it, I didn't want to read it. It turns out that when I read some of those introductions I sneered at years ago, I probably should have read them. Not all scholars are useless.

But I read like everybody in my generation. We tried to out-read each other—it was like a reading contest. From 1957 to somewhere in the sixties there was a mad rush to read more than everybody else. But I can't spin out a list of narrative sources.

Horvath: No. I just wondered if you were intent on not being, say, the next John Updike.

Sanders: What was that novel … *Couples*! I got viscerally angry reading that. No, I didn't have anything in mind other than wanting to do an act of imagination. I had my typewriter there on Avenue A, had just broken up the Fugs, and didn't have anything to do, so I started that novel.

Horvath: I have the impression you are impatient with what's going on with literary criticism.

Sanders: I don't know anything about it. What I know I've learned from visiting people like you and reading what you have lying around your house and office, which I do all the time. I go to colleges all over America and always spend a couple hours studying the books in professors' offices. I was just up at Union College in Schenectady studying the books. Professors always have great books. What we need is a website listing the books in every decent professor's office.

Horvath: What's going on in current fiction that you like?

Sanders: I read in a very specialized way. I live in my own little maelstrom. I don't keep up on what's being written, and I don't follow the rebirth of narrative, although I think that is happening. Because what is needed now are pathways through the chaos, and writers can be helpful. Who knows what's going to happen? Whatever it is, it will be unusual, and the task of the writer will be difficult—creating virtual rooms to sit in and participate. Whatever happens, narrative will still be required, and a lot of negative capability, a lot of "just say no." In a fact-suffused universe, saying no is very important.

What the writer does is, I think, vitally important, although I could be wrong. I do think good writing is still the most intimate way of describing reality. However, I'm fifty-eight years old, don't have the time to figure out what's going on in literature, and am going to let others do this new thing that's going to happen. I have my march orders.

One Busy Fug

Bob Reidel

Originally published in Beat Scene, *no. 48 (Summer 2005): 47–49. Reprinted by permission of* Beat Scene.

Last fall, I let my 14-year-old son skip school for a couple of days so we could drive to the city to see a reunion of the Fugs, the proto-folk-punk band formed in 1964 by Ed Sanders and Tuli Kupferberg, at the Knitting Factory. The musicians were in fine form, cranking out two sets of updated oldies and new material; Kupferberg, now in his 80s and leading candidate for Oldest Living Rock Star, was spry as all get-out. My most vivid memory, though is of the band's live debut of Sanders's song "Impeach George Bush" ("Drive him from power/Just like we drove the malevolent Nixon back to San Clemente/Whoa-oh … "). At one point Sanders muffed the words a bit, but at my side I could hear an adolescent voice singing them straight through. My son had downloaded Sanders's solo recording from Thurston Moore's Protest Records website, and had the lyrics down cold. So much for dinosaurdom.

Read anything about Sanders, and you'll likely be treated to a hyphenated appellation along the lines of "poet-journalist-inventor-publisher-novelist" or some such, by way of introduction. But as Robert Creeley once noted, "It would be altogether pointless to divide Edward Sanders into categories: Poetry, fiction, music," and that attempts to pigeonhole his work into separate genres "seem now useless echoes of an isolating taxonomy of a century ago."

Whether noodling on his Talking Tie, writing a verse biography of Chekhov, or publishing a small-town newspaper, there is always a distinctive Sanders stamp on the work, and a natural continuity from one form to another.

That work's latest manifestation is the newly completed and vastly enlarged *Tales of Beatnik Glory* (Thunder's Mouth Press, $16.95), a 784-page slab of fictive Beat Hip-era revelry, drawn on the author's own experiences in the 1960s, when a friendly new world disorder seemed possible, and the Lower East Side provided a mixing bowl for whipping up impromptu festivals of life. Sanders's first 17 Tales came out in 1975, and an expanded edition, with a second volume added, was published in 1990. The new completed tome adds on the final two volumes, almost doubling the size, and expands the action into Midwest hippie communes and the psychedelic bastions of California.

But the crux of the interwoven lives of the characters is embedded in the area east of 5th between Delancey and 14th Streets, where Sanders himself stomped throughout the '60s. Much of the action takes place in Lower East Side hot spots—some real, like Stanley's Bar and Sanders's own Peace Eye Bookstore, and in others, like the House of Nothingness Café and the Luminous Animal Theater, that Sanders says "should have existed, but didn't." In much the same way, the characters drift, drive, or are driven through real-world events of the '60s—the assassinations, the Freedom Rides, the Cuban missile crisis—as well as playing key roles in some that weren't, but should have been. (Oh, to have been present at the Great Tompkins Park Beatnik-to-Hippie Conversion Ceremony …)

Bob Reidel: [I caught up with Sanders to talk about the book, by phone, at his home up in Woodstock.] Congratulations on the finished product.

Sanders: Yeah, I'm glad it's out, after such a long period of creation. It took 30 years because I thought initially that there'd only be one volume, and then as I indicated in the final story in the book—

Reidel: Where the characters all get together and try to talk you into writing more …

Sanders: They come around and tell me, "What is this, Sanders? Let's go—we have longer lives, more stuff to do—why don't you write about us?" That's sort of the way it was. When you create characters as vivid as Uncle Thrills or Sam Thomas or John Barrett or Louise Adams or Claudia Pred or any of these archetypal denizens of the civil rights/peace/underground/mimeograph revolution/filmmaker generation, they have a vitality of soul that made them the sort that wanted to live on and on. Other books intervened, but I always kept ideas and notes for stories. And all my other researches were of use. My researches for the book on Chekhov helped provide insight into these characters in *Tales of Beatnik Glory*; the same thing with my long poem "Yiddish-Speaking Socialists of the Lower East Side," which sort of led to the story "Farbrente Rose" in volume two.

I kept getting invited to Kerouac events over the years, so I started studying his life, which led to the story "The Ghost on 20th" in volume 4. My work with the Fugs in touring California and playing the psychedelic light shows—the Kaleidoscope in L.A., the Avalon Ballroom in S.F., playing for the hippies outdoors in Golden Gate Park, experiencing Topanga Canyon in the '60s, Malibu, Hollywood—led to some of the stories in volume four, the one about Johnny Ray Slage, the story about Debbie Harnigan … well, it's a group of people you obviously enjoyed hanging out with. I knew them. I knew them in my soul, so I could easily write about them. I realized Debbie had fatal flaw and a death wish, that this charismatic, wonderful singer should have a hunger for oblivion at the same time. So I have her dying of an overdose as her helicopter takes off out of Giants Stadium with the people still on their feet applauding. It's a long way from hanging out on Avenue B.

Reidel: You must have seen people live that rags-to-riches-to-ruin story.

Sanders: Janis [Joplin] was a good friend. I saw her not long before she died.

Reidel: And you must have known older leftists who were a lot like the character Rose Snyder.

Sanders: When I came to Woodstock, there was some mild muckraking and reform after Nixon fell, so in the late '70s there was a resurgence of activism. And the leaders were older, in their 60s and 70s. There was a guy up here running the consumer movement who had once chained himself to the Statue of Liberty in protest against the House Un-American Activities Committee. There were a number of older women, especially, who had been socialist activists in the '30s. Rose is modeled on some of these women I met up here, but also some women in the early Southern Tenants Farm Workers Union and in the early needle trades unions, especially after the Triangle Shirtwaist fire in 1911. Clara Lemlich is one of them—she was one of the *farbrente maydlach*, the "burning young women," and Rose Schneiderman.

I didn't get Rose Snyder from Rose Schneiderman, though there's a similarity in the name. Rose Snyder has a little bit of the very young Dorothy Day before she became saint-like. And there are nonviolent activists like Barbara Deming and Marjorie Swann, many women with fierce personalities who are sort of melted together into the character of Rose, who exists throughout the book as a leitmotif of "never give up on the beliefs of your youth"—they're just as valid when you have a walker and are half-blind as when you're young and can run 15 miles a day.

Reidel: You quote from the preamble to the IWW [Industrial Workers of the World] constitution, about building a "society in which it is easier to be good," and that seems to be a through-line.

Sanders: Yeah. A peaceful society without war, where nations get along, there are no border disputes, where there's cradle-to-grave health care and everybody has a six-week paid vacation, and people can change careers without worrying about their future. That's the biggest thing now—people get these jobs and they're trapped forever. It's the same way with the downside of rent control. You get these apartments, and where are you going to move?

You're trapped in the same house your whole life and the same career. People in America, even in the professions, don't take more than a week's vacation—there's no downtime, there's no goof-time. We need a society where it's not only easier to be good, but easier to take time off and goof around, study things and engage in strange research.

Reidel: There are a couple of verse sections, like "Sappho on East Seventh."

Sanders: I was experimenting with the mixing of verse and text—which is right out of William Carlos Williams' *Spring and All.* That's where the poem

> so much depends
> upon
> a red wheel
> barrow
> glazed with rain
> water
> beside the white
> chickens

is, so I realized you could embed poetry inside of a prose text pretty easily. I'm supposed to be part of an international avant-garde, so I figured, well, this is part of it. I'm going to read one sentence from volume three: "In Apollinaire's *Vie Anecdotique*, anecdotes crowd the life-track like layers of feathers on a hawk's wings and one anecdote is barely under way when the next one begins."

Reidel: Did you find that was true for the whole book? That a bit of one story would lead into another one?

Sanders: That's kind of the way it is with life situations. My first conscious encounter with that phenomenon came when I became close with Charles Olson, who was my mentor beginning in '62 till death in '69. He would be in the middle of an anecdote, and then all of a sudden another one would sprout out, so they were like layered anecdotes. Very interesting. I guess he could only do it with people that he felt could follow it—you had to have your wits about you to follow that kind of thing. And is an anecdote ever fully told? There are always aspects that you can't include in the anecdote for whatever reason. So they do layer together. And the book is a big system—people may like it or not like it, but it is a metaphysical system It was constructed with care. Some people are not going to be able to leap into it to the depth they could, but it is right there, waiting.

Reidel: When we were setting this interview up, you mentioned you were getting involved in the Ohio count-the-vote effort.

Sanders: I've joined a group of investigators called Crisis in Voting, and we've opened up a website. Information on the two other investigators is on the website, crisisinvoting.org. One of them is my friend Larry Larsen, with whom I worked investigating the Manson family and who has for years been a very prominent private investigator in Los Angeles. This whole election thing is going to die down, and everybody's going to say—not everybody, but many people will say, including the liberal establishment—that it was fairly won. But our group is going to do a much deeper investigation into this than what's going on. It may take years. I'm going to devote significant time to it during the next year or two to interview people and to really take a look at electronic voting, the issue of long-distance hacking of computer systems.

Reidel: Well, maybe you'll get help from Senator Boxer.

Sanders: She was brave. But the liberals and the Democrats are going to be so occupied saving Social Security and preventing a gutting of social programs and stopping, say, the next invasion, the imposition of the draft, so they can do more invasions. We have to stop the imposition of the draft so they won't be able to do so many new wars—you know: "Four more wars, four more years." So the right wing is very cunning. They know the whole Democratic apparatus will have to swing into action. I mean, their fight is still against FDR. It's very Middle-Eastern—these right-wingers have kept these grudges for 80 years now.

On the other hand, if there has been enough massive high-tech vote fraud, it won't matter who the Democrats run. They could run the reincarnation of John Kennedy, and he'd lose because they'd steal it. So we're going to take a look at that. We're keeping an open mind and not jumping to any conclusions, and we'll see where it stands, but we're going to do a severely serious investigation of the current voting situation. Here in New York state, the state's under mandate—they've gotten a year's extension, to 2006—under the Help Americans Vote Act, to institute an electronic system. New York state, since 1896, has had a very accessible, very viable, very accurate, very useful, and very honest system of mechanical voting. It works. We know the results almost as quickly as with an electronic system, maybe quicker. So what's the deal? Why should New York state have to go on something where they can be hacked by right-wing nuts? Anyway, I'm raving on. But that's what I'm involved in.

I'm [also] tooling up my life now for volume four of *America: A History in Verse*, which will cover the fall of Nixon up through the rise of Reagan. So I'm working on that, and this Crisis in Voting project.

Reidel: I have to ask you about another Ohio controversy. The Fugs still aren't in the Rock and Roll hall of fame in Cleveland. What's up with that?

Sanders: It's a disgrace. I see to my horror that Jackson Browne—is Jackson Browne in there?—the Eagles are in there, Bruce Springsteen's in there. Hey, we're waiting for the phone call. Is it still Ahmet Ertegun that's the controlling factor, or Jann Wenner? Come on Jann! Come on Ahmet! They could give Tuli and I those honorary things that they give to pioneers. We helped pave the road for HBO. It's true! The producers of *Gone With the Wind* paid a $5,000 fine, as I talk about in volume one of *America: A History in Verse*, for Clark Gable saying "damn" in 1939. Speed forward to Lenny Bruce in '64 getting arrested at the Cafe Au Go-Go. And then the Fugs broke in on the scene and helped to change it so that Tony Soprano could utter his foul-mouthed expletives to millions of people. I mean, Tony Soprano would've been there in jail with Lenny Bruce. It's a shame. It's crying shame, Ed. It's Johnny Ray shame. It's a "Mood Indigo" shame. It's a "Tears on my Pillow" shame. It's "Cry Baby Cry" shame. It' a "Heartbreak Hotel" shame. It's a … it's a … waiting-for-the-call from Cleveland … [*sounds of sobbing*] … Ed, you OK? You have some tissues there? … waiting for … a vindication of my youth … [*sniffles*] …

Reidel: Are you doing any appearances down in New York related to the book?

Sanders: I have Rapidograph, will sign. I've told them I'm willing. But you know, the thing about when a book like this comes out is, it's a 30-year book—it's going to take a while for it to settle in, given the circumstances. It is a universe of itself, and it requires study and getting into it. So anytime in the next five years is pub date.

An American History, Line by Line
An Interview with Edward Sanders

Steve Paul

An American History, Line by Line: An Interview with Ed Sanders" and "Introduction to Ed Sanders" by Steve Paul. This first appeared in New Letters 76, no. 1, 2009. *It is printed here with the permission of New Letters and the Curators of the University of Missouri-Kansas City. Permission also granted by Steve Paul.*

Ed Sanders shares his small home at the base of Mead Mountain in Woodstock, NY, with his wife of nearly 50 years, Miriam; two chirping parakeets; countless books and magazines stacked on almost every flat surface; and a crowd of orchids queued up in sunny windows. Outside, his wooded yard is populated by what, on an early spring day, must be the friendliest herd of deer around.

A small stream runs behind the house and near it lies an array of gray stones in the strokes of a Chinese character that Sanders placed as a prayer for ailing fellow poet Gary Snyder, who once wrote, "each rock a word." Snyder, of course, is among the last of a generation of poets pinned loosely with the label of Beat, an association that comes more by friendship and influence rather than aesthetic stance. Although Sanders, a decade younger, caught the attention and friendship of the likes of Beat icons Allen Ginsberg and William S. Burroughs, he considers himself a kind of tweener: too young to be a Beat and too old to be a flower-carrying hippie child in the 1960s. Nevertheless, he was present at enough important poet-activist culture clashes of the decade that he, too, seems now like the elder statesman of the crowd: the march on Washington (1963), the Pentagon march and "exorcism" by music (1967), the siege of Chicago (1968), the set of William F. Buckley's *Firing Line* with a drunken Jack Kerouac (1968), the bloody wake of the Manson family murder spree (1969), which he corralled into a still-vital work of narrative nonfiction, *The Family*.

Sanders, who turned 70 on August 17, 2009, had planted himself in the New York alt-culture landscape of the early 1960s, steeped in ancient Greek verse, poetry pamphleteering, Bohemian bookselling, and the wild musical satire of the band he co-founded, the Fugs, specialists in songs of dope and sex. (At the time I dropped in, Sanders had been tinkering in a recording studio, refining some new Fugs tracks he'd made with band co-founder, Tuli Kupferberg, now 85.)

Over the course of two March afternoons, Sanders talked about his evolution as a poet, from the rhyming formalism of his English class at Blue Springs (Missouri) High School to the Charles Olson-inspired practice he developed and labeled "Investigative Poetry" in the mid-1970s to the extensive immersion in history that underlies his ambitious and long-running project—recounting the history of America in verse. Sanders's poetic history of the United States in the twentieth century spans five volumes, not counting a separate book entirely devoted to 1968, and lately he's been filling binders, reading, and making progress on the previous three centuries.

Sanders also is the author of a sprawling fictionalized memoir, *Tales of Beatnik Glory*, which has been optioned by Hollywood, as has *The Family*, his nonfiction investigation of Charles Manson and "family."

In the fall of 2009, Coffee House Press issued a two-volume collection of Sanders's poetry, the first half being a revised edition of *Thirsting for Peace in a Raging Century*, his selected poems from the 1960s, '70s and '80s, the second an all-new selection from the last two decades. The latter, *Let's Not Keep Fighting the Trojan War*, owes its title to Simone Weil, who made a similar declaration in an essay after the outbreak of the Spanish Civil War.

Sanders has an impish sense of humor and a mellow demeanor that would suggest an unruly absent-mindedness if he weren't so focused on making things right in the world and on the page. What else is a poet to do?

"Basically," he told me, "I hate to say it, but no one reads poetry. Nobody reads history. I write history and poetry. Therefore, what?" Here's what.

Steve Paul: Everyone comes from somewhere, of course, so maybe it's of interest only to those of us in the Midwest that you hail from Blue Springs, Missouri, a Kansas City suburb. But how did that contribute to your development as a poet?

Ed Sanders: I was raised in Missouri. All my poetry was rhymed until I came to New York.

Paul: It rhymed because you were raised in Missouri?

Sanders: I had this great English teacher who taught us about the silver age of literature and the golden age of literature. We read William Cullen Bryant. We memorized Poe, and "The Cremation of Sam McGee," "The Road Not Taken," Shakespeare's sonnets. We memorized a lot. All my poems rhymed. So I realize now, as I'm getting on, I'm starting to rhyme again.

My friend Robert Creeley, a rock-ribbed New Englander from Worcester—his late poems started to rhyme, too. Rhyming is a well of the muses a poet can drink from later in life. Look at Thomas Hardy, at those beautiful, rhymed poems he wrote in his 80s. Some of his best work was when he was older. The rhyming circuits are the last ones to go in a poet's mind, I think.

Some people have rhymophobia. But rhyme was as American to me as my aunt's homemade ice cream. Everything was rhyme.

Paul: So you were actively writing poems in high school?

Sanders: Oh yeah, sure. I have all my life's poems arranged in three-ring binders in one of my storage sheds. I got all my stuff returned from one of the heirs to my English teacher, Mrs. Hall, Lecie Hall, in Blue Springs. I was quite religious once. She, herself, was religious. She would read some of my high school poems to her Sunday school class, and this was after the Fugs, too, when I was writing erotic stuff. She forgave me some of my transgressions. I always visited Lecie Hall when I went back there.

If it weren't for her, I probably wouldn't have been a poet. She saw my wild, Poe-like, strange mindset, and she encouraged me. Under her tutelage, I started shifting away from rhyme, and I became aware of Dylan Thomas and Ezra Pound. I began reading modern poetry in high school.

Paul: In *Tales of Beatnik Glory*, you write about the period in your senior year in high school after you discovered Ginsberg's *Howl* and went wild over it.

Sanders: I bought *Howl* at the University of Missouri bookstore, and I memorized it. I used to shout it out to my beer-drinking buddies as we drove around the Independence courthouse square drinking Griesedick Brothers beer. They ignored me. But they let me do it.
[Note: Sanders attended the University of Missouri for a year before transferring to New York University. Following his late mother's advice to learn from the classics—she died during Sanders's senior year in high school—he studied Greek. By the early 1960s, he had settled into the bohemian district of lower Manhattan, opened the Peace Eye Bookstore, and published broadsides and stapled, mimeographed booklets of poetry.]

Paul: How did you end up in Ginsberg's circle and getting noticed in general?

Sanders: I used to go to readings of beatnik poets in the coffee houses on Bleecker Street. I wouldn't have dared to introduce myself. A fellow needed to write something worthy of my generation. Finally, I wrote "*Poem from Jail*" (City Lights, 1963). I sent it to Ferlinghetti. And I started writing to Ginsberg. I started to put out *Fuck You* magazine, and I sent it to my heroes: Beckett, Picasso, Castro, and I sent one to Allen Ginsberg in India. He wrote back. I sent one to Charles Olson. They all started writing back. All of a sudden I had more fame than I should've had. I was still in college.

I opened the store in the fall of '64. Allen lived nearby. Jack Kerouac used to walk by my store on his way to visit Allen. So I was a wild, young man in the midst of all that when I got out of college. But then I became their friend because I started writing things worthy of my generation.

Paul: Being up here in Woodstock, NY, as long as you have, how does it, as a place, contribute to your writing? Is it any different than writing in the city?

Sanders: It's pretty good to write here because people leave us alone. No one would dare call me before noon. I'm usually up at 6:30, and I write till noon. Then I do community work—fund-raising for causes, raising money for gravestones for writers, auctions. I was a key person in writing a Woodstock zoning law, a ban on aerial spraying, a pesticide law. I'm very controversial locally. I'm always trying to protect the water. I was a Yippie, after all, so I can be controversial. In a small town, it becomes a matter of personality … but Miriam and I have many, many, many friends. We don't want malls here. We biased the hotel economy toward bed and breakfasts, and no Motel 8s.

Paul: And you also published a newspaper.

Sanders: For eight years we did a biweekly newspaper, the *Woodstock Journal*. Now it's a desultory Web site. It was a little bit like military duty. It paid for itself. It was a lot of work. I was touring, traveling all the time, sometimes editing the paper from a hotel in Vienna or Frankfurt or Rome in the middle of the night. I did it for eight years, then decided I couldn't do it anymore. At the same time, I was writing a verse biography of Chekhov, a verse biography of Ginsberg, and the first three volumes of *America: A History in Verse*. I could feel my hair turn whiter each day. Running a newspaper—all the anguish, dealing with advertisers, proofreaders, getting honest distributors. It's like running a rock band. It's full of hundreds of details that no one knows anything about.

Paul: Your concept of "investigative poetry" (see *Investigative Poetry*, City Lights, 1976) is much like the practice of journalism or history, involving research and exploring facts, though with an attention to the poet's craft, of course. Is that what drives your American history project?

Sanders: My mentor Charles Olson urged us to find out for ourselves. I have taken ten years to build a library of hundreds of books, some of them very old. You open up their pages and make notes. You try to make accurate chronologies, and I list sources for each assertion.

When I was writing the Manson book, in 1970 and '71, I had pages all over the floor of our big loft in New York City, and a transcriber who transcribed my tapes. I found myself writing text in clusters, so for this new version of *Thirsting for Peace in a Raging Century*, I decided to transcribe my note pages as when I was writing the Manson book. It's a poem called "The Road to Investigative Poetry." I described the scene as police arrived. I wrote it in the short lines that I was typically writing at the time. And I realized as I did this back then, even though these were typed up in regular paragraphs, I originally wrote it in line breaks. That gave me the idea of investigative poetry, which I wrote four years later.

Paul: How do you turn what is essentially nonfiction, or history, into poetry? I mean, the project could end up fairly dry, right?

Sanders: Nonfiction is a kind of map of fragments of information sequenced together, like an elegant baklava with layers of meaning. You have to think of different arrays of sequencing information. If you want to entice a reader not to put down the book and turn on the television, you need to make it interesting, but you have to be true to the material. It's about data clusters and pathways to sequencing information. It's extremely important not to get trapped in a certain array. I used to encounter people in rock 'n' roll who would say, "I wrote those lines and I can't change it." I'd say, "What do you mean you can't change it?" I call it a lame-o lyric lock. You get locked into a lame-o lyric sequence. It's the same for nonfiction writing or playwriting or in putting together a sequence of stuff. It's important not to get frozen into a certain array, but to do some experimentation on the data.

The postmodern negative capability comes into play. I could write a biography of you; I could probably write 15,000 pages on you. But in nonfiction you have to say no to hundreds of things. You have to make an apt choice, or an artistic choice, or an aesthetic choice about what you put in—and what you leave out. It's an art form when to say no. Especially in investigative poetry, it's a mission.

Then the double problem is to make it euphonious, eurhythmic, to have emotive power and to have the structure of poetry. That is not easy. It's not only "first thought best thought" in investigative poetry. There's a lot of elbow grease.

Paul: What did you accomplish today?

Sanders: Well I got up [*laughs*] about 6:30 a.m., and as I was doing yesterday, during my four or five hours of writing, I was working on *America: A History in Verse, the 18th Century*. Today I've been researching things like Thomas Paine's quarrel with George Washington. This was when he was in prison under the Terror in Paris, and Paine felt that Washington should have worked harder to get him out.

I did some research to try to figure out those years, but I was also writing a draft of the first 30 pages, up through the Tuscarora Wars. The Tuscarora was a tribe in North Carolina, which battled German, Dutch, and British settlers. The early part of the eighteenth century is very complicated and interesting. So that's what I did this morning, I wrote and printed out 30 pages of the eighteenth century. Then I switched to my local political role. I'm refereeing some disputes in local government as a town father.

Then I printed out some poems.

Paul: I wanted to return to something you said yesterday, an offhand comment speculating as to whether you were literary enough for a literary quarterly. What did you mean by that?

Sanders: I was more or less jesting. I did not follow an academic career. I was offered all kinds of jobs as a professor, which I turned down. I have by my bed Aeschylus in Greek. My Greek is still pretty good. I always read quite a bit of Greek, but I am not up on postmodernist theory. So I was joking. I don't write for *The New York Review of Books*. I'm not much of a careerist. I don't go out of my way to get published in the right venues. There are in-crowd places. I used to try to do that, to write stuff for the *Village Voice* or *Paris Review*. I don't know the answer to forging quote a career unquote. So I deliberately didn't take a faculty position. I wanted the personal freedom of seven-hour writing days or really writing around the clock if I wanted to.

Paul: I was hoping you'd talk about your Greek studies.

Sanders: Well, the lead poem in my new collection is my translation of that new Sappho poem that was discovered in 2004. They matched two pieces of papyrus, and they pulled out the texts using modern technology. It was underneath something, some kind of commercial text. I translated that. This particular poem by Sappho, which I translated a couple of years ago, is written in a meter called choriambics. Choriambics is long-short-short-long.

It's a beautiful meter, which I found in Eliot, in "Four Quartets." I like to parse poems that I like, such as the "Four Quartets" or Whitman's "Out of the Cradle Endlessly Rocking." Out of the cradle endlessly rocking—it's like a metrical phrase that repeats: OUT of the CRA-dle, ENDlessly ROCKing. To me those are matching metrical units.

So this Sappho is beautiful. Once I realized that it was choriambics, I decided to translate it. When you translate Sappho on a religious topic, you have to explain the mythic theme, so you have to add stuff. I added a few lines to explain the story. She brings up her own aging. She says she used to dance light-legged like gamboling fawns. She says you can't live forever, then she tells this story of Eos, the Greek goddess of dawn, who fell in love with a Trojan prince, Tithonus. The Greek gods liked to date humans, which is one of the key differences between Christianity and the ancient religions. Tithonus was mortal, and Eos was kind of randy; she went to Zeus and said please, daddy, make Tithonus immortal. But she forgot to ask, as Sappho points out in the poem, to keep him from aging, so Tithonus kept getting older and older and older and older. Goddesses are eternal beauty queens, but he aged on her. I guess you can't go back to Zeus and ask again. So that's the poem by Sappho, on that legend and her own story of aging.

So I keep my hand in. I go to all these conferences. I'm the only beatnik who can yodel. No, I'm just kidding. I always tell that to European interviewers, especially in Austria. I yodeled on Austrian state TV.

[All of this was introduction to Sanders's impromptu performance, sitting on his couch, of the poem. He walks off and returns with a small stringed instrument.]

I have set this to music. I put a melody to it because Sappho, just like William Blake or Robert Burns, they [always] set themselves to music. That's how I discovered it was choriambic. I figured out the long and shorts as best I could, then I just kind of breathed into it. Just like Yeats, I guess. Yeats, when he was polishing his poems, kind of beat time with his hands, singsong it, until he'd get the sound. It's the same way working with Greek texts, to try to figure out the meters for complicated texts or to get the melody lines. I play the Sappho with this little three-stringed dulcimer-like instrument.

I genuinely try to give the flavor of what the Greek was like. Of course, no one really knows how the Greek was pronounced. Until they work out time travel, we'll never really know. So I do the best I can. I give it a little Missouri protestant hymn inflection.

Paul: Considering the way you've immersed yourself in the metrics, are you conscious of metrics as you write, or are they so internalized you don't need to think about it?

Sanders: Sometimes the metrics seem internalized. I tend now to write more in rhyme, but it's a difficult thing. All metrics are a sequence of vowels and consonants. It's a sequence of stops. The vowels carry the melody, and consonants are kind of the drums of poetry. Basically, the music in a line comes from vowels, or diphthongs, and consonants, and you bring to it meaning and sequence.

Everybody writes in meter. You can take any well-known poem and break it down into Greek meters. If you memorize those, or internalize those, and then you read Eliot or Ezra Pound or Robert Lowell or especially the most dense and open-field writers like Robert Duncan or Charles Olson, you can break their lines down into ancient meters—the iambs and the trochees and the dactyls—but also the anapests (dada dah), the spondees (two longs, dah dah) or various combinations of the basic meters. But how do I arrive at my lines? Well, the first thing a professor points out, line breaks are important. [Sanders recites William Carlos Williams' short poem "The Red Wheelbarrow": So much depends / upon / a red wheel / barrow / glazed with rain / water / beside the white / chickens.]

I think it was Yvor Winters who pointed out that if you just ran this out as a couple of lines, ho hum. It was in the line break where the genius came forward. I grew up on Allen Ginsberg and Ezra Pound and Robert Duncan and decided to use a lot of line breaks. I have a lot of indented lines in my work so I pay attention to that.

Paul: That's what is interesting about *America: A History in Verse*. This could be prose, except for how you distill it and distribute the words.

Sanders: I really work to make it poetry. I rewrite and select. First, I didn't want to write a kind of verse that's difficult to understand. I didn't want it like an ancient dithyramb, which is like the ancient Greek method of writing poetry that was difficult to understand. I wanted people to understand what I was saying. Yet I wanted it to have mystery and be referential and wanted to encourage people to explore for themselves. True, it's not prose. It is carefully chosen, and I work on it over and over again trying to breathe life into it, breathe the spirit of the bard into it. It is true you could take all of Shakespeare, run it together, run all his sonnets into prose. I use line breaks to facilitate the verse. It's true, I could break it into prose.

Paul: Is the breath important in where you make those breaks?

Sanders: Olson said this: "from the breath to the line." And Duncan, too: the state of your body, the breathing apparatus, your heart—he called it body tones—gave meaning to the way you write, and breathing had something to do with the length of the line. Allen Ginsberg had really good lungs, and he could write these 10-league lines that went on and on and on.

In the actual writing, sometimes you get poetry like Rilke's *Duino Elegies*, where it was kind of dictation from the sky. In that case, you're a transcriber, and you write it down. That's a graceful form of poesy. However, more often than not, you get an idea and then it's bardic elbow grease. You have to write it and rewrite it and polish and listen to it. It has to thrill the eye. It has to have intellectual content, but it has to thrill the ear, too. So, like Yeats, beating the time and chanting, I try to see what it sounds like.

Paul: It occurred to me that when I write about this book, *America: A History in Verse*, it would be useful to compare your project to conventional history.

Sanders: The thing about it, I've learned, is that historians are not a violent group, but they're contentious. Each point in history can be debated. There's a fact blizzard, an unbelievable amount of facts in the timelines of history. There's an unbelievable number, trillions of factional units one can choose. Then your own taste and your own abilities, your own historical outlook, your own politics, your own ethics, your own set of what's right and wrong, your own beliefs about the goodness or badness of something, your upbringing, your belief in spirituality and the afterlife, your non-belief in spirituality and the afterlife, your education, and everything comes into play as you choose to pluck the heart of your verse with all those possible notes. So in writing my history, I reject a lot of stuff. I agonize about this stuff. You have to say no. Like when you're selecting poems for a book. You're always breaking the hearts of your poems, if they were alive, when you don't put them in a book. It's the same way with history.

The biggest problem is converting thought and passion into poetry. That's where it all lies. I do my best. I work hard at it. Was it Olson who said, there are no weekends for poets? That I know.

Ed Sanders in Conversation

Markus Brandstetter

Originally published in Stadtbekannt Wien, *October 8, 2011, https://www.stadtbekannt.at/Edward-Sanders-im-Gesprch/. Reprinted by permission of* Stadtbekannt.

Edward Sanders was part of several cultural epicenters (such as literary and musical). The poet, author, musician (the Fugs), activist, publisher, and inventor (to name only some of his occupations) would often be called a connecting link between the Beat generation and the hippie generation. The poetry collection *Poem from Jail*, his work on "Investigative Poetry," as well as his book about the Manson Family, *The Family: The Story of Charles Manson's Dune Buggy Attack Battalion*, are among his most famous works. At present, Sanders is in Vienna, where he is giving the course, "The Poetry and Facts of the Final Months of Jim Morrison 1970–1971" at the *Schule für Dichtung*. [He is] performing June 17th at the Radiokulturhaus. Edward Sanders in conversation with Markus Brandstetter about poetry, lyric poetry, the Beat Generation and much more. [Title and introduction translated from German. The interview was published in English.]

Markus Brandstetter: In the documentary film *What Happened to Jack Kerouac*, Gregory Corso claimed that he wouldn't consider people like Jim Morrison or Bob Dylan as poets—he was strongly against that notion, drawing some of kind line. What is your opinion about this line between lyrics and poetry?

Ed Sanders: Well, some lyrics are not poems, and some poems are not lyrics. Lyrics are of themselves, and as for Jim Morrison: I wouldn't call The Doors's songs poems. But he kept notebooks and was trying to write what I call poems that stand apart from music. He was encouraged to do this by the Beat poet Michael McClure, who read through Jim's notebooks and said, "all right, these are good enough to publish." Morrison put together a book in 1969—and then kept struggling. My class this week will deal with that struggle: of someone writing, who is a famous star, like a Dionysos, or a Bacchus, who had all these groupies, who was very wealthy and controversial—who had people following him around, stopping him the streets. But he was at the same time carrying around his notebook, trying to write interesting lines of poetry that weren't songs. They were poems. So I tip my hat to that. So, who's to say?

Gregory Corso was a pure poet who didn't need music, who recited his poems. Very good poems, they were just black on white on a piece of paper. Words on paper, and that's a valid stance. But Shakespeare's "Under the Greenwood Tree" is a great poem and a song. So, it's hard to say. Also Bob Dylan: not all of his songs are poems, but there are some [that] will stand as literature. There are whole books written about Dylan's lyrics as if they were poems. And the same way with Jim Morrison: there are several books analyzing his poems as worthy. So I'm accepting his attempt: that he wanted to write poetry, wanted to get inside his head and write poems based on his final days, his final month—where he was drinking too much, taking too much cocaine, winding up drunk at the floor at night. But at the same time, during the day, he would sit at a Café at the West Bank, trying to write his poetry.

Brandstetter: You often have mentioned that the poem "Howl," and Allen Ginsberg in general, has been a major influence. You have been, so to say, at the very epicenter of various counter-cultural movements. Speaking about our time: do you think that poetry still has the ability of the social significance and power and change that it obviously had during those days? How do you see this role of poetry?

Sanders: It can be as powerful as the text of the poem. "Howl" was a unique explosion from a long time ago, from 1959, over 50 years ago. There *can* be a modern "Howl." Poetry as a form has the power to inflame and inform to rouse up. Now it's combined a lot with music, chanting, and performance. It has a power to make the walls of the city shake. There is a Fugs song: "When the mode of music changes, the walls of the city shake." And it's the same way with poetry: we write a great new poem and send it out into the world—it has secret ways to making its power known. It goes forward, and it influences one, it influences two, it influences three. It has a way of helping change the world.

Brandstetter: You are often times called a "bridge" between the Beat Generation and the hippie movement. Now there was a time when the Beats became the beatniks, a popularization of a subcultural movement. How did you experience that time when the Beats became the beatniks and then later on developed into the hippies?

Sanders: Throughout the late '50s and throughout most of the early '60s, people would call you a dirty beatnik. "Look at that beatnik!" Then, in 1967, all of a sudden it was "look at that dirty hippie!" It was like a change: if people wanted to put you down, you weren't a beatnik anymore, you were a hippie. That was in '67, the summer of love, the year of love. The year of the great be-in, the year of psychedelia, psychedelic music. That was when people stopped wearing all black and started wearing wildly colored robes, necklaces, letting their hair grow. The beatniks didn't have long hair. Beatniks had regular cut hair, but all of a sudden you let your hair grow.

Brandstetter: So it was just a flow from one movement into another.

Sanders: Yeah.

Brandstetter: There was this talk show where Kerouac was already in a terrible shape, drunk, cursing about what became of the Beat movement—calling them "hoodlums," and even harshly talking about his peers such as Ferlinghetti, yourself (who was on the podium), and Allen Ginsberg who was in the audience …

Sanders: That was the William Buckley Show, September 1968. Well, he [Kerouac] was very drunk. He was wearing the same jacket that he was buried in a year later. He was drinking too much, so much that he fell off the stage and landed on his back. Buckley tried to throw him off the show and put Allen in his place, but we said "no." I had told him beforehand that I didn't want to fight with him, that I respected him a lot. He couldn't handle fame well. He was a famous writer, and, as they say in the States, he couldn't do fame. He didn't accept that well, he was drinking too much and lived with his mother, who was a very right-wing Catholic. Very, very conservative—and she hated Allen Ginsberg. Kerouac loved Allen, but out of respect for his mother, he put Allen down. He had a double mind, he loved Allen and he hated Allen—in the same psyche. But after the William Buckley show, we went out to a bar, Kerouac and I, and we drank and had a good time.

Brandstetter: He said—and I can only paraphrase that—"In my mind the movement was always pure," and people like Ferlinghetti brought in the political perspective Kerouac disliked, calling them "communists."

Sanders: Kerouac was a Republican, Ginsberg was a Democrat. Kerouac voted for Richard Nixon in 1960, while Ginsberg voted for John Kennedy. So there was this split: the conservative wing in the Beats was Kerouac, and the liberal wing was Ginsberg. Kerouac was very conservative.

Brandstetter: If I may ask, are you still in contact with your peers Gary Snyder and Lawrence Ferlinghetti?

Sanders: Ferlinghetti, yes: I perform with the Ferlinghetti now and then. He's quite old, gee, but he still gets around. Gary Snyder lives in Northern California, Nevada City, and I am in touch with him by letter and by email. He's an old friend. They say, we're becoming geezers. In the USA they say, we're old, they're geezering up.

Brandstetter: And with Michael McClure?

Sanders: Yeah, Michael—he just sent me a poem he dedicated to me. We keep in touch, he calls me every now and then. The University of California Press has just published his collected poems. So he's doing all right, he must be in his late 70s too. So yes, we're in touch, he's an old friend.

Brandstetter: You're also famous for your inventions for musical instruments, for instance the Talking Tie. Can you tell us a bit about that?

Sanders: The Talking Tie is a pressure-sensitive switching membrane. It's a membrane mounted onto a clip-on tie, and then I use computer cables to go out on the array of the keyboard on my tie. The switching array goes by a multi-colored computer ribbon to a little synthesizer, and I can look at the audience and play with my tie while performing songs. The other instrument I am known for is one where the keyboards are mounted to my fingers by means of gloves. I close the circuit by having a metal ring on my thumb, and I touch the bars on my fingers. I can wave my hand around, gesticulate and make music at the same time. And recite my poetry. I also have an instrument called the Lisa Lyre, which is like an ancient lyre, only instead of strings it has infrared beams. When my fingers break the beams, it goes through a switching matrix and again through a computer cable to a synthesizer. And when I break the beams, it creates those sounds. It looks like passing through air, but through the light beams, interrupts them and biases the current to turn on the synthesizer note.

Brandstetter: Sir, thank you so much for taking the time. It was a great pleasure meeting you.

[Note MB: I would like to take this opportunity to thank the Schule für Dichtung, especially Harriet Nachtmann, for facilitating this conversation.]

Ed Sanders on His New Memoir, *Fug You*, and the East Village of the '60s and Today

Daniel Maurer

Originally published in The Local East Village, *December 7, 2011, http://localeastvillage.com/2011/12/07/ed-sanders-on-his-new-memoir-fug-you-and-the-east-village-of-the-60s-and-today/. Reprinted by permission of Daniel Maurer.*

Out this month, poet Ed Sanders's memoir of the 1960s, *Fug You*, serves as a veritable who's-who of the characters of the beatnik, hippie, and yippie scenes: splitting his time between playing with his satirical rock group the Fugs (first at local spots such as the Bridge Theater at 4 St. Marks Place and then around the world), publishing one of the East Village's most influential alternative journals, and operating the iconic Peace Eye Bookstore (first at 383 East 10th Street and then at 147 Avenue A), Mr. Sanders crossed paths with the likes of Andy Warhol, Jimi Hendrix, Janis Joplin, Abbie Hoffman, and Timothy Leary, among others. Jonas Mekas and Harry Smith inspired him to experiment with underground filmmaking, and another close friend, Allen Ginsberg, joined him in attention-grabbing stands in support of drug legalization, pacifism, and first amendment rights.

Interspersed with Mr. Sanders's memories of publishing everything from mimeographs (many of which are reproduced in the book) to some of Ezra Pound's "Cantos" out of his "Secret Location" on Avenue A (at one point, the $27.49-a-month apartment was raided by the FBI as they sought a roommate rumored to have knowledge of Lee Harvey Oswald) are his recollections of recording with the Fugs, defending himself in court against charges of obscenity, and also defending himself on television against a drunk and surly Jack Kerouac, who had grown conservative in his later years. ("During the show," writes Mr. Sanders, "I was very tempted to mention his daughter Jan, who'd come to many Fug shows. I remembered how the owner of the Astor Place Playhouse had come on Jan and a Fugs guitarist making it on the drum riser one midnight.")

The Local spoke with Mr. Sanders, who now lives in Woodstock, over the telephone earlier today.

Daniel Maurer: As you put this memoir together, did you find gaps in your archives due to some of the police confiscations you describe in the book?

Ed Sanders: I have a vast archive, and it's pretty well organized—I keep a lot of files in bankers boxes in my barn out back. The only things they confiscated were my underground films, which they took in their entirety from my secret studio on Avenue A. And when they raided my bookstore in early 1966, they took some publications, but not all of them.

Maurer: When you started the book, did you have any inkling, as you wrote about the many demonstrations that you participated in, that your story would be so relevant now in light of Occupy Wall Street and the Arab Spring?

Sanders: I didn't do it to be timely. I just thought I had a varied career and I had met an enormous panoply of Americans, Europeans, writers, artists and fellow rock people, so I just dipped into those memories and into those files and old leaflets. I didn't mean to be *au courant*. The book is out to the public right at a time when protest has come back like it does every 30 or 40 years, going back to the revolution of 1805.

Maurer: What do you think of Occupy Wall Street, anyway? As the '70s set in and you began working on a book about the Manson family, you seemed to be gaining a new appreciation for authority.

Sanders: I think [Occupy Wall Street] is great. I'm a little too creaky to go camp out somewhere, but I certainly appreciate their struggles. There are such a vast variety of issues now that I think they're correct in not focusing on one specific issue, but to have 100 or 200 issues they bring up.

Maurer: You were involved in quite a variety of issues yourself. Where do you think you were most effective?

Sanders: I guess I'm proudest of the ability to take a stance for a right cause in the face of great hostility and to use the nonviolence of Gandhi and Dr. King to present controversial issues. I raised my banners and helped exorcise the Pentagon and the grave of Senator McCarthy, took part in the Chicago riots of the summer of '68, tried to get into Czechoslovakia to sit in front of Soviet tanks as part of the Fugs tour. And I was part of a generation that helped expand constitutional freedoms.

Maurer: Occupy Wall Street has reminded us that police work can sometimes still come up against the work of the press. Back then, was there an us-vs.-them mentality as far as the Ninth Precinct went?

Sanders: I was never really specifically bothered by the police in the Ninth Precinct, but during the Summer of Love in 1967, they had a captain down there who did a lot of what I thought were unconstitutional drives against crash pads and urban communes, and virtually stifled them. The police were pretty vicious against smoke-ins and certain activities in Tompkins Square Park. The only problem I had was with one sergeant who raided my bookstore in '66 and kept showing up at our concerts. During one in Tompkins Square Park, there was a bomb scare and he came backstage, looking through our bags. I think most cops probably just want to uphold the law as they see it and don't want to reach out to squelch personal freedoms.

Maurer: One gets the sense while reading this book that the East Village was a very tight-knit community back then. It didn't take long for you to befriend some of your heroes, like Allen Ginsberg.

Sanders: It was all contained in a few blocks where everybody could live because that's where the rents were affordable thanks to rent control. There were a lot of bars and bistros and cafes and hangouts and art galleries and stores where you met. I was part of what they called "the mimeograph revolution" so I was always, always printing flyers and pamphlets, and setting up poetry readings. I was pretty active in my milieu of writing, art, and music, and we had a lot of benefits for people arrested for pot or to help raise money for issues. There was a sense of camaraderie and community among the partisans in the 1960s. You could still get an apartment for $20 or $30 a month—the rent control didn't start corroding until the '70s and '80s.

Maurer: But things got darker as the '70s began. In the book, you write about the infamous murder of Groovy, who briefly ran Peace Eye as a sort of community center.

Sanders: In my mind, it began in 1969. There was a lot more violence in the street. We lived on Avenue A and 12th and there was a tailor across the street. Some kids came in and [bashed] his head in with a brick and ran away. He died. There was a woman late in '69 who was just stabbed to death in the street outside our house. She was screaming for her life as she fell down to the cobbled streets. I put it in my book: it could be late '60s paranoia, but after Nixon came into office, there seemed to be a lot more heroin on the Lower East Side. There were a lot more muggings. I was mugged. That's one reason we decided to move.

Maurer: Peace Eye was clearly a tremendous asset to the community, much as the St. Mark's Bookshop is considered to be these days.

Sanders: I called it a scrounge lounge. I always had places for people to sit and chew the fat, and I always had a free mimeograph—I printed lots of street leaflets for all kinds of groups. For a while I was helping with the underground railroad to help soldiers escape the war and get up to Canada. They'd come into my store and leave their uniforms and we'd give them clothing and they'd head out and I'd have to figure out ways of discarding their uniforms in nearby waste cans. A lot of people came in and out of the store in both locations. It was a kind of hangout.

Maurer: What did you think of that other pioneer in the underground press, the *East Village Other*?

Sanders: They did a good job. They advanced design—they had Bill Beckman and others who helped design their format. They did some investigations. We had some good times. I moved Peace Eye Bookstore in 1968 to the old *EVO* office on Avenue A because they moved over to Yoko Ono's loft on Second Avenue. We were friends. Walter Bowart [a founder] was a bartender at Stanley's which was the prime watering hole for the East Village art, poetry, revolution crowd in the late '60s.

Maurer: It's funny, the blog Ephemeral New York just linked to a *New York Times* item from 1964 that referred to the changing demographic at Stanley's. Did you feel that the bar and the neighborhood around it became more upscale while you lived there?

Sanders: Stanley's always stayed pretty funky. I did notice the East Village going upscale. First of all, there was no East Village—we called it the Lower East Side, and the *Village Voice* and *EVO* started calling it the East Village for commercial reasons. There were more tie-dye shops and the Psychedelicatessen on Avenue A where you could buy psychedelic candles and acid. A lot of commerce developed on the Lower East Side and it became more of a tourist mecca. People tended not to live there forever—it was more of a transient neighborhood. You got a pad while you were in college and then moved on after a couple of years.

Maurer: Do you go back to the neighborhood these days? What do you make of it?

Sanders: I always stop in and sit there in Tompkins across from the old bookstore, which is now a coffeehouse [Cafe Pick Me Up]. It's all right. It's nice to go in May or April when the fruit trees in Tompkins are still in bloom. There are still a lot of rats in the park. I take part in the Ginsberg festival every now and then, and I'll walk around the nabe, go to Odessa.

Maurer: As an NYU graduate, what do you say to people who think it's the scourge of the neighborhood? Is it responsible for ruining the neighborhood by flooding it with students, as some have said? Or has the East Village long been a neighborhood of young transients?

Sanders: It's been that way since the overcrowding after the War of 1812 when they first made those tenement buildings. It's been a transient phenomenon. I don't feel a resentment against NYU—it has expanded, like a lot of these colleges. NYU is expanding and it's gotten more upscale. It was a little more proletarian when I went there, and they've raised their standards quite a bit. It's still a desperate-search-for-some-meaning-in-life college and it's all right.

From Turbulent '60s to Turbulent Teens
A Q&A with Ed Sanders

Marc Schultz

Originally published in Publishers Weekly, *December 9, 2011, http://www.publishersweekly.com/pw/by-topic/authors/interviews/article/49799-from-turbulent-60s-to-turbulent-teens-a-q-a-with-ed-sanders.html. Reprinted by permission of* Publishers Weekly, *permission conveyed through Copyright Clearance Center, Inc.*

Ed Sanders, 72, is a storied icon of the 1960s counterculture, an author-poet-scholar-activist-musician-bookseller-underground publisher with feet in both the Beat and hippie generations: he started a mimeographed avant-garde arts journal called *Fuck You,* where he published (among much, much more) the work of his good friend Allen Ginsberg; he founded pioneering folk-rock band The Fugs, before the term "folk-rock" even existed; he opened a "vegetarian literary zone" called Peace Eye Bookstore in the East Village; and helped found the Yippie anti-party, all while agitating (nonviolently) for the end of the Vietnam War, the expansion of civil rights, and the social safety-net envisioned in Johnson's Great Society. His latest, *Fug You: An Informal History of the Peace Eye Bookstore, the Fuck You Press, the Fugs, and Counterculture in the Lower East Side* (Da Capo), is a memoir of the '60s that ties in all of Sanders's favorite preoccupations. He spoke with Tip Sheet from his home in Woodstock, NY, about his book, the state of the nation, and his advice for today's young and increasingly visible social activists.

Marc Schultz: How did this memoir come about?

Ed Sanders: Well, I began in 2009 in the summer and finished the first draft in 2010, turned in a final draft early this year. I'm a pack rat, I have an archive of 500 bankers boxes organized alphabetically and chronologically, so I've been going through a long and arduous process. I'm trained to write chronologies, I have a life-in-verse of Allen Ginsberg and Anton Chekhov, so I decided to turn my investigative skills on myself. I went through all my boxes, got help from libraries that keep my work, debriefed various friends. When I put it together and sequenced it, it turned out over 400 pages.

Schultz: Do you know of any bookstores or publications carrying on the radical tradition of the Peace Eye Bookstore or Fuck You Press?

Sanders: Well, rent for bookstores [today] is really skyrocketing. I had the advantage of very low rent, it was in a former kosher meat market, I left the words "Strictly Kosher" on the front and put up the Peace Eye sign next to it. Rent was $50 a month.

Fuck You was the equivalent of rebel publications on the internet—I'm not sure there are any mimeograph machines being built now. You can get some used ones, but that technology is basically gone, though there are Kinkos and other offset publishing sources. People put their publications in my hand when they see me, and I get a lot of stuff in the mail. 8.5" x 11" publications are flooding the post office as we speak.

Schultz: How would you compare the current moment of civil unrest to the 1960s?

Sanders: There's a lot more issues now than we felt in the '60s. Then, the Great Society had just begun, and we thought that the social safety net would grow and grow, and by the time we were old everything would be taken care of. Occupy [Wall Street] has so many fragmented issues to face. [In the '60s,] we just had war, and freedom of expression, and partying—a lot of partying. Now it's a serious thing, kids with huge debt and unable to find jobs, more and more wars, drones. The kids in Occupy Wall Street have a noble mission to try to transform the economic injustice that's going on but, boy, it's going to be tough. Police come on the scene like Darth Vaders, coordinated nationally, raiding Occupy encampments all over the Western hemisphere. It's a peculiar situation we face: the militarization of the police, the desperation of poor people, the decimation of pensions and savings. It's gonna become like a Dickens novel, baby.

Schultz: Do you think the pendulum of political America is currently making a significant swing back toward the left?

Sanders: I've been around a long time, seen a couple pendulums swing back and forth, but I think maybe the pendulum is a broken metaphor now. It's just a swing out to less and less, widening this abyss between people who can pay $300 for a shirt and those who get by with a $10 tee. I don't know what's going to happen: we could all wind up in the gutter, eating dog food quiche on an encampment under the freeway somewhere. There's no safety net anymore except for people who have strong family ties and families that have money. Like in a Chekhov short story, where you have some out-of-work uncle living well in the manor house of a wealthy family member. I thought that when I was old that social democracy would have grown up in the United States, and my heart is broken that it hasn't.

Schultz: How does *Fug You* fit into the current political landscape?

Sanders: *Fug You* is built on that vision, of America growing out of the Great Society—the good side of the Johnson administration—building on that, defeating the war party and the war interests, creating an equal society, a William Morris-like vision of a social paradise. But it didn't happen. [*Fug You*] is a truthful story of a ten-year swatch of time, when I was a young semi-idealistic college grad trying to survive in the turbulent '60s. Now we have the turbulent teens, it's sort of the same in a way: same turbulence confronting war and social inequality. We went down to the South to get black people the right to vote, now 25 states have passed laws making it harder for them to vote. It's a little bit like déjà vu.

Schultz: Do you think things are better or worse than they were in the '60s?

Sanders: I think in some ways it's better now, there's more personal freedom. The producers of *Gone with the Wind* paid a fine when Clark Gable uttered the word "damn," but thanks to the fight for personal freedom from my generation or the Beat generation, you have HBO and the *Sopranos* and a richer [popular arts] landscape—the comedy channel can pretty well say whatever it wants. So there's gluts of freedom, there's just no social safety net. Paul Goodman said, "In America, you can say anything you want, as long as it doesn't have any effect." Bless his soul.

Schultz: What advice do you have for today's crop of young activists?

Sanders: Become a scholar-activist. That is, study issues and create research and don't hesitate to get out into the street and raise the banners of your concern. You've got to have one foot in activism and one foot in scholarship.

Peace Eye! Fug! A Long Talk with Ed Sanders

Alan Bisbort

Originally published in Literary Kicks, *January 3, 2012. https://www.litkicks.com/EdSandersInterview. Reprinted by permission of* Literary Kicks *and Alan Bisbort.*

Ed Sanders has been a cultural force in America for the past half-century. Arguably best known for his satirical 1960s rock band The Fugs and his perennially wide-selling 1971 book *The Family: The Story of Charles Manson's Dune Buggy Attack Battalion*, Sanders's appeal to readers is also grounded in his deep Beat Generation roots. As a high school senior in Missouri, he read Allen Ginsberg's *Howl* and then, after a failed attempt at a college education in Columbia, Missouri, hitchhiked east to see what all the Beat commotion was about.

Sanders was founder of a legendary literary "scrounge lounge," the Peace Eye Bookstore, remembered as a Greenwich Village version of San Francisco's City Lights Books during the hippie era; editor of the seminal *Fuck You/A Magazine of the Arts*; publisher of works by Charles Olson and Ezra Pound; underground filmmaker (*Amphetamine Head*); prose author (*Tales of Beatnik Glory*); poet (*America: A History in Verse*); anti-war and anti-nuclear activist; he also seems to have known anyone and everyone affiliated with the American underground.

In his new book, *Fug You: An Informal History of the Peace Eye Bookstore, the Fuck You Press, the Fugs, and Counterculture in the*

Lower East Side, Sanders ties all of his earliest threads—up to 1970—together in the most engagingly idiosyncratic memoir of the new year. Helpfully subtitled "An Informal History of the Peace Eye Bookstore, the Fuck You Press, the Fugs, and Counterculture on the Lower East Side," *Fug You* comes at you from all sides of this complex, rugged individual who appeared on the cover of *Life* magazine in 1967, emerging from splatters of Pollock-like paint as "a leader of the Other Culture."

Still placing his shoulder to the cultural wheel, Sanders, 72, is today the strongest living link between the Beat Generation, the hippies and all other underground currents that have trickled along the countercultural pipeline since then. Sadly, his partner in Fug crimes, the irreplaceable Tuli Kupferberg, died in 2010 after 86 years of stirring up trouble and mirth.

On November 17, 2011, I spoke with Sanders by phone at his home in Woodstock, N.Y., where he lives with Miriam Sanders, his wife of more than 50 years.

Alan Bisbort: The events you describe in the new memoir are so rich in detail that many of the chapters and sometimes even individual paragraphs would be worthy of entire books. Did it seem this complex at the time or is this true only in retrospect? In other words, did you just get up every morning and do all these things on instinct and now look back, and you can't believe all the ties to all the things and people?

Ed Sanders: I was very young, had a lot of energy, didn't need to sleep a lot. Plus, I really believed that I was helping to make fundamental changes in the ways the economy works, in spiritual and personal freedom. Even though there were all those deaths and assassinations, the countercultural activities fueled the idea that there was a lot of hope throughout these years up to the early 1970s, which is where I stopped the book.

Bisbort: It's a good stopping point. It makes sense. It's at the end of the first phase of the Fugs, and just after the big moratoriums against the Vietnam war and Woodstock and I think, but I could be wrong, before Altamont …

Sanders: No, Altamont was in December 1969. But I didn't go to Altamont.

Bisbort: One thing the book reminded me of was that your roots were firmly in Beat culture. In the book, you talk about coming to New York City partly, or primarily, because you had read the Beats in high school, in particular Ginsberg's *Howl*. And you wanted to head east to see where they action was. You felt the clarion call.

Sanders: I don't know if I put it in the book, but in early 1958 I applied to UC Berkeley and New York University simultaneously, and NYU answered right away. I hitchhiked from Missouri to New York in the summer of 1958. I wanted to be a rocket scientist. It was the era of the Mercury program. NYU had a good engineering department, and initially I was going to study mathematics and was thinking of joining the Mercury program. But I'd read *Howl* and was fascinated by the Beats in New York City and soon I began frequenting the Greenwich Village bookstores and buying more and more Beat literature. Then in 1958 and 1959, I began going to Beat poetry readings. I saw Gregory Corso and others at the Living Theater [another major Beat launch pad, run by Judith Malina and Julian Beck].

So my future wife [Miriam] and I would roam around lower New York City bohemia, and I got more and more attracted to poetry and the Beats. Meanwhile, I switched my major over to Greek and Latin. My mother had said that a gentleman knows Greek and Latin. She died when I was a senior in high school. And in her honor I took a beginning Greek class in 1958, and that's where I met a blonde girl from Queens named Miriam. Three years later, we were married. And, she's still here, with me, in this house.

Bisbort: You quickly entered the Beat inner circle. It might be partly due your personality, genial and respectful of your elder Beats, but pretty quickly (and, I might add, enviably) you were rubbing shoulders with your heroes.

Sanders: Well, I wrote them all. When I started publishing my magazine *Fuck You/A Magazine of the Arts*, I sent out copies to all the Beats. I sent one to Allen Ginsberg, but also to Nikita Khrushchev, Fidel Castro, Pablo Picasso and Samuel Beckett. I had kind of catchy title for my journal and so I attained a sort of instant status and began getting quality manuscripts from my heroes. I sent a copy to Ginsberg in India. I had gotten his address from the owner of the Eighth

Street Bookshop, who told me he was depressed. So I sent him a copy of the magazine and an upbeat letter. He responded and later told me that my magazine had helped pull him out of his depression. Anyway, when he got back to New York from India, in 1963, we became friends, and then really were good friends for many years up to his death.

Bisbort: I wrote Ginsberg a couple of times and he always responded with fairly long, thoughtful letters. And I had a nice long phone interview with him that ended up in my book, *Beatniks: A Guide to an American Subculture*. He really opened some doors, he was a real facilitator …

Sanders: That's right. I miss him a lot. He and I talked a lot over the years and saw a lot of capers together [*laughs*]. [Among the funniest of the capers, which is described in the book, was an exorcism rite that Sanders and Ginsberg performed at the grave of Senator Joe McCarthy, not to mention the exorcism that they performed at the Pentagon, which Norman Mailer wrote about in *Armies of the Night*].

Bisbort: Getting back to *Fuck You/A Magazine of the Arts*, have you thought of putting together an edition of all the back issues, partly to save people like me hundreds of dollars trying to get them on eBay? I mean, the contributors' list is a real who's-who of American culture and literature, and the writing quality was as good as any journal of its day. Better, in some ways, because of the unrestrictive editorial policy.

Sanders: I have had offers, for facsimile editions. I don't know, I've turned all of them down so far, but I might think about it. Someone is coming up here to see me in a couple of weeks and I think one of the proposals will be for an edition like that. I don't know, we'll see.

Bisbort: I don't want to get sidetracked, but it strikes me that that journal and all your other endeavors, the underground film, the Fugs, your so-called "mimeograph revolution," all of it was sort of a precursor to the punk movement. You wanted to meet your heroes. What better way than to start a magazine and have them contribute!

Sanders: Right.

Bisbort: It created almost a maelstrom, a sort of one-man revolution.

Sanders: It was a very intense set of years. Of course, you get into your 70s, I'm 72, and you realize that you don't have the energy to stay up three straight nights, party, publish, drink, smoke pot, forget about sleep …

Bisbort: You mentioned that you knew you had entered the Beat inner circle when several things happened. Among these is that you were propositioned by Allen Ginsberg [respectfully unrequited] and were conned out of some money by Herbert Huncke, who was sort of the quintessential Beat, having provided that word to Kerouac, "beat."

Sanders: Yes, to both of those.

Bisbort: But you were also given a rather harrowing ride by Mr. Neal Cassady, weren't you?

Sanders: Oh yeah … he took Peter Orlovsky and I down to La Honda to Ken Kesey's place—

Bisbort: Cassady always ends up behind the wheel! It's just amazing …

Sanders: Yeah, we had a Volkswagen bus that we, meaning the Fugs, were traveling around in, all five of us. Neal had stopped by my bookstore in September, just before the band went West on tour. He pulled up at the curb in front of Peace Eye Bookstore in a small Studebaker that only had a second gear.

Bisbort: What had he done to that poor car!

Sanders: [*laughing*] I had a friend who had some amphetamine, and Cassady traded the Studebaker for an ounce of amphetamine. Anyway, a couple months later, we were in San Francisco and Neal was there. He said he'd drive us down to Kesey's commune in La Honda. Oi, oi! He was pretending he was like Sterling Moss, going into a power slides around hairpin turns along the coast.

Bisbort: Were you on Pacific Coast Highway, going through Big Sur?

Sanders: Yes.

Bisbort: Holy shit.

Sanders: Yeah … hairpin turns on the outside lane … no guardrails … whew … but you know Neal was a good driver and he got us there safely.

Bisbort: People tend to think that the Beat Generation just sort of petered out and was replaced, or subsumed, by the hippie generation.

Which really wasn't true, especially in New York. It seemed that all the same people simply walked forward into the hippie scene, Allen Ginsberg, Peter Orlovsky, Gregory Corso, William Burroughts, etc. They were all there, just another wave of fashion … the best part is that the Beat sensibility brought an active rather than passive sensibility, or infusion, to the hippies.

Sanders: They brought some good writing, too. Hippies could be pretty vaporous in their literature. You know, I figure it must have been around February 1967 that we began to see the changeover. Instead of someone sneering at you and calling you "a dirty Beatnik," they were now calling you "a dirty hippie." I remember when Allen Ginsberg came over to our house on Avenue A around this time and said, "Now I guess we're going to have to be hippies." Miriam wasn't even sure what he was talking about.

It was a mysterious switch over. It went from tire-soled sandals to Merlin curved-toe shoes and gowns, and men wearing necklaces, which was a big deal for a man. Suddenly you have to wear a necklace, toe ring or go barefoot in the street, and burn incense. It was pretty strange. But the Beats ultimately prevailed. There are still conferences on the Beat Generation where young people come dressed all in black. It's very interesting.

Bisbort: Yes, I've written about, collected and studied the Beats and the hippies. I co-wrote a book with my old college pal and longtime collaborator Parke Puterbaugh about the next generation, the next wave, so to speak, *Rhino's Psychedelic Trip*. I only bring that up to show how interwoven the roots of these two so-called subcultures really were. The tapestry is so rich. It's not as simplistic as people want to make it. You saw this graphically in the transcript of the William F. Buckley *Firing Line* show that you provided in the book. I have never been able to find full footage of the show, only snippets are included in documentaries about Jack Kerouac. But to read the entire show in its full context, wow, a new meaning emerges.

Sanders: I put additional information about that in my book [*Fug You*] because I was there and I remember this stuff so clearly. It was indeed a strange hour or two of life.

Bisbort: It's taken on an iconic life in documentaries. But the whole thing was staged by Buckley to set up a false argument, between conservatives and "the hippies." And Kerouac was like his little pet salvation project, the prop to prop up his specious arguments.

Sanders: Right, exactly.

Bisbort: To pit an icon of the Beats against a so-called hippie. And I guess you were the one he had on to represent the hippies.

Sanders: Well, in the middle of the show, Kerouac fell off the riser. He was drunk, really drunk. He had come down from Lowell with a couple of old friends and they had been drinking the whole way. This happened in an early section of the show and Buckley threw up his hands in frustration and said, "That's it, that's it" and they thought they would try to get Allen Ginsberg, who was in the audience, to come up on the set to replace Kerouac. To substitute for Kerouac, who they thought could not go on. And we all shouted, "No, no, let him do it." Kerouac was one of my heroes.

Bisbort: Oh my gosh. It's heartbreaking, really, to think about it. You spoke for all of us when you told Kerouac "It's all your fault," meaning that he helped open the door, in a good way … and "you're a great poet." Essentially, you were thanking him for what he did in his writing and showing your sorrow for the way he ended up, this bloated, red-faced drunk sucking up to the likes of the viperous William F. Buckley. Or so it seemed to me.

Sanders: The Beats were divided into Democrats and Republicans. And Kerouac voted for Nixon in 1960 and again in 1968. Ginsberg was of course a very liberal sort of Democrat. This was a cultural divide in the Beats. And, of course, Kerouac had this ultra-right-wing mother.

Bisbort: She was a piece of work.

Sanders: She was always there … always there hovering in the background.

Bisbort: That weird divide in the Kerouac family still extends to this day. Just to get permission to quote some short parts from his work in my book, it cost me the bulk of my allotted expenses. And this was money going to people who had no blood connection to Kerouac.

Meanwhile, they did everything in their power to deny money to Jan Kerouac when she was near destitute and terribly ill.

Sanders: She ultimately got a good slice of it. Now I think her cousin has the estate.

Bisbort: Good, at least it is going to the Kerouac bloodlines …

Sanders: Yeah, they proved that his will was forged. Or, rather, his signature on the will was forged. And they worked out a deal.

Bisbort: Can we talk a bit about the Fugs?

Sanders: Sure, go ahead. I'm enjoying this.

Bisbort: Are you familiar with the website Pandora? You key in a musical artist and they compile a playlist based around that artist.

Sanders: No, don't know about it.

Bisbort: Well, out of curiosity, I decided to key in "The Fugs" and see what the great Internet swarm locks on to as your kindred spirits. Oddly enough, they play a couple of Fugs songs from compilation albums then stuff like early T. Rex, the 13th Floor Elevators, Lovin' Spoonful, the Yardbirds, all of which is fine, of course, but it doesn't seem to be the kindred spirits I would choose. I would think more in line with bands like the Mothers of Invention and Country Joe and the Fish. Did you feel you had kindred spirits?

Sanders: We did gigs with the Mothers of Invention. I remember Dick Clark yukking it up when he introduced the Mothers and the Fugs … "uhhh, I guess that means they're Motherfugs" yuk yuk … " and Frank [Zappa] was a friend. We played theaters near each other in 1967. Mothers played the Garrick Theater and the Fugs were at the Players Theater in Greenwich Village and we'd hang out after the shows. We were at the Essen Song Festival in 1968 together. We were not close to the whole band but very friendly. Everybody knew everybody then. I knew Jim Morrison, saw Jimi Hendrix a lot, was pretty good friends with Janis Joplin.

Bisbort: Yes, in the book, you mention you even tried to set Joplin up with your hero Charles Olson the great poet.

Sanders: Right. I tried to be a matchmaker there but it didn't quite work out. I was acquainted with so many people on the music scene. When you are caught in a band, you travel in a vortex and you are pretty much confined to who is connected to that band. All other connections go by the wayside.

Bisbort: In those days, they would put together these bills that seemed just random combination, disparate bands, you know. You can see the ads in the old underground papers for shows at the Fillmores and other rock 'n' roll venues and music clubs. I was talking to Bert Jansch awhile back and he remembered The Pentangle being on a bill with Canned Heat and Rhinoceros. Can you imagine? That seems so random, but so great, in a way.

Sanders: It wasn't computerized then. Every band had a Rolodex with all the promoters in it. The managers would make calls and try to patch together a tour and the Rolodexes would commingle. I can remember when Fleetwood Mac was our opening act on a Scandinavian tour in early 1968. Fleetwood Mac opening for us, imagine that.

Bisbort: That was the good Fleetwood Mac, though, fronted by Peter Green.

Sanders: Right. Peter Green was quite a guitar player ... You never knew who you'd be billed with. For example, our last gig in the 1960s was with Grateful Dead and Velvet Underground.

Bisbort: What a bill, that's unbelievable!

Sanders: That was an intense night. Of partying, too.

Bisbort: Did Lou Reed deign to speak with you?

Sanders: Oh, no. I didn't know him well. But I went to see the Velvet Underground in the early days when they were totally undiscovered, playing the Café Bizarre in the Village [before Mo Tucker joined the band, when Angus MacLise was the percussionist]. Summer of 1965, must have been. And then they were with Andy Warhol. Nico would hang out at my bookstore. And I knew Andy pretty well. He made the banners for my bookstore. He came to some Fugs shows. There was a kind of cross pollination.

Bisbort: You had an affinity with bands. I mentioned the Mothers of Invention, but I would think Country Joe and the Fish would be a pretty good fit for the Fugs.

Sanders: Oh yes, we played with them on their first performance in the fall of 1965. We were billed with his band and Allen Ginsberg.

Bisbort: I think Country Joe deserves much more credit that he's given. First of all, his band was great, but he also took strong antiwar stands, wore military fatigues, and really took chances at a time when it was physically dangerous to say and do and wear the stuff he did.

Sanders: Yes, true. And he's still here. I did a gig with him in Detroit a couple of years ago. He's out there playing. He's a big collector, I understand. He has a big collection I've heard of underground and psychedelic ephemera and posters.

Bisbort: You were friends with Phil Ochs, one of my other heroes.

Sanders: Phil was a good friend of mine. We had some capers together.

Bisbort: As we said before, the Fugs had some strange bill sharings, but I can't imagine a less likely pairing than the gig you mention in the book, with Little Anthony and the Imperials, at the El Patio Beach Club. Where was that place?

Sanders: Oh, yeah! It was in Queens. Again, it was the battle of the Rolodexes. We were pretty popular then. We were selling out our off-Broadway show [at the Players Theatre] and had other offers around the New York area. But it was relentless, being in a band. You had to get up, write a song, write a press release, get on the phone, etc. Every day.

Bisbort: You and Tuli Kupferberg had these other aspects of your creative impulses outside the band that must have felt somewhat thwarted or confined by the endless touring and promoting. Among many other things, you were ahead of the curve on underground film. You describe in great detail films like *Amphetamine Head* and some "blue movies," which you made "at a secret location on the Lower East Side." You were also an early promoter of underground commix, plus trying to run a bookstore. The cartoonist Spain Rodriguez helped you out with your store.

Sanders: Yes, Spain made the banners in front of the store. Spain is still alive and working, out in California.

Bisbort: At some point you knew that the Fugs had to step up the game musically, so to speak.

Sanders: That was part of my early agenda, to step it up. I ended up in San Francisco in fall of 1965, played Café au Go Go, and then kept running into all these bands who were so tight, like the Blues Project, the Youngbloods, Howlin Wolf's band, Richie Havens. So we were dumbfounded and amazed at the quality of people like the Blues Project. And we realized we had to bump up the quality of our music after that first album [*The Fugs First Album*, released on Folkways in 1965]. So I started just collecting musicians, trying to put together a really topnotch band.

Bisbort: You had some great musicians filter through the Fugs, beyond the core group of you, Tuli and Ken Weaver. Danny Kootch, for one.

Sanders: Yeah, Kootch was an important player for us. He really bumped up our quality.

Bisbort: Did Bob Dylan ever come see the Fugs?

Sanders: Yes.

Bisbort: Did he give you any feedback?

Sanders: No, he swooped into a show one night and took a listen. There were a lot of people did the same, Keith Richards, a lot of people came to the shows.

Bisbort: The funniest thing in the book and one of the funniest things I've ever read is a description by Elizabeth Hardwick. She came to see The Fugs and wrote up her impressions for the *New York Review of Books*. I could picture her sort of standing in the back holding her nose while she jotted notes. She wrote a piece that was mostly favorable—for the breaking of cultural taboos that the band was doing—but she referred to you as "a sort of foul Bob Hope." In a way, it's like the greatest backhanded compliment of all time.

Sanders: She [*laughs*] … yeah, it was a real moment.

Bisbort: Hardwick was actually indirectly responsible for me writing a book. I came across a collection of her essays a while back and found in it an essay about the execution of Caryl Chessman. It really stopped me in my tracks. I had long heard about Chessman but I really hadn't done any research. After reading her piece, I was moved to answer the question, "What ever happened to Caryl Chessman?" Well, we know what happened. He was executed in May 1960. But what happened to his legacy and his writing? He was once on the cover of *Time* and *Life* magazines. He wrote and published four books in his Death Row cell, three of which became international bestsellers. I ended up getting access to his papers and writing a biography of Chessman and his legal struggles.

Sanders: Oh, you did? You wrote a book about it?

Bisbort: Yes, I found his literary executor in Florida. Joseph Longstreth, a wonderful man. He gave me everything. Chessman had a cottage industry on death row for 12 years. Tons of unpublished manuscripts and letters, which formed the basis for my book *When You Read This, They Will Have Killed Me*. What sparked this digression is that you, in your new book, are the only chronicler of the 1960s who made the obvious point of how significant the Chessman execution was to the decade.

Sanders: Marlon Brando was there. Abbie Hoffman was there. Shirley MacLaine. I took part in a protest walk past the Plaza Hotel in New York. It was a tense moment. It was ghastly. I wrote a short story about Chessman's execution in *Tales of Beatnik Glory*. Yeah, it was a real change in my life.

Bisbort: I mentioned in the book, and it struck me talking to people who lived through it and knew Chessman. In a way his execution so tainted Jerry Brown's father, Pat Brown, then governor of California, who claimed to be anti-death penalty but allowed Chessman's execution to go forward, that he was persona non grata at the Democratic Convention that fall. He really wanted to be nominated as the presidential candidate. Instead, a little known, or lesser known, Senator from Massachusetts got the nomination.

Sanders: He didn't get the nomination because of Chessman, you think?

Bisbort: I believe so. I've never had that disputed. I talked to Brown's granddaughter who was making a documentary about her grandfather and she wanted to interview me for the film, but when I started in with this line of talk she dropped me like a hot potato. Never heard from her again. And yet, there it is. His handling of the Chessman execution essentially ended Pat Brown's political career. He eventually drifted back into private practice as a lawyer.

Sanders: Miller Leavy was a prosecutor at the end against Chessman, and he was involved in the prosecution of the Charles Manson family. I used to see him around the court house when I was working on *The Family*, and he reminded me of J. Edgar Hoover, kind of dour, bloodless.

Bisbort: Yes, that sounds about right for that guy. I got to know Chessman's lawyer, George Davis, who sent me a lot of good material for the book, lived into his 90s and died a couple of years ago in Hawaii. Davis was the one who got the last-minute stay from the judge but they didn't make the phone call to San Quentin in time and the execution went forward when, in fact, it should have been stopped and the chamber cleared. I think it was deliberate foot dragging. They wanted Chessman dead, they didn't care. He was a pain in the ass to them, a thorn in their side, a reminder of the capriciousness of the death penalty. Anyway, Chessman and the wave of protests that accompanied his execution provides a fascinating door into the 1960s and I was so glad to see that you had written about it in that way, too. Just look at the photographs of the protesters at Chessman's execution in May 1960, and then look at the photographs of the protesters in Chicago in 1968. It's like the same group of people. The hair is growing out, there are moustaches and beards, military fatigues, desert boots, etc.

Sanders: One of my favorite historians Richard Drinnan was there, very involved in trying to save Chessman's life. Well, I don't know … you'll just have to find a good home for that Chessman archive. That's important stuff.

Bisbort: I wanted to ask one final thing about the legendary episode that took place up here in Connecticut. You once tried to board a nuclear submarine in 1962?

Sanders: It was 1961 in Groton [home of the U.S. Naval Submarine Base].

Bisbort: Did you dive into the Thames River and swim toward the damn thing?

Sanders: Yes, I tried twice. Once in June and once in August. Both times it involved swimming in the Thames River outside the shipyard. I was a good swimmer then. But the frogman they sent after me was wearing flippers and caught me and I was hauled off onto a barge. I wasn't able to get on board the submarine. The workers were throwing bolts at us in the water. There were a few of us doing this. It was frightening. We were going to stand up on top of the submarine tower in protest.

Bisbort: You may not have stopped the nuclear proliferation, but it did lead to your first book, *Poem from Jail*, in 1963.

Sanders: Yes. [Lawrence] Ferlinghetti published that book on his City Lights imprint.

Still Happening
A Conversation with Ed Sanders

Jennifer Seaman Cook

Originally published in Los Angeles Review of Books, *July 18, 2018, https://lareviewofbooks.org/article/still-happening-a-conversation-with-ed-sanders/. Reprinted by permission of* Los Angeles Review of Books *and Jennifer Seaman Cook.*

Known for his role in the avant-garde mimeograph revolution, New American Poetry, '60s social justice movements, and his intermedia Beatnik-proto-punk band, the Fugs, Ed Sanders weds political pragmatism with media shamanism. As we celebrate the anniversary of May 1968 and the release of Sanders's new "investigative poem," *Broken Glory: The Final Years of Robert F. Kennedy*, his reflections offer insight for our hyper-militarized and hyper-mediatized political moment. The following conversation was recorded at the Burchfield Penney Art Center on April 12, 2018, where Sanders premiered a new musical play based on Cassandra, the prophetess of the Trojan War that no one would listen to. The transcript has been edited and rearranged.

Jennifer Seaman Cook: It's interesting that you started talking about access to the mimeograph as new, but not complicated, technology, because the first question I had was how you are considered part of the mimeograph revolution and what you really think that did.

Ed Sanders: Well, access to these small, portable mimeograph machines that were mainly used by churches and peace groups in the early '60s—in the Ban the Bomb movement it was very big, the civil rights movement, Congress of Racial Equality, and Student Non-Violent Coordinating Committee—they all had mimeograph machines in their offices, which could quickly turn out leaflets and brochures and pamphlets and time schedules right away. There was no photocopying then; it was before photocopying, and there were no cassette tape recorders back then, so the mimeograph was the current, state-of-the-art way of producing quick leaflets and flyers. So I was hanging out at the Catholic Worker in 1962. My friends worked on the Catholic Worker newspaper, and in February of '62 I purchased a $39 or $40 Speed-o-Print mimeograph machine—a real small thing. I had an apartment in the lower east side that had the bathtub in the kitchen. There was a porcelain cover over the bathtub, and that's where I put my mimeograph machine when I bought it in February 1962 and started publishing a mimeograph magazine, which I typed up at the Catholic Worker because I didn't have a good enough typewriter to type stencils.

So I borrowed the Catholic Worker's typewriter and started putting out a magazine and started mailing it out all over the world, and it became quite famous in its day. So that was the state-of-the-art technology. A few years later, when what they called the underground press started, there were printing facilities in many cities that printed used car bulletins and flyers for supermarkets, but they were willing to sell you a little space, a little slot in their printing schedule. So all across America grew up this thing called the underground press. Web press, they called it, and they printed off big rolls of newsprint, and it made possible the underground press because you could rent a two-hour slot at these web press sites. In between their car ads and their newspapers [that] they were already printing, you could put your radical and revolutionary underground press, such as the *Los Angeles Free Press* or the *Berkeley Barb*.

Cook: So a lot of the early alternative press movement ... actually was in part this convergence of the counterculture and the actual structural aspects of classified ads, which I think is very interesting. I'm thinking back to when you published the "Vancouver Report" ...

Sanders: I gradually converted from my little handheld mimeograph to an electronic mimeograph when I opened up to the Peace Eye Bookstore in early 1965. I'd printed little publications, such as the 1963 "Vancouver Report," which was a report on a literary festival held in late '63 in Vancouver that featured Allen Ginsberg, Robert Creeley, Charles Olson, and many other poets, Robert Duncan, I guess, too.

Cook: Do you think that part of the mimeograph revolution that you're credited for was seen as the socializing media of the mimeograph and bringing it to socializing poetry, or a cultural movement? How do you see it now versus what you were thinking of doing with it in the moment?

Sanders: We were interested in nonviolent revolution, you know. We thought that when we were old we could forge change in the United States, so that there was universal health care for everybody, guaranteed annual income, good pension, a month's paid vacation. You know, in Europe if you work for McDonald's in Sweden you get a month's paid vacation. Very few people get a month's paid vacation in the United States. Anyway, we thought all these changes would come. We were kinda wrong, but we had youthful hope that it would lead to vast change.

Using mimeograph machines and later web presses, and with the advances in recording from two to four to eight track, [it] mirrored what we were doing in the mimeograph revolution—they were going from two track to four track. The Beatles recorded most of their main albums on four track, and it was only at the end of their career in the late '60s that eight track and then finally 16-track recording came in. So there wasn't all this technological … movies: they were using 16 mm cameras—the Bell and Howell, and Rolex—and Andy Warhol shot in 16 mm film mostly, and only gradually at the end of his career did 35 mm, professional, Hollywood-level shoots, but most of it was stuff you bought cheap, at Willoughby's … or, there were a lot of camera stores in New York City—Willoughby's and others where people bought their cameras.

Cook: That brings me to how you were, in your work with the Fugs, establishing these relationships between music and experimental poetry, New American Poetry, and what would now be considered avant-garde print media—which, really, we're talking about avant-garde uses of alternative press media. I was wondering if, at the time, you saw the work as part of the larger social possibilities of the mediums, or if were you trying to just build something around you, expression, a community? Did you see art and poetry as being able to shape something within a social movement alongside alternative press media, or did you see it as happening organically, almost as if you were documenting all this intermedia mixing that was happening organically?

Sanders: Well, the civil rights movement, the antiwar movement, the Ban the Bomb movement, and the general pro-pot movement, and various other movements were forming … and there was the happening movement, where you could rent a storefront and you'd get a bunch of people, you'd get someone to take off their clothes, and you'd get a stock tank full of grapes, and you'd get people to dance on the grapes, and have somebody reading poetry, and you'd bring in a cow and paint it, and you'd call it a work of art. And you could charge admission, so the issue was making a living through your art.

So the happening movement coincided with the civil rights movement, all these great songs like "We Shall Overcome," and "Down by the Riverside," and "I Ain't Gonna Study War No More"—all these great civil rights anthems—combined with the fact that, in these apartments where I lived in the Lower East Side, there was usually a guitar in the corner. People always sang together. There were all these three-chord songs. You'd sing Joan Baez songs but also civil rights songs, and then, finally, when the Beatles showed up in 1964 you could sing Beatles songs, and guys like Richie Havens and The Lovin' Spoonful. There were various groups that led this thing that became folk rock around 1965, 1966, and Jimi Hendrix burst forward in '67. He got one of the first wah-wah pedals, which was an American invention—a guy invented this way of modulating a guitar—and I was around when Hendrix got his first wah-wah pedal and he took it over to London in late '66 and the rest is history. He made musical history.

Right at the same time as Hendrix was first using the wah-wah pedal, eight-track and then 16-track recording was coming, so that you could overdub. Early jazz players like Charlie Mingus and Charlie Parker didn't have a chance to overdub, so it was part of this culture of spontaneity, all these great jazz albums … they were one take only, or they'd do two takes for the whole album and pick the best one. By the late '60s, you could overdub. The Beatles could slow stuff down and add drones, and add Indian instruments and experiment with overdubs.

So it was quite experimental, and people would feed off the films, would feed off the music, the music would feed off the Happenings, then there was the modern art ... Willem de Kooning, Warhol were great innovators. Andy Warhol used to come to Fugs shows all the time. He was always out there to get ideas, and he made the banners for the opening of the Peace Eye Bookstore. He silkscreened his flowers, his famous flowers from 1964. So Warhol was a friend of the Fugs, and it was a lot of cross-pollination between the civil rights movement, the happening movement, the mimeograph movement, the rise in recording technology, and also the rise in sound reproduction. In order to do Crosby, Stills, Nash & Young in '69, they had to develop a whole new generation of speakers, because the four-part harmonies were blowing out all the speakers, and they would play big halls but also became so popular they could play big outdoor places.

So the technology to reproduce sound grew, which made possible the Woodstock festival of 1969—this new technology where you could play rock 'n' roll for 500,000 people and not blow out the speakers. So there was all this technology rising at the same time as artists were rising.

Cook: You're describing this culture of spontaneity coming out of both access to amateur media and the time and space for experimentalism. But it seems like you're also describing developments tied to intention ... toward creating spaces and events of collectivity, creating alternative economies that connect the cultural movements to the social movements, and also organizing important protest events. I'm thinking of your time with the Fugs and how you were part of several important public countercultural events in 1967 that arguably mobilized national and transnational political resistance, and arguably contributed to the momentum of the revolts in 1968. I'm thinking specifically about Perception '67 ...

Sanders: Oh, Toronto?

Cook: Yes, and I'm thinking of your exorcism as part of the March on the Pentagon, and I'm thinking about the Angry Arts Week, and, again, all the intermedia movements that were part of Angry Arts Week. So I was wondering what you had to say about this network of artists and activists, artists as activists ... what you think was accomplished versus what you had hoped would be accomplished because we're upon an anniversary of 1968. It's seen as a kind of culminating period of what happened before 1968 and also this kind of wave cresting, the decline of movements afterward, but maybe you reject this idea.

Sanders: 1967 was an interesting year. It contained this interlude called the Summer of Love, where in San Francisco and New York City—but also places in the Midwest where the Fugs toured—there were these love-ins. We would go to little towns in the Midwest on tour, and there would be a crowd of younger people who were holding a love-in. And there was a love-in in Central Park. Then came the fall of '67 and the war wouldn't end. The CIA killed Che Guevara in early October in Bolivia, and the war wouldn't end. So we decided to hold a demonstration at the very heart of the war—that is, right at the Pentagon. And the Fugs were charged with organizing an exorcism of the Pentagon—which we did—which involved members of the Diggers movement in San Francisco such as Michael Bowen and others. I wrote a ceremony to exorcise the Pentagon. You know, "Out, demons, out. Out, demons, out. Out, demons, out," and we chanted it over and over in front of the Pentagon, and it became a world-famous event.

To this day, I have camera crews who want to come from Europe to talk about this exorcism that my band did on October 21, 1967, but I point out that, yeah, we did levitate the Pentagon—it worked—but we forgot to rotate it. And the war went on for another five years. So the Vietnam War didn't end until 1975, so our exorcism was symbolic, but not really efficacious. But it helped trigger off [other movements]—of course Martin Luther King Jr. had come out against the Vietnam War in 1967, and was leading a lot of the religious aspects of the American social movement to come out against the war. Most Americans still approved of the war in Vietnam when we did the exorcism in October '67, but by '68 the movement against the war was rising ever higher.

Then, of course, Martin Luther King Jr. was assassinated in April and Robert Kennedy was assassinated on June 5, 1968, which put an end to a lot of the momentum of the '60s. They always say Charles Manson ended the '60s, but what ended the '60s was the evil assassination of Martin Luther King Jr. and the evil assassination of Robert Kennedy. If they had lived, America would be different now. The war would have ended much sooner, and over 20,000 American boys wouldn't have been killed, the number of those who died between 1968 and the end of the war.

It's a terrible thing that happened in 1968, but there was the big rise up in Paris, the big, big, big, big student revolt, and also the farmers demanded better pay in France, and they won concessions from the de Gaulle government. Then there was a huge riot in the streets of Chicago during the Democratic Convention, mainly in response to the assassination of Robert Kennedy and the futility of what the Democrats were doing. The Democrats were—like they are now—they were supportive of war, in good part. So Robert Kennedy was part of the antiwar Democrats and he was assassinated, which gave the pro-war Democrats the upper hand. In 1968, though, there were a lot of great things, a lot of wonderful music and jazz, cultural festivals.

I remember going in '67 to the Toronto Perception, and just as we were landing at Toronto the captain came on and said, "It's minus five in Toronto," so it was very cold.

Cook: And this wasn't really an opportune time to have a festival, but wasn't it in response to the Expo '67?

Sanders: Right. So it was okay. Timothy Leary was there. The Fugs gave a good show, and we had a lot of partying and fun.

Cook: This was more of a lysergic acid festival than it was a protest?

Sanders: Yeah, it was more of a cultural event than a protest event.

Cook: But you bring up the assassinations of MLK and Robert Kennedy, and one of the questions I have is whether you see their assassinations as instrumental in cutting off a timeline of possible progress in the United States, not just because of their antiwar positions, but because they were profoundly invested in bigger conceptions of a non-instrumentalist society, culturally and socially and politically.

Sanders: I agree.

Cook: It ties into a lot of these artists' movements.

Sanders: Right. Now, they were a part of the good side of America. America is a great nation, and has many wonderful things about it. One of the unfortunate aspects of America is that it has a military-industrial complex that Eisenhower spoke about in his final speech. And this military-industrial complex that he complained about in his final speech is still running a great part of the show. We live here in peace (from war). None of us invade any countries, none of us drop napalm, none of us drop defoliants. It goes back to the generals demanding to drop the A-bomb on Hiroshima and Nagasaki in 1945. That's the source of a lot of the evil aspects of the United States. I mean, I call myself patriotic because there are many things about my nation that I love. Those things that I abhor I have to struggle against nonviolently, because I grew up in the nonviolent struggle of the early '60s that Martin Luther King was a great example of—he called it "unearned suffering," the realization that you have to suffer in order to try to do good.

Angry Arts was well organized in New York City. They had committees and they put out really good literature, good schedules.

You know there's that line in Allen Ginsberg's *Howl*—"I saw the best minds of my generation." And that was part of the marching orders of my group in the '60s, to find the best minds and cross-pollinate with them. Find the best dancers. Find the best guitarists. Find the best artists. Find the best writers. Find the best leaders. Find the best activists. Find the best technicians, sound recording people, recording studio people, movie people. Find those and cross-pollinate and see what you can come up with. And Angry Arts was a result of this: a lot of active people who were angry about the war in Vietnam and decided to take a stance against it.

But there was also, in New York City, a tendency to ban certain cultural events. There was a law that prevented poets from reciting in restaurants. There was a cabaret card that you had to get in order to perform at nightclubs where there was drinking. So Lenny Bruce lost his cabaret card. Billie Holiday lost her cabaret card. And, then, before the World's Fair of 1965, the city government of New York decided to clean out its counterculture and to clean out poets who read in coffee shops. There was a whole group of city bureaucrats who were trying to stop coffee shops from having poetry readings. This was what we learned later was an attempt to clean up the city preceding all the tourists that would come for the World Fair in 1965. So we had to fight against that. We had picket lines and protest lines and letters to the editor and we were all trying to stop this squashing of poetry readings in coffee houses. You know, it was ridiculous.

And then there were movies. Jack Smith, *Flaming Creatures* (1963), and there were other movies ... a Jean Genet movie that was censored. So they were always trying to censor. And my magazine, *Fuck You/A Magazine of the Arts*, was [censored]—my bookstore was raided in early 1966, and I had to get the New York Civil Liberties Union to handle my case, and finally I won a year later, but I had to [go to] court like 10 times to get a victory against the police who raided my bookstore and carted away a whole bunch of my magazines, including the "Vancouver Report" and other publications I put out. I finally won, but it took a lot of effort and fundraisers. I had to raise money to pay for my defense and so forth.

So it wasn't automatic, you know. You didn't succeed. It wasn't a cream-puff gig. It was a difficult march, a difficult progress in the '60s to prevail, to open up voting. After the death of Kennedy, the Civil Rights law was passed, and Johnson passed the Medicaid law and the various Great Society legislations, and this all came about after the assassination of Kennedy, these social laws to quell and keep down social revolution, because there was danger of outbreaks of violence. So they passed these laws to calm down the masses.

Cook: I'm thinking of the political threat of counterculture to social norms that you're describing ... the threat of reciting poetry in a cafe ... or I'm thinking about the extreme hostility during the trial of the [Chicago] Eight after the Democratic National Convention. Allen Ginsberg, when he's on the witness stand, when he's asked to recount what happened, starts going into a chant—his Om chant—and how threatening the courtroom found that, that he was doing a poetic demonstration in the courtroom. These kinds of counterculture [activities] are political in a way because they keep social norms fluid. It reminds me of Ezra Pound, how he wrote in the *ABC of Reading* that what literature does versus journalism is that literature stays news. He says "literature stays news," and that what poetry does—or you could argue poetics, media poetics, intermedia does—is that it keeps subject matter from becoming history and it keeps it immediate and it keeps it circulating. And maybe this has to do with the way we almost erroneously see this separation between cultural and social movements, or maybe what was successful and what failed.

Sanders: Yes, Pound says poetry is news that stays news, and there's some truth to that. He also had the phrase "make it new." Well, you make it new, but you keep the roots of the good part of the past alive too.

Cook: In 1976, you wrote a manifesto for Investigative Poetry, published with City Lights books. Do you see a kind of renewed value for Investigative Poetry in our time in this so-called crisis of fake news? I'm specifically thinking about how we have some of this fallout from media decentralization. Maybe it does have something to do with the alternative press movement, but it's led to ideological thinking along the lines of very anti-democratic communities. So we're talking about threats to some of the important traditions of our institutions, and we have reports … opinions toward journalism and hostility to free press threatens to dissolve rather than reform or change institutions. So I guess it's also a question about not just levitating, but rotating something, maybe.

Sanders: Well, there's a basketball term about throwing it up for grabs. I guess it's called the "alt-right." I don't pay much attention to the alt-right, but they want to throw it up for grabs and create a more rigorously right-wing republic, and do away with democracy, in a way … keeping voters from voting, and keeping blacks from registering to vote, and keeping poor people from registering to vote. When the republic was formed, only male landowners were able to vote, and that's probably what some of the alt-right would like to have happen, just a bunch of guys getting in a smoke-filled room and voting, but that won't happen. There's too many people who believe in the American Constitution to allow this decimation of voting. Voting is very important, and sometimes, as happened in 2016, somebody weird can get elected. We all just have to rise up and deal with the weirdo that gets elected now and then—not always, but billionaires pour hundreds of millions of dollars into American elections, so it's remarkable they don't elect Mussolini, you know?

Look, kids don't know Allen Ginsberg now. I gave a talk at the University of Michigan a couple years ago, before 200 people … and I talked about 1968, and I talked about the Yippies and the riots in Chicago and this and that. I talked about the revolution in France.

And this guy comes up to me after my presentation, he says, "Professor Sanders, Allen Ginsberg, he was one of the lawyers at the O. J. Simpson trial, right?" And I say, no, wrong, and I explained who Allen was. He was a young kid from the Midwest, and he had not been taught about it. We lost the battle of the textbook, I guess that's what I'll say. Allen Ginsberg and the Beats, they are a presence in American education, but they're not featured in the expensive textbooks that high school kids buy.

Cook: Do you think cultural institutions have an ability to compete with this kind of political money anymore, compared to the really robust funding we had when a lot of the new Americanist poets came through really well-funded public universities? This is just an example. Maybe if we can't compete equally in terms of resources, in terms of the structure of campaign financing, can we turn back to relationships between art and politics, between cultural life and social life?

Sanders: It's hard to know what could happen. As we sit here talking, Trump is threatening to shoot missiles at Syria. And Russia has said it will respond to any of their soldiers being killed by targeting the sources of American missiles, submarines, and destroyers located in the ocean. So if America bombs Assad from American ships and Russia attacks and destroys American ships, does that mean World War III will happen? And that could happen this evening as *Cassandra* gets performed. So nothing is certain. It's a very perilous time, and the Military-Industrial Surrealists—I call them—the Military-Industrial Surrealists are threatening World War III. So we're in a comfortable meeting room in a nice cultural center waiting for my play to be performed tonight with the world holding on the balance of survival.

Cook: I'm thinking about how we got here and I'm thinking about something we were talking about earlier, off tape, these audio interviews that no one listens to, and the need to go back and transcribe these things. Marshall McLuhan described World War III as a mass information war where there's no distinction anymore between the public and the military. Is part of what's going on with the threat of nuclear war tonight that war of information or a war over people caring about it?

Sanders: There's been a big militarization of the United States, jet flyovers of football games. Up where I live in Woodstock, New York, there are billboards: "Help the army win." Big, huge billboards. There's a huge militarization going on, plus the defense budget … they can't possibly pay for it so they just borrow money to pay the American military with bases in 500 countries or 500 bases here and there …

Cook: In 1961, you wrote "Poem from Jail" on a piece of toilet paper. There's this trajectory of you going from this—what's considered one of your first significant poems — to *Fuck You*, and later, writing a history of America in verse that was distributed on CD. Does that legacy of something that started on a piece of toilet paper say something in the face of this massive information war that Allen Ginsberg was talking about in "Wichita Sutra Vortex," which is this inability to deal with the ideological war machine on the radio?

Sanders: Well, I wrote it on toilet paper because the jail in Connecticut wouldn't allow paper, so just like the mimeograph was the method of publishing at a certain time in my life, so too writing on toilet paper was a method of taking down my thoughts and laying out a poem I was writing. It's so long that the toilet paper was hundreds of feet long and I wadded it up and smuggled it in my tennis shoe in the jail because they didn't allow you to write. They didn't allow you to have pencils. They didn't want us to talk about conditions in the jail.

You use the tack you can, that you have. I suppose if there was no paper I'd get a piece of crayon and write on the sidewalk like they do in Paris, street poetry, street art.

Index

www.ingramcontent.com/pod-product-compliance
Lightning Source LLC
Chambersburg PA
CBHW030632110726
47901CB00002B/414